teach yourself...

WordPerfect

for Windows

Susan Rothenberg
and
Phyllis Romanski

First Printing 1992
ISBN: 1-55828-122-3

10 9 8 7 6 5 4 3 2 1

Printed in the United States of America
MIS: Press books are available at special discounts for bulk purchases for sales promotions, premiums, fund raising, or educational use. Special editions or book excerpts can also be created to specifications.

For details contact:

> Special Sales Director
> MIS:Press
> a subsidiary of Henry Holt and Company, Inc.
> 115 West 18th Street
> New York, NY 10011

TRADEMARKS
AutoCAD is a trademark of Autodesk, Inc.
DisplayWrite is a trademark of International Business Machines Corp.
DOS is a trademark of Microsoft Corporation
DR. Halo is a trademark of IMSI
Excel is a trademark of Microsoft Corp.
GEM Draw is a trademark of Digital Research, Inc.
GEM Paint is a trademark of Digital Research, Inc.
Hewlett-Packaard Graphics Language Plotter is a trademark of Hewlett-Packard Co.
IBM DCA/FFT is a trademark of IBM Corp.
IBM DCA/RFT is a trademark of IBM Corp.
Lotus 1-2-3 is a trademark of Lotus Development Corp.
MacPaint is a trademark of Claris Corporation
MS Word is a trademark of Microsoft Corporation
Multimate is a trademark of Ashton-Tate
Multimate Advantage II is a trademark of Ashton-Tate
OfficeWriter is a trademark of
PC Paintbrush is a trademark of Z Soft, Inc.
PC Paint Plus is a trademark of Mouse Systems Corp.
PlanPerfect is a trademark of WordPerfect Corp.
Postscript is a trademark of Adobe Systems, Inc.
Quattro Pro is a trademark of Borland International, Inc.
Windows Paint is a trademark of Microsoft Corp.
Windows 3.0 is a trademark of Microsoft Corp.
Word for Windows is a trademark of Microsoft Corp.
WordPerfect is a trademark of WordPerfect Corp.
WordStar is a trademark of Micro Pro International
XYWrite III Plus is a trademark of

Dedication

This book is dedicated to Uncle Joe, who hates computers.

Acknowledgments

We would like to thank all of the people who have helped to make this book happen:

Stefan Romanski, our graphics master and general assistant, who captured all of the screens, proofread the manuscript, and ran errands.

The support staff at WordPerfect, who answered our innumerable questions with unflagging courtesy and patience.

Our literary agent, Matt Wagner, at Waterside Publications, who remembered us when he needed an author for a WordPerfect book.

Our publisher, Steve Berkowitz, and our editor, Mia McCroskey, for their patience, guidance, and understanding.

Our lawyers and friends, Paul Landsman and Joe Gruner, for their friendship and multifaceted support.

Our friend and neighbor, Andy Craig, Photographer Extraodinaire, who took the pictures in the beginning of the book.

Our friend, Lois Karp, for her ever-constant friendship and support of all of our endeavors.

And, last but not least, all of our clients, who put up with being put off while this book was being written.

Contents

INTRODUCTION 1

A Word About Mice 2

Exciting New Features in WordPerfect for Windows 2

    Graphics 2

    Character Sets 2

    Button Bars 2

    Ruler 3

    Convert 3

How this Book is Organized 3

Additional Information 4

CHAPTER 1:

   GETTING STARTED 5

What You Will Learn in this Chapter 5

An Introduction to Your System 6

Let's Talk About Hardware and Software 6

A Few Words About Your Disk Operating System (DOS) 11

A Few Words About Windows 12

Installing WordPerfect and Windows 13

Starting the Program from Windows 13

The Title Bar 16

The Menu Bar 16

Dimmed Menu Items 17
Ellipses 18
Triangular Arrows 18
Checkmarks 18
Shortcut Keys 19
Dialog Boxes 19
Text Box 20
Check Box 20
Option Buttons 20
Command Buttons 21
List Boxes 21
Drop-Down List Boxes 21
Scroll Bars, Scroll Buttons, and Scroll Boxes 22
Minimize and Maximize Boxes and Control Boxes 22
The Mouse 22
Drag 23
Click 23
Double-click 23
Triple-click 23
Quadruple-click 23
The Template and Keyboard Layout 24
How to Use the Template 24
Exiting the Program 25
Review Exercises for Chapter One 26
Before You Go On… 26

CHAPTER 2:
CREATING AND EDITING A SIMPLE DOCUMENT 27
What You Will Learn in this Chapter 27
Typing a Document 28
Scrolling Through the Document 33
Adding and Deleting Text 34
Adding and Deleting Characters 34
To Add a Character 35
To Delete a Character 35
Adding Blocks of Text Using Typeover and Insert Modes 35
Using Select to Delete Larger Blocks of Text 37
Deleting Words with the Mouse 37
Deleting Words with the Keyboard 38
Deleting Sentences with the Mouse 38
Deleting Sentences with the Keyboard 39
Deleting Paragraphs with the Mouse 39
Deleting Paragraphs with the Keyboard 40
Deleting to the End of a Line 40
Deleting Other Blocks of Text 40
Deleting Blocks of Text with the Mouse 40
Deleting Blocks of Text with the Keyboard 41

Recovering Deleted Text Using Undelete (Alt+Shft+Bkspc) 42
Using Undo (Alt+Bkspc) 44
Using Reveal Codes 44
Saving the Document and Exiting WordPerfect for Windows 46
Review Exercises for Chapter 2 48
Before You Go On… 48

CHAPTER 3:
SAVING, RETRIEVING, AND PRINTING DOCUMENTS 49

What You Will Learn in this Chapter 49
A Word About the Features Covered in this Chapter 50
Saving Your Documents 50
    A Few Things You Should Know About Saving 50
    Naming Documents 51
    Using the Save Command (Shft+F3) 52
    Using the Save As Command (F3) 54
    Using the Close Command (Ctrl+F4) 55
    Using the Exit Command (Alt+F4) 56
    Saving a Block of Text to a New Filename 57
    Using Original and Timed Backup 58
        Original Backup 58
        Timed Backup 59
Retrieving Your Documents 61
    Using the Open Command (F4) 61
    Viewing a Document 62
    Using the Retrieve Command 63
    Using the New Command (Shft+F4) 65
Printing Your Documents 65
    Using the Print Command (F5) 66
        Printing a Page 67
        Printing Multiple Pages 67
        Printing a Document from Disk 68
        Printing Multiple Copies 69
        Selecting a Different Printer 69
Review Exercise 71
Before You Go On… 71

CHAPTER 4:
BASIC TEXT FORMATTING AND TYPING ENHANCEMENTS 73

What You Will Learn in this Chapter 73
Changing Left and Right Margins (Ctrl+F8) 74
Changing Line Spacing 77
Working with Tabs 78
    Position from Left Edge or Left Margin 79
    Types of Tab Settings 80
        Left Align Tabs 80
        Center Tabs 80

Right Align Tabs 80
Decimal Align Tabs 81
Dot Leaders 81
Setting Tabs 81
Clear All Tabs 82
Set Default Tabs 82
Evenly Spaced Tabs 83
Using Hard Tabs 83
Using the Margin Release Key (Shift+Tab) 84
Using the Indent Keys 85
Left Indent (F7) 85
Double Indent (Ctrl+Shift+F7) 86
Hanging Indent (Ctrl+F7) 86
Centering Lines of Text 87
Centering Text Between the Left and Right Margins 87
Centering Text at a Specific Location on a Line 87
Ending a Center Code 88
Centering Text With Leader Dots 88
End Centering in the Middle of a Line 88
Centering Existing Text 89
Centering Multiple Lines of Text 89
Using Flush Right 89
Using Flush Right with Leader Dots 90
Flush Right Aligning Existing Text 90
Flush Right Aligning Several Lines of Text 90
Aligning Text with Justification 90
Left Justification 91
Right Justification 91
Full Justification 92
Center Justification 92
Setting Justification 92
Enhancing Words with Bold, Italics, and Underline 94
Bolding Your Words 94
Deleting Bold Codes 94
Italicizing Your Words 95
Deleting Italic Codes 95
Underlining Your Words 95
Deleting Underline Codes 96
Double Underlining Your Words 96
Deleting Double Underline Codes 96
Underlining Spaces and Tabs 96
Converting Case 97
Using the Date and Time Feature 98
Inserting Date Text 98
Inserting a Date Code 98
Changing the Date Format 99
Using Hyphenation 101
Inserting Soft Hyphens 102

Hyphenation Zone 103
Auto Code Placement 104
The WordPerfect Ruler 104
Setting New Left and Right Margins 105
Deleting and Setting Tabs 107
Deleting Tabs 108
Inserting Tabs 108
Changing Line Spacing 108
Changing Justification 109
Using Reveal Codes 110
Using the Ruler with Fonts 110
Using the Ruler with Styles 110
Using the Ruler with Tables 111
Hiding the Ruler 111
Review Exercises for Chapter 4 112
Before You Go On… 112

CHAPTER 5:
WORKING WITH MULTIPLE PAGE DOCUMENTS 113

What You Will Learn in this Chapter 113
Creating a Two-Page Letter 113
Working with Headers and Footers 114
Creating a Header or Footer 116
Odd and Even Pages 117
Editing a Header or Footer 119
Discontinuing a Header or Footer 119
Suppressing a Header or Footer 120
Using Page Numbering 120
Page Numbering Position 122
Page Numbering Styles 123
New Page Number 124
Accompanying Text 124
Forcing Current Page Number 125
Inserting Page Numbering 125
Discontinuing Page Numbering 126
Suppressing Page Numbering 126
Changing Top and Bottom Margins (Ctrl+F8) 127
Centering Text Between Top and Bottom Margins 127
Hard and Soft Page Breaks 128
Using Conditional End of Page and Block Protect 130
Conditional End of Page 130
Block Protect 130
Widows and Orphans 132
Getting Around in Multiple Page Documents 132
Using Movement Keys 133
Using the Scroll Bar 133
Using Go To 134

Position 135
Last Position 135
Review Exercises for Chapter 5 136
Before You Go On… 136

CHAPTER 6:
ADVANCED EDITING FEATURES 137

What You Will Learn in this Chapter 137
Cutting, Pasting, and Copying Blocks of Text 138
Selecting More than One Window of Text 138
Cutting Text (Shft+Del) 138
Pasting Text (Shft+Ins) 139
Copying Text (Ctrl+Ins) 139
Cutting, Pasting, and Copying a Rectangle 140
Working with Multiple Documents 140
Copying or Moving Text Between Documents 142
Appending to File 142
Using Search (F2) 143
Searching for Text 143
Searching for Codes 144
Using Search and Replace (Ctrl+F2) 145
Draft Mode (Ctrl+Shft+F3) 147
Document Comments 147
Creating Comments 148
Converting Text to Comments 148
Converting Comments to Text 149
Editing a Comment 149
Document Initial Settings (Ctrl+Shft+F9) 149
Using the Help Feature (F1) 151
Index 152
The Command Buttons 152
Index 152
Back 153
Browse 153
Search 153
File 154
Edit 154
Bookmark 155
Help 156
Keyboard 156
How Do I 156
Glossary 157
Using Help 157
What Is 157
About WordPerfect 157
Review Exercises for Chapter 6 158
Before You Go On... 158

CHAPTER 7:
USING THE SPELLER AND THE THESAURUS 159

What You Will Learn in this Chapter 159
Using the Speller (Ctrl+F1) 160
    Manually Editing a Word During Spellcheck 162
    Suggest 163
    Add 163
    Skip Once 163
    Skip Always 163
Looking Up a Word Phonetically 163
Speller Menu Bar Selections 164
    Dictionary 164
    Edit 165
    Options 165
        Words with Numbers 165
        Duplicate Words 165
        Continue 166
        Delete 2nd 166
        Disable Checking Duplicate 166
        Irregular Capitalization 166
        Continue 167
        Replace 167
        Disable Checking Capitalization 167
    Match 167
Using the Thesaurus (Alt+F1) 169
    Looking Up an Existing Document Word in the Thesaurus 169
    Looking Up a Word Before You Type It 170
    How the Thesaurus is Organized 170
    Finding Additional Alternatives 170
The Thesaurus Menu Bar 172
    Dictionary 172
    Edit 172
    History 172
Review Exercises for Chapter 7 173
Before You Go On… 173

CHAPTER 8:
SYSTEM AND DOCUMENT MANAGEMENT 175

What You Will Learn in this Chapter 175
Using File Manager 177
    Using the Navigator and the File Viewer 177
    Creating a Directory (Ctrl+T) 180
    Changing Directories (Ctrl+G) 181
    Deleting Files (Ctrl+D) 182
    Deleting Several Files at Once 183
    Copying a File (Ctrl+C) 183
    Copying Several Files at Once 184

Moving/Renaming a File (Ctrl+R) 185
Moving Several Files At Once 186
Renaming a File Without Moving It 187
Printer Setup in File Manager 188
Printing a File (Ctrl+P) 188
Printing a List of Your Files 189
Running Another Program from File Manager 189
Accessing the Windows Clipboard through File Manager 190
Copying to the Clipboard (Ctrl+Insert) 190
Appending to the Clipboard (Alt+Insert) 191
Using the File Manager Search Feature 191
Searching for a Document Containing a Word 191
Adding a Directory to the Quick List 193
The File Manager View Feature 194
What the Info Windows Tell You 195
The Applications Feature 195
Setting Preferences in File Manager 196
Changing Your Default Directory 197
Saving to Floppy Disks 198
Opening or Retrieving a Document from a Floppy Disk 198
Setting Passwords for Your Documents 198
Deleting a Password 199
Review Exercises for Chapter 8 200
Before You Go On… 200

CHAPTER 9:
OUTLINING, PARAGRAPH NUMBERING,
AND FOOTNOTING **201**
What You Will Learn in this Chapter 201
Defining a Numbering Style 202
Creating and Turning On an Outline (Alt+Shft+5) 203
Turning Outline Off 206
Using Paragraph Numbering (Alt+F5) 206
Footnotes in WordPerfect 208
Setting Footnote Options 208
Creating a Footnote 210
Editing a Footnote 210
Deleting a Footnote 211
Copying or Moving a Footnote 211
Renumbering Footnotes 212
Endnotes 212
Review Exercises for Chapter 9 213
Before You Go On… 213

CHAPTER 10:
CREATING NEWSPAPER AND PARALLEL COLUMNS **215**
What You Will Learn in this Chapter 215

Working with Newspaper Columns 216
    Creating Newspaper Columns 218
Moving from Column to Column 219
Turning Columns Off 220
Working with Parallel Columns 220
    Creating Parallel Columns 221
    Redefining Columns 225
Copying, Deleting, or Moving Column Groups 225
Parallel with Block Protect 225
Using the Ruler with Columns 226
    Defining Columns with the Ruler 226
    Turning Columns On and Off with the Ruler 227
    Adjusting the Column Widths Using the Ruler 227
Review Exercises for Chapter 10 229
Before You Go On... 229

CHAPTER 11:
WORKING WITH TABULAR COLUMNS AND TABLES,
IMPORTING SPREADSHEETS 231

What You Will Learn in this Chapter 231
Setting Up Numeric Columns (Shift+F9) 232
Copying or Moving Text within Tabular Columns 233
    Changing the Value of the Decimal Align Character 234
    Adding Headings to Your Table 235
    Using Dot Leaders 235
Creating Tables (Ctrl+F9) 237
    Formatting the Data in Cells 238
    Changing One Cell in a Column 240
    Setting Lines Per Row and Row Height 241
Naming and Identifying a Cell by Its Position in a Table 243
Adding and Deleting Rows 243
Adding and Deleting Columns 246
Changing the Width of Columns 247
Entering Math Formulas in a Table 248
    Recalculating Totals When You Have Changed a Number 250
Using the Subtotal, Total, and Grand Total Functions 250
Joining Cells 251
Splitting Cells into Rows or Columns 251
Locking and Unlocking Cells 252
    Locking a Cell 253
    Unlocking a Cell 253
    Disabling Cell Locks 253
Using Headers in Tables 254
Controlling Page Breaks in Tables 255
Designing Table Formats 255
Setting Up a Keyboard Merge in a Table 256
Converting Existing Tabular or Parallel Columns into Tables 258

Converting Tables into Text 259
Creating a Table Within a Graphics Box 260
Importing and Linking Spreadsheets 261
    Importing a Spreadsheet 261
    Linking an Imported Spreadsheet 264
    Importing and Linking Simultaneously 265
    Editing a Link 265
    Deleting a Link 266
    Manually Updating Multiple Links 266
    Manually Updating a Single Link 267
    Linking Options 267
    Linking Three-Dimensional Spreadsheets 268
The DDE Link 269
Creating a DDE Link 269
Review Exercises for Chapter 11 271
Before You Go On… 271

CHAPTER 12:
MASS PRODUCING WITH MERGE
AND DOCUMENT ASSEMBLY **273**
What You Will Learn in this Chapter 273
Planning and Creating a Secondary File 274
Creating a Primary Merge File 277
Merging a Primary File with a Secondary File 282
Merging Directly to the Printer 286
Stopping a Merge 287
Preventing Extra Lines when Merging Blank Fields 288
Preventing Extra Spaces when Merging Blank Fields 292
Merging to a List 295
Doing a Keyboard Merge 298
Merging a Primary File with the Keyboard 300
Creating a Boilerplate Document 301
Building a New Document Using Boilerplate Text 302
Review Exercises for Chapter 12 304
Before You Go On… 304

CHAPTER 13:
SORT AND SELECT **305**
What You Will Learn in this Chapter 305
Doing a Line Sort (Ctrl+Shft+F12) 306
Doing a Paragraph Sort (Ctrl+Shft+F12) 309
Doing a Merge Sort (Ctrl+Shft+F12) 312
Doing a Table Sort (Ctrl+Shft+F12) 314
Sorting by Date (Ctrl+Shft+F12) 315
Selecting (Ctrl+Shft+F12) 315
Using Global Select (Ctrl+Shft+F12) 316

Review Exercises for Chapter 13 317
Before You Go On… 317

CHAPTER 14:
WORKING WITH REFERENCE AIDS 319
What You Will Learn in this Chapter 319
What Are Reference Aids? 320
Creating an Index 320
    Creating a Concordance File and Marking Text for an Index 321
    Defining the Index 322
    Generating the Index 324
Creating Lists 324
    Marking Text for Lists 324
    Defining Lists 324
    Generating Lists 325
Creating a Table of Contents 326
    Marking Text for a Table of Contents 326
    Defining the Table of Contents 326
    Generating the Table of Contents 327
Creating a Table of Authorities 328
    Marking Text for a Table of Authorities 328
    Editing the Full Form 329
    Defining a Table of Authorities 330
    Generating a Table of Authorities 331
Editing Reference Aids 332
Cross-Referencing 332
    Marking Text For Cross-Referencing 332
    Marking Reference Only 332
    Marking Target Only 333
    Marking Both Reference and Text 334
    Multiple Targets 334
    Generating Cross-References 334
Document Compare 335
    Removing Markings 336
Using Master Document 336
    Creating a Master Document 337
    Expanding a Master Document 338
    Condensing a Master Document 339
    Saving a Master Document 339
Review Exercises for Chapter 14 340
Before You Go On… 340

CHAPTER 15:
WORKING WITH STYLES 341
What You Will Learn in this Chapter 341
Styles Versus Macros 342
Types of Styles 342

Creating a Paired Style (Alt+F8) 343
Creating an Open Style 345
Turning a Style On 346
Turning a Paired Style Off 346
Editing a Style 346
Changing a Style Type 347
Deleting a Style 348
Creating a Style Library 349
Retrieving a Different Style Library 350
Review Exercises for Chapter 15 350
Before You Go On… 350

CHAPTER 16:
USING PRINTING ENHANCEMENTS 351
What You Will Learn in this Chapter 351
Using the Control Printer Dialog Box 352
Selecting a Paper Size Definition 354
   Adding a Paper Size Definition 356
   Editing a Paper Size Definition 358
   Deleting a Paper Size Definition 359
   Copying a Paper Size Definition 359
Working with Multi-Bin Printers 360
Using Line Numbering (Shift+F9) 362
Using Print Preview (Shift+F5) 364
Using Advance 367
Using WP Characters (Ctrl+W) 368
Using Fonts to Enhance Your Text 369
   Selecting Fonts 370
   Using Font Attributes 371
      Multiple Attributes 371
      Using Redline and Strikeout 372
Selecting Fonts from the Ruler 373
Using the Typesetting Command 375
Changing Line Height 376
Common Printing Problems 378
Review Exercise for Chapter 16 378
Before You Go On… 378

CHAPTER 17:
CREATIVE DOCUMENT PROCESSING WITH GRAPHICS 379
What You Will Learn in this Chapter 379
Appearance Options 380
   Border Style 381
   Border Spacing 382
   Gray Shading 382
   Minimum Offset from Paragraph 382
   Caption Numbering 382

First Level 383
Second Level 383
Style 383
Caption Position 383
Position and Size Options 384
Box Type 384
Anchor To 385
Number of Pages to Skip 385
Wrap Text Around Box 385
Horizontal Position 385
Page 386
Paragraph 386
Character 386
Vertical Position 386
Page 387
Paragraph 387
Character 387
Size 387
Setting Horizontal and Vertical Position and Resizing Graphics with a Mouse 388
Caption Editor 389
New Number 389
Creating a Figure Graphics Box 390
Graphic Images You Can Use with WordPerfect 392
Creating Text Boxes 393
Creating User Boxes 394
Creating Equation Boxes 394
Editing Graphics Boxes 396
Editing Appearance Options 396
Using Graphics Lines 397
Editing a Line 397
Editing a Line with the Mouse 398
Using Line Draw 398
Review Exercises for Chapter 17 400
Before You Go On… 400

CHAPTER 18:
SPEEDING THINGS UP WITH BUTTON BARS AND MACROS 401
What You Will Learn in this Chapter 401
What Are Button Bars? 402
Displaying the Default Button Bar 402
Hiding the Button Bar 404
Creating a New Button Bar 404
Selecting a Button Bar 405
Editing a Button Bar 406
Assigning a Macro to a Button 407
Saving the Button Bar to a New Name 408
Using the Options Feature 408
Category Markers 409

What Are Macros?...411
    A Note to WordPerfect 5.1 Users 411
    Recording Macros (Ctrl+F10) 412
    Pausing While Recording a Macro 414
    Playing Macros (Alt+F10) 414
    Editing a Macro 415
    Programming and Command Language 416
    Using the Mouse with Macros 416
    Converting 5.1 Macros 416
    Assigning Macros to the Macro Menu 417
    Editing a Macro Menu Item 418
    Deleting a Macro Menu Item 419
Review Exercises for Chapter 18 420
Before You Go On... 420

CHAPTER 19:
    USING WORDPERFECT WITH WINDOWS **421**
What You Will Learn in this Chapter 421
A Word About the Program Manager 422
Switching Between Two Open Applications 423
Switching Between More than Two Open Applications 424
Accessing DOS Using the Windows Shell 426
Multitasking in Windows 426
A Word About Memory Problems 427
The Windows Swap File Feature 427
When You Get an Unrecoverable Application Error Message 428
Review Exercises for Chapter 19 429
Congratulations! 429

APPENDIX A:
    INSTALLING AND CONFIGURING
    WORDPERFECT FOR WINDOWS **431**
System Requirements 431
    Hard Disk Requirements 432
    Floppy Disk Requirements 432
    Memory Requirements 432
    Mouse Requirements 433
    Software Requirements 433
Installing WordPerfect for Windows 433
    Basic Installation 434
    Custom 434
    Printers 434
    Cartridges and Soft Fonts 436
        Cartridges 436
        Soft Fonts 436
        Initializing Printer 437

Configuring WordPerfect for Windows 437
    Backup 438
    Date Format 438
    Display 438
    Document Summary 438
    Environment 438
    Equations 439
    Initial Codes 439
    Keyboard 439
    Location of Files 439
    Merge 440
    Print 440
    Table of Authorities 440

APPENDIX B:
   CONVERSION **441**
Converting a File to WordPerfect Format 442
Converting WordPerfect Files to Another Format 443
A Few Words About Converting 444

APPENDIX C:
   INITIAL SETTINGS **447**

APPENDIX D:
   EQUATION PALETTE **451**

APPENDIX E:
   CODES IN REVEAL CODES **457**

INDEX **469**

Introduction

WordPerfect is the most popular word-processing program in the world. Its flexibility and array of features exceed those of all other word-processing packages available today. With WordPerfect for Windows, the WordPerfect Corporation has taken a giant leap forward. Even if you are a seasoned WordPerfect user, you will be thrilled at the exciting new features offered by the program. Beginners will love the fact that it is the most user-friendly version of WordPerfect ever produced. Either way, you are in for an exhilarating experience when you begin to work with this program.

This book is written for beginner and intermediate-level users. Even if you are a complete novice on computers, you will be able to master the program comfortably and painlessly. The approach used in the book reflects the hundreds of hours of training we have done in WordPerfect. We have anticipated the most common questions and problems, and have presented the material in a logical, easy-to-master format. The book starts with the basics and gradually builds up to the more complex features.

Readers who are familiar with another version of WordPerfect will be able to use this book to learn the new features and become comfortable with the new graphical, mouse-based environment of WordPerfect for Windows.

A Word About Mice

You can operate WordPerfect for Windows without a mouse, but the program really is designed to be used with a rodent. If, like many people, you have an aversion to rodents, this may be a problem. We strongly suggest that you force yourself to use the mouse as much as possible in the beginning. Eventually, you will find it faster and easier than the keyboard.

Exciting New Features in WordPerfect for Windows

Graphics

For the first time ever, WordPerfect users can view graphics and fonts right on the screen. You can use your mouse to move and size graphics without having to go into the graphics menus.

Character Sets

Previously, you either had to have a phenomenal memory or a list of character sets handy to access characters like paragraph and section signs. But the old days are gone. Now, with the click of your mouse, you can view and select any character you want right on the screen.

Button Bars

Button bars made us flip! You can set up a button bar to do just about anything WordPerfect can do. You can even set up button bars to do macros. All you have to do is click on the button, and the commands are executed. Button bars can make it possible for you to never use your menus again.

Ruler

You can set and change all of your tabs without ever having to go into Format. You can even realign columns while you are in the document, by dragging the column margins in your ruler.

Convert

You can now convert documents right in WordPerfect when you retrieve or save them.

How this Book is Organized

This book is organized into two parts. Chapters 1 through 7 cover the basics. You will learn basic information about your computer and how it interacts with WordPerfect for Windows. You will create several documents and learn how to use basic editing and formatting features like margins, tabs, copying, deleting and moving text, indents, line spacing, justification, headers and footers, page numbering, page breaks, and hyphenation. You will learn how to save, retrieve, and print files. You will begin using simple print enhancements like bold, italics, and underline. Special features like Reveal Codes, Speller, and Thesaurus will be covered.

Chapters 8 through 9 cover system and document management and complex document formatting. You will learn advanced formatting features like columns, tables, and graphics, and how to use advanced word processing features like print enhancements, multiple document processing, merge, sort and select, styles, reference aids, macros, button bars, and spreadsheets. You will learn how to manage your system using the File Manager. A special section on Windows features will help you learn how to work with several windows, switch between applications, and use the Windows Program Manager.

Each chapter begins with a list of what you will learn in the chapter. At the end of the chapter are review exercises to reinforce what you have learned. Following the review exercises is a "Before You Go On…" section, which details all features you should know before you move on to the next chapter.

Additional Information

Key combinations on the PC keyboard are indicated with a plus sign (+). For example, "Alt+F10" means that you should hold down the Alt key while pressing the F10 function key.

Throughout the book there will be sections that require special attention. The following icons will be used to mark these sections:

 Indicates that you should take note of the information. This symbol may indicate a helpful hint or a special condition.

 Indicates that you can perform an action more quickly by using shortcut keys or by following the suggestion in the text.

 Indicates cautionary information or warnings. This symbol often provides a warning that you may lose data if you perform an action incorrectly.

 Indicates a serious warning. Data may be lost or the system may hang-up or crash. A misuse of these functions may seriously jeopardize your data, disk, or system operation.

Indicates a particularly useful feature or usage. This is also used to indicate an exceptional suggestion for a procedure or process.

Chapter 1

Getting Started

What You Will Learn in this Chapter

- ◆ How to identify parts of the computer
- ◆ How the basic parts of the computer interface
- ◆ Why DOS is necessary
- ◆ Some facts about Windows
- ◆ How to start WordPerfect for Windows
- ◆ How to identify parts of the window
- ◆ How to work with menus
- ◆ How to use a mouse
- ◆ How to use a template

An Introduction to Your System

If you have never worked with a computer before, you might find your first experience somewhat intimidating. We hope this section will put your mind at ease and answer your most important questions.

A computer system consists of two basic elements: **hardware** and **software**. The hardware consists of the physical components of the system, which break down and decode instructions. The software consists of the programs, which transmit instructions to the computer. There are many different software programs available for your computer. WordPerfect is an example of a software program.

The **Disk Operating System** (DOS) is a software program that acts as a link between the hardware and the software. In a sense, it is the brain of the computer, and is responsible for translating software instructions into language that will be understood by the hardware. DOS is explained in more detail later in this chapter.

Let's Talk About Hardware and Software

It helps if you can identify all of the basic parts on your computer, as shown in Figure 1.1, and understand what they do.

Figure 1.1—A typical PC.

Let's start with the big box, otherwise known as the **chassis**. The chassis contains most of the parts necessary to make the computer work. If you open it up, as shown in Figure 1.2, you will see several **boards,** or cards with futuristic-looking paraphernalia called **chips** and **circuits**.

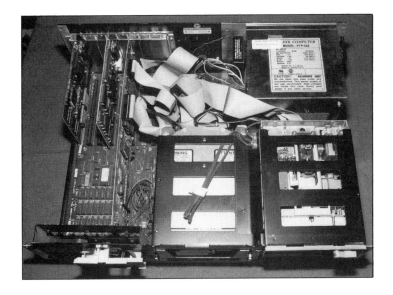

Figure 1.2—The inside of a typical PC.

These are plugged into a master board appropriately called the **motherboard**. Also on the motherboard is the CPU, or **central processing unit**, chip. This is the most important chip in the computer. The CPU controls the operation of the computer, and is the part of the computer that performs logical operations and decodes and executes instructions. The circuitry on this chip also determines, to a large extent, the speed of your computer.

You will also see a bunch of cables that look more like wide ribbons and twisted pair wire. These connect the battery, floppy disk drive(s), hard drive, power pack, and other **peripherals** to the motherboard, either directly or through another board. These basic parts are essential to the operation of your computer, but they operate behind the scenes, and it is rarely necessary for the user to have to deal directly with them.

Also in the chassis are your **hard drive** and **floppy disk drive(s)**.

These parts are of more interest because you must interface directly with them. The hard drive is really a large, high capacity storage device that is used to store software and data. It is sometimes called a **fixed disk** because, unlike floppy disks, it is permanently fixed inside the chassis of your computer. The hard drive has many advantages over floppy disks. The most obvious advantage is that it can hold much more data. Also, it is not as subject to damage as a floppy disk. Hard drives come in many sizes, but most hold anywhere from 20 megabytes (20 million characters) to several hundred megabytes. On a really large system, you might have a hard drive that can store hundreds of gigabytes (billions of characters). Like any large area of space, hard drives must be organized to work efficiently. Chapter 8, *System and Document Management*, explains how to organize your hard drive into directories for better management.

On one or more of the boards inside the chassis are chips known as **RAM chips**. These chips determine how much information can be held at a time in a temporary buffer called **Random Access Memory** (RAM). Usually, when you execute a program (such as WordPerfect), all of the instructions necessary to operate the program are loaded into RAM, as well as the data you are creating while using the program (such as documents). If you have enough RAM, you can operate more than one program at a time. Programs like Windows create a shell, allowing the user to execute more than one program at a time and then switch back and forth between them. Or, you could have a program running in background (such as indexing on a database) while concurrently operating another program, such as WordPerfect, in the foreground. This is known as **multitasking**. The key elements in this type of operation are speed and RAM. If you are using WordPerfect for Windows, you should have at least 2 megabytes (2 million bytes) of RAM in your computer. This allows enough space to accommodate DOS, Windows, and WordPerfect, all of which are in use at the same time in WordPerfect for Windows. Additional RAM can be added to a computer by purchasing more RAM chips or, in some cases, a RAM board (refer to your computer manual for information on how to add RAM to your computer). The more programs you plan to operate concurrently, the more RAM you will need.

Information loaded into RAM is temporary. When you exit a

program, all information relating to that program is deleted from RAM. When you reboot or turn off the computer, all information in RAM is deleted. Any information that has not been stored to the hard drive is lost.

Floppy drives are accessible to the user from outside of the chassis. They are the small slots into which you insert your floppy disks. **Floppy disks** are storage devices used to hold software and data. They hold much less data than a hard drive. There are two sizes of floppy disks, as shown in Figure 1.3, that are used with most computer systems: 3.5" and 5.25".

Figure 1.3—3.5" (left) and 5.25" (right) floppy disks

The larger 5.25" floppy disks are available in two densities: **high-density** (or quad-density) and **low-density** (or double-density). High-density 5.25" floppy disks hold approximately 1.2 megabytes (or 1.2 million bytes) of information. Double-density 5.25" disks hold approximately 360 kilobytes (360,000 bytes) of information. If you have a 5.25" floppy disk drive on your computer, and your system is a 286 or higher, you probably have a high-density disk drive.

You may have a 3.5" disk drive on your computer; 3.5" disks also come in high-density and low-density. A 3.5" high-density floppy disk holds approximately 1.4 megabytes (1.4 million bytes) of information. A 3.5" low-density floppy disk holds approximately 720 kilobytes (720,000 bytes) of information.

Floppy disks must be **formatted** before they can be used. The process of formatting initializes the floppy disk so that it will be recognized by DOS. Different versions of DOS require different procedures to format floppy disks. Refer to your DOS manual for the correct instructions for your system.

When you turn your computer on, several lights appear on the front of the chassis. One of these lights is attached to the power pack, and indicates that power is being received by the computer. Another light is attached to the hard drive, and indicates that the hard drive is receiving power from, and is recognized by, the system. The remaining lights are attached to the floppy disk drive(s), and indicate that they are receiving power from, and are recognized by, the system.

Another peripheral that is attached to the computer by a cable is the **monitor**. This is sometimes called the **CRT**, which means Cathode Ray Tube. This is a scientific term that indicates how patterns are actually formed on the monitor. Although there are other types of monitors, the term CRT has become so widespread that it is frequently (although incorrectly) used to describe all monitors.

Monitors come in many different sizes, and can be either monochromatic, monochromatic with gray tone, or color. The clarity, or resolution, of the monitor depends on the type of monitor you are using and the video interface card it is plugged into. If you are using a color monitor, you will be able to configure your software to reflect your personal color preferences (within the color limitations of your monitor). Some monitors have knobs that allow the user to adjust light and contrast, as well as horizontal and vertical position and size. Refer to your manual for information on how your monitor works.

Keyboards are plugged into the chassis and are used to transmit text and instructions to the computer. Two basic styles of keyboards are used with IBM or IBM-compatible computers; standard and enhanced. The standard keyboard usually has 88 keys and contains 10 function keys, which are located on the left side of the keyboard. The enhanced keyboard usually has 101 keys with 12 function keys, which are located across the top of the keyboard. The type of keyboard you use is a matter of personal preference.

The **mouse** is another kind of input device that is rapidly gaining popularity, and is desirable for working in the Windows environment.

Unlike the keyboard, where you "key" or type in instructions, the mouse is a pointing device. You point to an instruction or **icon** (picture) on the screen, and then click a button on the mouse to execute the command or activate the icon. Some mice have two buttons and some have three that perform various functions. As with the different types of keyboards, the number of buttons on the mouse is a matter of personal preference.

You probably also have a **printer** plugged into your computer. The printer is an output device that is used to print text and graphics sent to it from the computer. Instructions are transmitted from the computer to the printer through parts of programs called **printer drivers**. Most software programs come with their own printer drivers, and allow you to configure the software to communicate with your particular printer. Appendix A, *Installing and Configuring WordPerfect,* explains how to configure WordPerfect for your printer. There are many different printers available, from inexpensive dot matrix printers to the most expensive laser printers. The type of printer you choose will depend upon your needs and budget.

You should refer to the manuals that came with your computer and printer for information on maintenance and use. If you take good care of your equipment and use it properly, you will avoid expensive repairs.

A Few Words About Your Disk Operating System (DOS)

When you purchased your system, you probably also purchased a software program called DOS. DOS is essential to the operation of your computer. It is the bridge between your hardware and other software programs. DOS is available in different versions and for different hardware systems. For example, this book is written for users with an IBM or IBM-compatible system, so your computer has IBM or Microsoft DOS. Users with an Apple system would have a different type of disk operating system. Software that is written for your computer is also written to interface with your DOS. When you purchase a software program, check to be sure it is compatible with the version and type of DOS you are using.

Different versions of DOS (such as DOS 3.x, 4.x, or 5.x) have slightly different command languages and may interface a little differently with other software. If DOS has been properly installed on your system, this should be no problem.

DOS is not a user-friendly program, which makes it difficult for beginners to use. With most versions of DOS, the command language must be memorized and typed in at the DOS prompt. Since DOS is essential to the operation of your computer, a certain amount of user interface cannot be avoided. Windows does away with this problem by providing a user-friendly interface between you and DOS. You use the mouse and keyboard to tell Windows what to do, and it communicates your instructions to DOS.

A Few Words About Windows

Windows 3.0 is a program developed by Microsoft, Inc. that makes your computer much easier to operate. In addition to providing an easy way to perform DOS functions (such as formatting a floppy disk or copying files), it also provides a shell that allows you to run more than one program at a time and switch easily between programs. Accessing programs, or **applications** (another word for software programs), is much easier in Windows. Because it is a highly visual program, beginners find it easier to use. People who are intimidated by computers are delighted to find that tasks can be accomplished by simply clicking a mouse on an icon. Experienced computer users will find many uses for the advanced features offered by Windows. On all levels, it is a program for all users.

Windows got its name because it runs programs in separate windows. You can switch back and forth between full screen windows, or you can reduce the windows and view different programs on one screen.

While working in Windows, think of the entire screen as your desktop. Each window on the screen or desktop represents a different project or task. You can switch back and forth between windows or tasks just as you would while working at your desk. If you think of Windows in these terms you will have a better understanding of what is happening on your screen.

While Windows can run both non-Windows and Windows programs, there is no question that programs designed to run under Windows best utilize its advantages. Also, because they have similar screens and commands to Windows, they are easier to learn for people who already know Windows. WordPerfect for Windows is a program designed to be used with Windows.

It is important to note that, while Windows can do away with the necessity for the user to interface directly with DOS, it does not replace DOS. Even if you have Windows on your computer, you must still install DOS.

Installing WordPerfect and Windows

WordPerfect for Windows is designed to be used with Windows. Therefore, Windows should be installed before you install WordPerfect for Windows. Refer to your Windows manual for instructions on how to install Windows. Instructions for the installation of WordPerfect for Windows can be found in Appendix A at the end of this book.

Starting the Program from Windows

Once you have properly installed Windows and WordPerfect for Windows, you are ready to begin operating the program. To start WordPerfect:

1. Start Windows following the instructions in your Windows manual. You should be in the Windows Program Manager.
2. Once inside Windows, look at the bottom of the screen for the WordPerfect Group icon, as shown in Figure 1.4. Double-click (click twice quickly with the left mouse button) to access the WordPerfect program group, as shown in Figure 1.5.

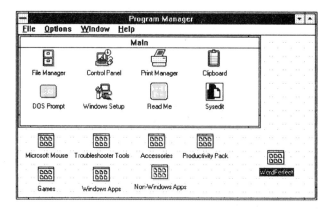

Figure 1.4—The Windows Program Manager with the WordPerfect Group icon selected.

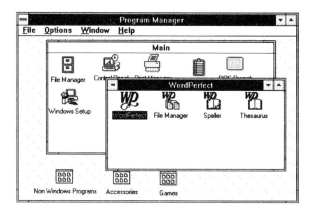

Figure 1.5—The WordPerfect program group.

3. Double-click on the WordPerfect Program icon. It may take a minute or so to execute the program (a small hour glass should appear on the screen, indicating that Windows is executing a command). The WordPerfect Document window is now on the screen, as shown in Figure 1.6.

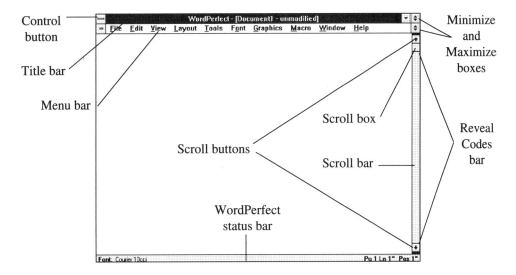

Figure 1.6—The WordPerfect document window.

4. The first time you start WordPerfect you will be asked to supply your license number. This is found on the Certificate of License Registration card that came with the program. Type in the number and click once on OK with the left mouse button.

If the WordPerfect Group icon does not appear on the screen while you are in the Windows Program Manager, it means that the WordPerfect program group is already on the screen. If you have more then one program group on the screen, you may not see the WordPerfect program group because it might be hidden behind another program group. To bring it to the forefront:

1. While in the Windows Program Manager, click once on the Window menu name in the menu bar. A list of program groups appears, as shown in Figure 1.7.

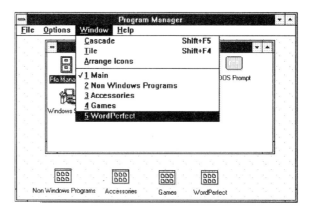

Figure 1.7—The Windows Program Manager window menu.

2. Click once on WordPerfect. The WordPerfect program group is now clearly visible on the screen (see Figure 1.5).
3. Double-click on the WordPerfect Program icon to open the WordPerfect Document window (see Figure 1.6).

If you are not familiar with Windows you should take some time to learn the various parts of the window. Figure 1.6 labels the basic parts of the WordPerfect Document window.

The Title Bar

The title bar appears at the top of each window, and contains the name of the program or application you are running in that window. Note that the title bar in WordPerfect also indicates the document and status: "Document1 - unmodified." The title bar also serves another purpose; when more than one window is displayed, Windows uses it to indicate which one is **active**. It does this by changing the color (or intensity, on monochrome monitors) of the active window.

The Menu Bar

The menu bar appears right under the title bar. The menu bar contains a row of words called **menu names**. There are two ways to open a menu. The best way is to just click once on the menu name with the left mouse button. You can also open a menu by pressing the

Alt key plus the underlined character in the word. For example, the File menu can be opened by typing Alt+F.

When you open a menu in a menu bar, a new menu appears. For example, if you click on File, the menu in Figure 1.8 appears.

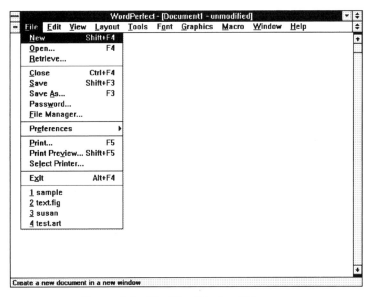

Figure 1.8—The WordPerfect File menu.

The new menu contains menu commands. There are three ways to select a menu command:

- Click on the menu command name; or
- Type the underlined letter in the menu command name; or
- Use the up arrow (↑) and down arrow (↓) keys to highlight the menu command, then press Enter.

Some of these commands (such as New or Close) perform functions immediately. Other commands appear with certain menu indicators that have special meanings.

Dimmed Menu Items

When a menu item is dimmed, the choice is not currently available. This usually occurs because there is no logical use for the menu item at that particular time. For example, if there is no text in the window, certain edit features (like Cut, Copy, and Paste) will be dimmed.

Ellipses

Menu items followed by an ellipsis (…) open a dialog box. A dialog box requests that the user provide additional information. Dialog boxes are explained in greater detail below.

Triangular Arrows

A menu item followed by an arrow (➤) opens a cascading menu. A cascading menu appears to the right of the previous menu item. You make a choice from the cascading menu the same way as with other menus. See Figure 1.9 for an example of a cascading menu.

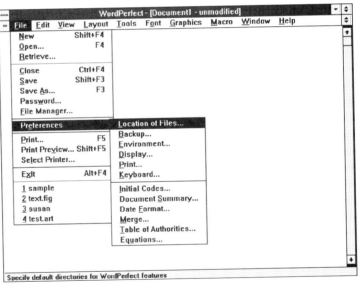

Figure 1.9—The Preferences cascading menu.

Checkmarks

A menu item preceded by a checkmark (✓) indicates the item is a toggle that is currently activated. A toggle item is one that is turned on or off each time you select it. It works like a light switch. If you select an item that currently has a checkmark, the item will be deactivated. To reactivate the item, select it again.

Shortcut Keys

Some menu commands are followed by shortcut keys in parentheses. These are keystrokes that can be used to choose the menu command instead of using the mouse. For example, in Figure 1.8, the menu command New is followed by the shortcut key Shift+F4. For convenience, throughout this book all shortcut keys will be listed in parentheses the first time the corresponding menu command is presented.

Dialog Boxes

As explained above, a menu command followed by an ellipsis (…) opens a dialog box. A dialog box appears in the window when WordPerfect requires information from you to complete the command (hence the name "dialog"). You may be requested to supply a name or make choices from a list. Some dialog boxes contain subboxes or submenus. In Figure 1.8, you will notice that the menu command Open is followed by an ellipsis. If you choose this command, the dialog box shown in Figure 1.10 will appear.

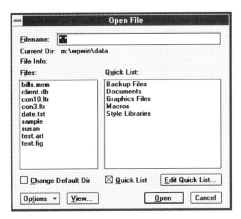

Figure 1.10—The Open File dialog box.

Most dialog boxes have more than one section. There are three ways you can move between the sections:

- Click on the section; or
- Use the Alt key plus the underlined letter to access the section; or
- Use the Tab key to move between sections.

There are six basic sections found in a dialog box: text box, check box, Option button, Command button, list box, and drop-down or pop-up list box. Not all sections are found in all dialog boxes. Information is supplied differently in the different sections.

Text Box

In a text box (for instance, next to "Filename" in Figure 1.10), you are asked to type in the required information. Usually when you open a dialog box, there is text already typed in the text box. If the text is correct, leave it as it is and go on to the next section. If the text is incorrect, click on the section or backspace to delete the old text. Then just type in the new text.

Check Box

A check box is a square that has an X marked in it when it is selected. These are used to allow you to select more than one option. For example, in Figure 1.10 you might want to change the default directory and/or view the quick list. To select a check box, click on the square. An X will appear. To deselect a check box, click on the box again. The X will disappear.

Option Buttons

Option buttons work differently than check boxes in that you can select only one option at a time. For example, in Figure 1.11 you may select only one print option. You select an option by clicking on the desired button, or circle, which will fill the circle. Only one button can be filled at a time. If you click on another button, the other option buttons will be automatically deselected.

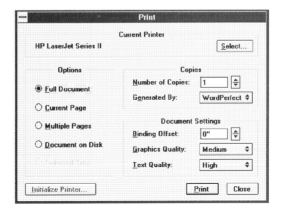

Figure 1.11—The Print dialog box.

Command Buttons

Command buttons are commands found inside rectangular boxes. Clicking on a Command button executes the command immediately. The most common Command buttons are Cancel and OK. If a Command button is followed by an ellipsis (see the Edit Quick List command in Figure 1.10), clicking on this command will open a new dialog box.

List Boxes

List boxes display lists of items you can choose from. For example, Figure 1.10 contains a list box with a list of files. To make a selection, click on the item in the list. If you are using the keyboard, use the arrow keys to highlight the item and press Enter to select it. If the list is too long to fit in the list box, use the scroll bar on the right-hand side of the list to see all the selections (scroll bars are explained below).

Drop-Down List Boxes

Drop-down or pop-up list boxes contain a small arrow to the right of the option (see the Options box in Figure 1.10, or Preferences in Figure 1.8). By clicking on the arrow you open a new list. You can select an item on the new list by clicking on it. Drop-down boxes are used when there are too many items to fit in the dialog box.

Scroll Bars, Scroll Buttons, and Scroll Boxes

Scroll bars, scroll buttons, and scroll boxes allow you to scroll up and down in windows. Use them to see information that cannot fit into the window. Figure 1.6 illustrates the location of scroll bars, scroll buttons, and scroll boxes. If you click on the scroll button with the up arrow (at the top of the scroll bar), the text will move down in the window, allowing you to view text further up in the document. If you click on the scroll button with the down arrow (at the bottom of the scroll bar), the text will move up in the window, allowing you to view text further down in the document.

The scroll box is the little empty box in the scroll bar. By moving this box up and down you can move your text up and down in the window. To move the scroll box, drag it up or down with the mouse. Notice that as you scroll with the scroll buttons, the scroll box automatically moves up and down as the text moves.

We will learn more about scrolling when we get to Chapter 5, *Working with Multiple Page Documents.*

Minimize and Maximize Boxes and Control Boxes

Your window also contains boxes that allow you to change the size of your window. These boxes will be covered in Chapter 6, *Advanced Editing Features*, and Chapter 19, *Using Windows with WordPerfect.*

The Mouse

A mouse is an input device, just as a keyboard is an input device. You use the mouse to send instructions to the computer. WordPerfect for Windows is designed to be used with a mouse. If you have never used a mouse before, it may take some getting used to, but it is well worth the effort. Using a mouse will allow you to operate WordPerfect for Windows at maximum efficiency.

Mice have either two or three buttons. As with different types of keyboards, the choice of which style mouse you use is a matter of personal preference. In WordPerfect for Windows we will be focusing primarily on the left button to perform the functions that follow.

Drag

You drag the mouse to select blocks of text or program commands. To drag with a mouse, bring the pointer (sort of a mouse cursor) to where you want to begin selecting or blocking information. Then press down, or **click**, on the left button and, while keeping the button down, drag the mouse in the direction you need to move to select or block the text or command. When you release the button, the text or command will remain highlighted.

Click

You click with the mouse to select an item or bring the pointer to a new location (called the **insertion point**). The instruction to click means that you click only once with the left button.

Double-click

An instruction to double-click means that you click the left button very quickly twice. If there is too much time in between clicks, WordPerfect will interpret it as two individual clicks.

Triple-click

An instruction to triple-click means that you click the left button very quickly three times.

Quadruple-click

An instruction to quadruple-click means that you click the left button very quickly four times.

Keep in mind that a mouse is primarily a pointing device. You use it to point to a particular location in the window, and then click to send an instruction to WordPerfect or drag to select text or an instruction.

The Template and Keyboard Layout

WordPerfect is shipped with a plastic **template** that contains all of the keyboard designations for both the CUA and WordPerfect 5.1 keyboard layouts.

The system defaults to the **CUA** (Common User Access) keyboard. The CUA keyboard layout closely matches the keyboard designations for Windows. Users familiar with Windows find it very easy to adapt to the CUA keyboard.

WordPerfect can also be set for the WP 5.1-compatible keyboard layout. This keyboard layout closely resembles the layout for WordPerfect 5.1.

Even if you are familiar with the WordPerfect 5.1 keyboard layout, we suggest that you use the CUA keyboard. Because WordPerfect for Windows is designed to be used with Windows, and because the screens and functions are patterned to work as closely as possible to the corresponding Windows functions, it is advisable to learn the Windows-related keystrokes.

When you installed WordPerfect for Windows, you were asked if you wanted to use the CUA keyboard. If you change your mind later you can change the keyboard designation (see Appendix A).

How to Use the Template

If you look at the template you will see that one side contains the layout for the CUA keyboard and the other side contains the layout for the WP 5.1-compatible keyboard.

Each function key has several functions listed in different colors, which indicate which key combinations to use with the function key. After the F4 key and the F8 key is a thin strip with the color codes. These codes line up horizontally with the corresponding functions. Use the following key combinations with the following colors:

Color	Key Combination
Black	Function key by itself
Green	Shift+function key
Blue	Alt+function key; or
Blue	Alt+Shift+function key
Red	Ctrl+function key; or
Red	Ctrl+Shift+function key

For example, on the CUA template, Select is F8. On the WP 5.1-compatible template, Select is Alt+F4.

Each template has Quick Keys on the left side. For example, on the CUA template, Ctrl+C is a Cut key.

Exiting the Program

To exit from WordPerfect for Windows:

1. Click on File.
2. Click on Exit. You have exited WordPerfect for Windows and are back in Windows.

Review Exercises for Chapter One

◆ Identify the parts of your computer.
◆ Start WordPerfect for Windows.
◆ Identify the parts of the window.
◆ Open the File menu. Identify the different indicators in the menu commands.
◆ Open a dialog box. Identify the parts.
◆ Practice dragging and clicking with the mouse.
◆ Use the template to open the Print dialog box. Click on the Cancel Command box to cancel the menu.
◆ Exit from WordPerfect for Windows.

Before You Go On...

Before you continue on to the next chapter, you should be able to start WordPerfect for Windows and exit from the program. You should be able to identify the basic parts of the window and the parts of a dialog box. You should know how to use a mouse and the template.

Chapter 2

Creating and Editing a Simple Document

What You Will Learn in this Chapter

- ◆ How to type a simple document
- ◆ How to scroll through the document
- ◆ How to add and delete text
- ◆ How to use Insert and Typeover modes
- ◆ How to use Select to delete text
- ◆ How to use Undelete to recover deleted material
- ◆ How to use Undo
- ◆ How to use Reveal Codes

Typing a Document

Now that you are comfortable with the Windows environment, you are ready to type a simple document and learn some basic editing features. Before you start typing, there are a few things you should know about WordPerfect for Windows and your document window.

If you have never used WordPerfect before, you will find that one of the advantages of using a word processing program instead of a typewriter is that you can see the text in the window as you work. This makes editing much easier. You can add, delete, and move text around at will without having to retype or erase it.

Another nice feature in WordPerfect is **wordwrap**. On a typewriter you must listen for a bell and then return the carriage to begin a new line. Wordwrap automatically wraps the text to a new line when you reach what is known as the **hot zone**. WordPerfect makes the decision on where to wrap based on the **font** (typeface) you are using, and the left and right margin settings. We are working with the default margins of 1" for the left margin and 1" for the right margin. The font you are using is the one that was set as the default during the installation process. (**Default** is the setting that the system automatically defaults to when you start up WordPerfect. Appendix A gives instructions on how to change the default settings in WordPerfect.)

If you have worked with previous versions of WordPerfect, you will notice some exciting display differences in WordPerfect for Windows. In previous versions, WordPerfect used a **text display**. The standard monitor has 80 columns and 25 rows. In a text display, the maximum number of lines and columns that fit on the screen is controlled by the number of columns and rows available on the monitor. This could be a problem if you used a font that fit more than 80 characters to a line (for example, most proportional fonts in a point size of 12 or less). If the text did not fit in 80 columns, it scrolled to the right of the screen, making it impossible to see all of the text at one time. Many users found this problem disconcerting. With WordPerfect for Windows, you do not have this problem. You will get an exact line-by-line display, no matter what type size or font you use. For those of you who went crazy trying to work in a small typeface or trying to see what you were doing while working in many columns, this is great news. (The number of lines that will fit in a window still depends on the font you use; the smaller the font, the more lines that will appear in the window.)

Another nice feature of WordPerfect for Windows is that you can see the differences in typeface on the window. For example, if you decide to italicize a word for emphasis, you will actually see the word italicized in the window as you type. (This might be limited by your hardware; if your video card and/or monitor are not sophisticated enough, they might not support this feature.)

Typing in a window is quite different from typing directly to a screen. It is a whole new visual experience. However, once you get used to the differences, you will really appreciate the visual sophistication and polish of WordPerfect for Windows. Going back to a regular typing screen from a window seems like switching from a modern sports car to a Model T.

Now that you are prepared for some of the immediate display differences in WordPerfect for Windows, let's type a simple three-paragraph document.

1. Turn on your computer and printer and access Windows.

2. Double-click the WordPerfect group icon to open the WordPerfect program group, as shown in Figure 2.1. (See the section in Chapter 1 entitled "Starting the Program from Windows" for more detailed information on icon groups.)

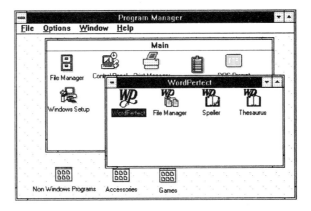

Figure 2.1—The WordPerfect program group.

3. Double-click the WordPerfect program icon. You are now in the WordPerfect-Document1 window, as shown in Figure 2.2.

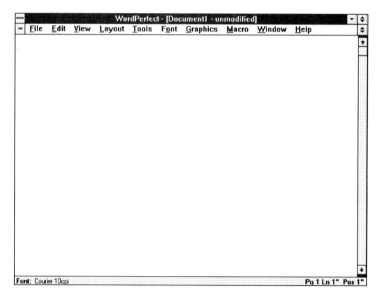

Figure 2.2—The WordPerfect document window.

4. You may start typing immediately. You will notice as you type that the text wraps automatically at the end of the line. Press enter twice at the end of each paragraph to start a new paragraph. If you make a mistake while typing, just backspace to erase it. Type the following text:

```
[TAB]In the year 1787 a convention met in
Philadelphia to revise the Articles of
Confederation. From May 25 to September
17, 55 men hammered out compromises that
would achieve a double objective: a
working government that would also be
acceptable to enough states to guarantee
ratification.[Enter][Enter]

[TAB]For almost four months, the most
talented statesmen in history labored to
form a government that would preserve and
enhance the independence so dearly won.
They set down the objectives of this
government in a famous statement known as
the Preamble to the Constitution of the
United States of America. It reads as
follows:[Enter][Enter]
```

[TAB]"We the people of the United States, in Order to form a more perfect Union, establish Justice, insure domestic Tranquility, provide for the common defense, promote the general Welfare, and secure the Blessings of Liberty to ourselves and our Posterity, do ordain and establish this CONSTITUTION for the United States of America."

Your window should now look like Figure 2.3.

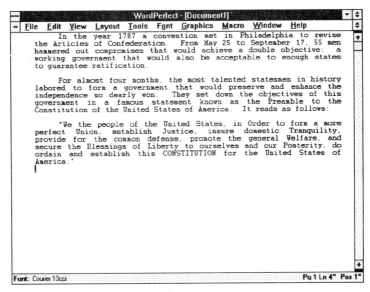

Figure 2.3—The WordPerfect document window with sample text.

Let's take a look at the window and review how to read the prompts provided by WordPerfect for Windows. Chapter 1, *Getting Started*, provides an in-depth explanation of all parts of the window. In this chapter, we will review only the portions of the window necessary to understand the applications currently being covered.

At the top of the Window is the **title bar**. This bar tells us the program we are working in (WordPerfect) and the document name (Document1). Remember: it is possible while working in WordPerfect for Windows to switch back and forth between applications (See Chapter 19, *Using WordPerfect with Windows*) and to work with more than one document at a time (see Chapter 6, *Advanced Editing*

Features). It is important to know which application you are working in and which document is in the active window—that is, the window you are currently working in. Note that the document still does not have a name—it is being referred to as Document1. When we name the document, Document1 will be replaced by the document name.

Right under the title bar is the **menu bar**. The menu bar contains the menus we will use to command WordPerfect to perform various tasks. To use the menu bar, click on the menu item to open it, then click on a menu command to select whichever function you want WordPerfect to perform. (See Chapter 1 for information on using keyboard commands to access the menu bar). Don't open any menus just yet; we will use them a little later in this chapter.

At the bottom of the window is the **status bar**, which provides you with information about the status of your document. Note the current status of the document. At the left-hand side of the status bar, the current font is displayed. In Figure 2.3, this is Courier 10cpi. This display will change to provide a brief explanation of selected menu commands or to reflect other changes in status. For example, press the Insert key on your keyboard. Notice that the prompt has now changed to Typeover. Press the Insert key again. The prompt has now changed back to reflect the current font.

At the right-hand side of the status bar is a display of the current position of the insertion point in the document. If you are at the very beginning of the text, and your left margin is set for 1" and your top margin is set for 1" (the system default), the display should read Pg 1 Ln 1" Pos 1". This status will change as you move the insertion point. For example, using your down arrow on the keyboard, move the insertion point down to the next line. Note that the Ln # has now changed. If you use your Right Arrow key to move the insertion point two spaces to the right, you will notice that the Pos # will change.

If you have never used WordPerfect before, you might be a little confused by the fact that your Ln # and Pos # are measured in inches and not in lines and spaces. The Ln # measures the position of the insertion point from the top edge of the page. The Pos # measures the insertion point from the left edge of the page. Therefore, if the Ln # is 1.78", it means that the insertion point is 1.78" from the top edge of the page. If the Pos # is 5.28", it means the insertion point is 5.28" from the left edge of the page.

In a sophisticated word processing package like WordPerfect, lines and spaces as they apply on a typewriter have no meaning. This is because WordPerfect assumes that you will be working with proportional as well as fixed fonts. When you work with proportional fonts, each character uses a different amount of space, depending upon the character itself (for example, a "w" might take up more space than an "i"); the typeface, or font, being used; and the point size. Since characters produced with proportional fonts cannot be measured in whole spaces or whole lines, the Ln # and Pos # will vary based on several conditions.

The Pos indicator also serves another purpose. If you press your CapsLock key, you will notice that it becomes all uppercase (POS). This is a handy way in which you can tell immediately if you are working in uppercase mode. If you press CapsLock again to return to lowercase mode, POS will return to Pos.

Scrolling Through the Document

The easiest way to move around in your document is to use the mouse. To get to a location in the text, simply point to the desired location and click once with the left button. For example, point the mouse immediately to the left of the "F" in the first word of the second paragraph. Now click once. Your insertion point is now right before the word "For." Practice locating different sections of the text with the mouse.

You can also use the mouse to scroll through documents that are too long to fit in the window (see Chapter 5, *Working with Multiple Page Documents*, for information on how to use the scroll bar), but for very long documents you might find it faster to get around in the text by using the movement keys on the right side of the keyboard. The following movement keys are available with the CUA keyboard (other keystrokes not related to movement are covered in other parts of this book; a list of all keystrokes can be found in the fold-out command card in this book):

Keystroke	Result
↑	Moves up one line
↓	Moves down one line
→	Moves one character to the right
←	Moves one character to the left
Ctrl + →	Moves one word to the right
Ctrl + ←	Moves one word to the left
End	Moves to end of the line
Home	Moves to beginning of the line
Ctrl + ↑	Moves to beginning of the previous paragraph
Ctrl + ↓	Moves to beginning of the next paragraph
Ctrl + Home	Moves to beginning of the document
Ctrl + End	Moves to end of the document
PgUp	Moves to beginning of the window
PgDn	Moves to end of the window
Alt + PgUp	Moves to first line of the previous page
Alt + PgDn	Moves to first line of the next page

Practice using the movement keys to move around in the document. If you have problems using combination keystrokes (such as Ctrl+Home or Alt+PgUp), keep working at it. The best way to press combination keystrokes is to press down the first key (such as Ctrl) and continue to hold it down while you press down the second key (such as Home). Then quickly release both keys.

On an enhanced keyboard, be sure the Num Lock is turned off if you plan to use the numeric keys as movement keys.

Adding and Deleting Text

A major advantage of using a word processing program rather than a typewriter is that you can edit the text without having to retype the entire document. In this section we are going to learn the most basic of all editing features: adding and deleting text.

Adding and Deleting Characters

The simplest form of editing is adding or deleting single characters. To add a character, put the insertion point one space to the right of where you want to add the character and type in the new character.

To delete a character, put the insertion point one space to the left of the character you want to delete and press the Del key.

To Add a Character

1. Using either the mouse or the movement keys, place the insertion point to the right of the letter "a" in the word "labored" in the second paragraph, second line.
2. Type an "s." The word now reads "lasbored." Notice that the new character appears to the left of the insertion point.

Let's add a character to another word.

1. Using either the mouse or the movement keys, place the insertion point at the end of the word "statement" in the second paragraph, fourth line.
2. Type an "s." The word now reads "statements."

To Delete a Character

1. Using either the mouse or the movement keys, return the insertion point to the left of the letter "s" in "lasbored" in the second paragraph, second line.
2. Press the Del key. The word again reads "labored."

Repeat the process to remove the "s" from the end of "statement." Practice adding and deleting characters until you are comfortable with this feature; then you can move on to more complex formatting.

Adding Blocks of Text Using Typeover and Insert Modes

In the previous section, when you added characters to words, you were instructed to bring the insertion point to the right of the location where you wished to add the character. This is because WordPerfect automatically defaults to **Insert mode**, which means that any text or codes added to a document are inserted to the left of the insertion point. Insert mode is safer to use because it inserts text without typing over existing text. Let's practice adding blocks of text in Insert mode.

1. Using either the mouse or the movement keys, bring the insertion point to the left of the letter "c" at the beginning of the word "convention" in paragraph one, line one.
2. Type in the words "revolutionary new" plus a space. This part of the sentence should now read "revolutionary new convention." Notice that we added the necessary space in between the words "new" and "convention." This is very important.

Let's insert some more words using Insert mode.

1. Using either the mouse or the movement keys, bring the insertion point to the space right after the letter "s" in the word "reads" in the second paragraph, last line.
2. Type a comma, then a space, then "in its entirety" followed by another comma. This part of the sentence now reads "reads, in its entirety, as...." Notice that it was not necessary in this case to add a space after the inserted words. This is because we added the segment of text immediately before the space that appears after the word "reads," so the space just moved over with the rest of the text after the insertion.

Practice inserting text and punctuation using Insert mode.

As we explained earlier, Insert mode is safe to use because new text is inserted without typing over existing text. However, there will be times when you want to replace segments of text with different text that uses the same number of characters. If you do this in insert mode you must first insert the new text and then delete the unwanted text. To avoid this extra work, WordPerfect allows you to work in **Typeover mode**, in which new text is typed over existing text. The danger in using Typeover mode is that you might forget it is turned on and accidentally type over text you wish to retain. Therefore, it should be used carefully and you must remember to turn it off when you are finished with it.

To switch from Insert mode to Typeover mode, press the Ins key. Notice that the Font designation in the status bar is now replaced by the word "Typeover." Let's replace some text using Typeover mode.

1. Using either the mouse or the movement keys, bring the insertion point to the left of the letter "f" at the beginning

of the word "four" in the second paragraph, first line.

2. Now press the Ins key. The Typeover prompt appears in the left-hand corner of the status bar.

3. Type the word "five." Notice that you have typed over "four" and replaced it with "five."

4. Press the Ins key again to return to Insert mode. The font designation prompt is back in the status bar.

Do not forget to return to Insert mode when you are through working in Typeover.

Using Select to Delete Larger Blocks of Text

It would be very inefficient to delete blocks of text one character at a time. Instead, WordPerfect offers faster ways to accomplish this type of editing. While there are some quick keystrokes to delete certain blocks of text, generally, deleting text blocks is achieved by first selecting the text to be deleted and then deleting the entire block. Text can be selected with the mouse or using keyboard commands. Both methods will be explained, but it is faster to use a mouse for editing.

Deleting Words with the Mouse

There are two ways to select a word with the mouse.

1. Point to the beginning of the word and drag the mouse through the word (be sure to include the space at the end of the word); or

2. Point to the beginning of the word and double-click (you can only select one word at a time this way; if you want to select more than one word, use step 1 above or see below, "Deleting Blocks of Text").

3. Once the word is selected, press the Del key to delete the word.

4. If you make a mistake while selecting the text, just click once and the text will be deselected.

Deleting Words with the Keyboard

1. Use the movement keys to bring the insertion point to the beginning of the word you want to delete.
2. Press F8, the Select key. The status bar will display the prompt "Select Mode."
3. Press Ctrl+→ to select a word.
4. If you wish to select more than one word, press Ctrl+→ again. Repeat this step until you have selected all of the words you wish to delete.
5. Press the Del key to delete the selected word(s).
6. If you make a mistake selecting the text, press F8 again to deselect the text.

Deleting Sentences with the Mouse

There are three ways to select a sentence with a mouse.

1. Point to the beginning of the sentence and drag the mouse through the sentence (be sure to include the period and space or spaces at the end of the sentence); or
2. Point to the beginning of the sentence and triple-click (you can select only one sentence at a time this way; if you want to select more than one sentence, use step 1 above or see below, "Deleting Blocks of Text"); or
3. Point to the beginning of the sentence and select Edit from the menu bar.
4. Click on Select (F8). A cascading menu will appear, providing further choices.
5. Click on Sentence (you can select only one sentence at a time this way; if you want to select more than one, use step 1 above or see below, "Deleting Blocks of Text").
6. Once the sentence is selected, press the Del key to delete it.
7. If you make a mistake while selecting the text, just click once and the text will be deselected.

Deleting Sentences with the Keyboard

1. Use the movement keys to bring the insertion point to the beginning of the sentence you want to delete.
2. Press F8, the Select key. The status bar will display the prompt "Select Mode."
3. Press the period to select to the end of the sentence. Then press the Right Arrow key (→) twice to continue to select the space or spaces after the period.
4. If you wish to select more than one sentence, press the period and Right Arrow key (→) twice again until you have selected all of the sentences you wish to delete.
5. Press the Del key to delete the selected sentence(s).
6. If you make a mistake selecting the text, press F8 again to deselect it.

Deleting Paragraphs with the Mouse

There are three ways to select a paragraph with a mouse.

1. Point to the beginning of the paragraph and drag the mouse through it (be sure to include the hard return at the end of the paragraph); or
2. Point to the beginning of the paragraph and quadruple-click (you can select only one paragraph at a time this way; if you want to select more than one paragraph, use step 1 above or see below, "Deleting Blocks of Text"); or
3. Point to the beginning of the paragraph and select Edit from the menu bar.
4. Click on Select (F8). A cascading menu will appear, providing further choices.
5. Click on Paragraph (you can only select one paragraph at a time this way; if you want to select more than one, use step 1 above or see below, "Deleting Blocks of Text").
6. After selecting the paragraph, press the Del key to delete it.
7. If you make a mistake while selecting text, just click once and the text will be deselected.

Deleting Paragraphs with the Keyboard

1. Use the movement keys to bring the insertion point to the beginning of the paragraph you want to delete.
2. Press F8, the Select key. The status bar will display the prompt "Select Mode."
3. Press Ctrl+↓ to select the paragraph.
4. If you wish to select more than one paragraph, press Ctrl+↓ again. Repeat this step until you have selected all of the paragraphs you wish to delete.
5. Press the Del key to delete the selected paragraph(s).
6. If you make a mistake selecting the text, press F8 again to deselect it.

Deleting to the End of a Line

Shortcut: You can delete from wherever your insertion point is located to the end of the line by pressing Ctrl+Del. This is one of the many Quick keys available in WordPerfect to speed up your use of the program. Many more will be discussed in Chapter 4.

Deleting Other Blocks of Text

The above examples explain how to delete particular segments of text; that is, a word, a sentence, a line, or a paragraph. Often the text you want to delete will not fall into any of these categories. This section will demonstrate how to use the mouse or the keyboard to select and delete any block of text.

Deleting Blocks of Text with the Mouse

This procedure will work to select and delete any block of text.

1. Point to the beginning of the text you want to delete and drag the mouse to the end of the block; or
2. Bring the insertion point to the beginning of the text you want to delete, and press Select (F8). Then hold down the

Shift key, bring the insertion point to the end of the block, and click.

3. Once the text is selected, press the Del key to delete the block.

4. If you make a mistake while selecting text, just click once and it will be deselected.

Deleting Blocks of Text with the Keyboard

There are several ways you can use the keyboard to select blocks of text to be deleted. One way is to tell WordPerfect to select through a particular character. For example, if you turn on Select mode and press a particular character, WordPerfect will select from the insertion point through the first occurrence of that character. If you then press another character, WordPerfect will continue to select through the first occurrence of that character. Let's try a practical application to see how this works.

1. Using our sample document, bring your insertion point to the beginning of the word "in" in the first line of the first paragraph.

2. Press F8 to turn on Select mode.

3. Press the Spacebar. WordPerfect will select through the first space to the word "Philadelphia."

4. Press the Spacebar again. WordPerfect will continue to select through the next space to the word "to."

5. Now press the Del key. WordPerfect will delete the selected text. This section of the sentence will now read "a convention met to revise."

Let's try another example.

1. Bring your insertion point to the word "From" in the first paragraph, second sentence.

2. Press F8 to turn on Select mode.

3. Press the Comma key. WordPerfect will select through the first comma ("17,") it encounters.

4. Now press the Spacebar. WordPerfect will continue to select through the first space it encounters. Your insertion point should now be to the left of the first "5" of the number "55."

5. Now press the Del key. WordPerfect will delete the selected text. The beginning of the sentence now reads "55 men hammered...."

You can also select segments of text using the movement keys listed earlier in the chapter. WordPerfect will select from the insertion point through the text indicated by the movement key. Let's try a few examples.

1. Bring your insertion point to the word "so" in the second paragraph, third line.

2. Press F8 to turn on Select mode.

3. Press Ctrl+→. WordPerfect has selected through one word.

4. Press Ctrl+→ again. WordPerfect has selected through the next word.

5. Now press the Del key. WordPerfect has deleted the two selected words. The text now reads "...enhance the independence won."

Let's try another example.

1. Bring your insertion point to the left margin of the third paragraph.

2. Press F8 to turn on Select mode.

3. Press Ctrl+End to select to the end of the document.

4. Press the Del key. All of the text between the insertion point and the end of the document has been deleted.

Recovering Deleted Text Using Undelete (Alt+Shft+Bkspc)

One of the handiest features in WordPerfect is the ability to recover text or codes accidentally deleted while working in the program. WordPerfect will hold the last three deletions in a temporary buffer. By accessing the Undelete feature, you can restore any or all of your last three deletions. WordPerfect will restore the text and/or codes at the insertion point. Remember, however, that if just one character is deleted, it will count as one deletion in your buffer zone. If you delete ten pages of text and then continue to edit your document, those ten pages will be lost if you have three or more deletions after the ten pages were deleted. A deletion is considered complete once the deletion is made and the insertion point is moved. Let's use the Undelete feature to restore a deletion.

1. Bring the insertion point to the beginning of the second paragraph.
2. Using the mouse or the keyboard, select the paragraph.
3. Press the Del key to delete the paragraph.
4. Click on Edit in the menu bar.
5. Click on Undelete. The last deletion will be highlighted at the insertion point and the Undelete menu will appear, as shown in Figure 2.4.

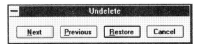

Figure 2.4—The Undelete menu.

6. Click on Restore. The text will be restored at the insertion point.

If you wish to restore a previous deletion, bring the insertion point to the location to which you want to restore the deletion. Follow steps 4 and 5 above. When the Undelete menu appears, click on Previous. Continue to click on Previous until the correct deletion is highlighted at the insertion point. Click on Restore to restore the deletion. Using this method, restore the last paragraph of the document, which you deleted earlier.

You can move back and forth between the last three deletions by clicking on Previous or Next. If you do not wish to restore any of the deletions, click on Cancel to exit the menu without restoring.

The following restrictions apply to the Undelete feature:

1. Text or codes deleted by using the Cut command (covered in Chapter 6) cannot be restored using the Undelete feature. You must use Paste.

2. Paired codes, such as [Bold On] [Bold Off] or [Und On] [Und Off], cannot be restored if they were deleted using the Bkspc or Del key unless they were selected first. If you delete such codes with text and do not select them before deleting, the text will be restored but not the codes.

3. When you delete text and codes using any other method, including shortcut keys, both the text and the codes will be restored.

Using Undo (Alt+Bkspc)

The Undo feature can be used to undo the last change made to the document. Undo will reverse typing, coding, and format changes. To use the Undo command:

1. Click on Edit in the menu bar.
2. Click on Undo, and the last change you made will be undone; or use the Quick key (Ctrl+Z).

Using Reveal Codes

Reveal Codes is probably the single most important feature in WordPerfect to master. If you cannot use Reveal Codes, you will never be able to operate the program properly. Unfortunately, it is also the feature that beginners find the hardest to use.

It may drive you crazy in the beginning, but stick with it. After a few days you will be able to read the Reveal Codes window as quickly and easily as you read straight text.

So far, we have worked only with straight text in the window. That is, we have inserted some simple codes in the document, but we cannot see or even locate them. In order to move, delete, or change codes, it is necessary to be able to locate them in Reveal Codes.

To access Reveal Codes, click on View in the menu bar, then click on Reveal Codes (Alt+F3). Your window should now resemble Figure 2.5.

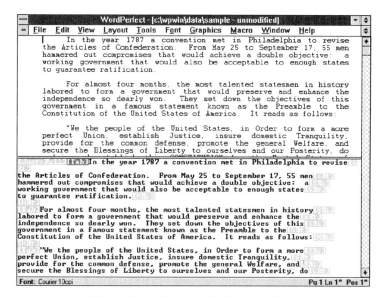

Figure 2.5—The Reveal Codes window.

You can also use the Reveal Codes bar (the black bar that appears immediately above and below the Scroll Up buttons on the scroll bar) to access Reveal Codes. Follow these steps:

1. Position the insertion point over the Reveal Codes bar.
2. When the insertion point changes to a double arrow, drag the bar as far up or down as you want to split the window for Reveal Codes. You can make the Reveal Codes screen larger or smaller, depending upon where you position the bar.

You will notice that there is a heavy, shaded line splitting the window in half. The top half of the window contains just the text you have typed; the bottom half of the window contains the text and the corresponding codes.

The codes are shaded and surrounded by brackets. For the most part, they are very logical and easy to understand. For example, [TAB] in Reveal Codes means a tab code. [HRt] means a hard return. [SRt] means a soft return. Appendix D contains a list of all of the codes used in Reveal Codes.

Notice that the insertion point is represented somewhat differently in Reveal Codes. Instead of being a vertical bar to the left of the character where it is located, it is represented as a shaded box directly on the character (the box is a different color or shade to make it stand out from the shaded codes). In this respect it looks more like a standard cursor than a insertion point.

You can add, delete, or format, or perform any WordPerfect command while in Reveal Codes. To delete text or codes in Reveal Codes, place the insertion point directly on the text or code you want to delete and press the Del key. For example, to delete the [TAB] code in the first paragraph of the text, place the insertion point directly on the [TAB] code and press the Del key. You can use either the mouse or the movement keys to move the insertion point in Reveal Codes.

To insert text or codes in Reveal Codes, bring the insertion point to the appropriate location and insert the text or code. For example, to reinsert [TAB] at the beginning of the first paragraph, bring the insertion point to the beginning of the paragraph and press the Tab key. [TAB] has now been reinserted.

It is a good idea to always work in Reveal Codes when you are editing. Otherwise, it is practically impossible to locate codes and properly format a document. This will become much more apparent when we get to more complex formatting and layouts later in the book.

To turn off Reveal Codes:

1. Click on View in the menu bar to open the View menu.
2. Click on Reveal Codes; or
3. Drag the Reveal Codes bar back to its original position.

Saving the Document and Exiting WordPerfect for Windows

Chapter 3 will cover all of the commands and features necessary to save a document. We will end this chapter very simply by saving our document and exiting from WordPerfect for Windows.

To save your document:

1. Click on File in the menu bar (Shft+F3).
2. Click on Save. The Save As dialog box appears, as shown in Figure 2.6.

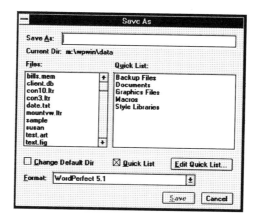

Figure 2.6—The Save As dialog box.

3. In the Save As text box, type SAMPLE.

4. Press Enter or click on Save.

5. The document has now been saved with the name SAMPLE.

To Exit WordPerfect:

1. Click on File in the menu bar (Alt+F4).

2. Click on Exit.

3. You have exited WordPerfect for Windows and are now back in the Windows Program Manager.

Review Exercises for Chapter 2

◆ Type a short document. If you make a mistake as you are typing, use the Bkspc key to erase the error.

◆ Turn on Reveal Codes. See if you can identify the codes.

◆ Move the insertion point around in the document and take note of the Ln # and Pos #.

◆ Scroll through the document using the mouse.

◆ Scroll through the document using the movement keys on the keyboard.

◆ Insert characters using Insert mode.

◆ Insert characters using Typeover mode.

◆ Delete one character.

◆ Delete a segment of text using Select.

◆ Use the Undelete command to restore the last deletion.

◆ Type a word and use the Undo command to undo the typing.

◆ Save the document and exit from WordPerfect for Windows.

Before You Go On...

Before you continue on to the next chapter, you should feel comfortable with simple typing and editing features. You should be able to scroll through a short document and use Reveal Codes. The window should now look familiar and you should be able to identify its parts.

Saving, Retrieving, and Printing Documents

What You Will Learn in this Chapter

◆ How to save your documents
◆ How to name your documents
◆ How to use the Save and Save As commands
◆ How to use the Close and Exit commands
◆ How to save a block of text
◆ How to use Original and Timed Backup
◆ How to retrieve your documents
◆ How to use the Open command
◆ How to use the Retrieve command
◆ How to use the New command
◆ How to print your documents

A Word About the Features Covered in this Chapter

Each of the commands reviewed in this chapter opens its own dialog box. Only the basic features included in the dialog boxes will be covered. Any features found in the dialog boxes and not explained in this chapter will be explained in other sections of the book. Saving, retrieving, and printing documents also can be accomplished in the File Manager, which is covered in Chapter 8.

Saving Your Documents

A Few Things You Should Know About Saving

Saving is the process of writing your document to a permanent storage device such as a hard drive or a floppy disk. If you wish to retain a permanent copy of your work, you must save it. If you do not save your document, you will lose it when you clear the window or exit WordPerfect. In order to fully understand the importance and mechanics of saving, you must understand how WordPerfect interacts with the computer to store documents.

While you are creating or editing a document in WordPerfect, your document is being held temporarily in a buffer called **RAM** (random access memory). But it is only when you save the document that it is permanently written (or stored) on a floppy disk or hard drive. Once you exit WordPerfect or clear the document from the window, the document is deleted from RAM. This means that if you do not save the document before clearing the screen or exiting WordPerfect, the document will be lost.

When a document has been stored to a floppy disk or hard drive, it remains there unless you delete it. Opening a document does not remove it from the drive, which means that if you open a document, but make no changes to it, it does not have to be saved again.

Naming Documents

When you save your document, you must give it a **filename**. The following rules and restrictions apply when naming a file.

1. You may use up to eight characters, followed by a period and an **extension**, which may contain up to three more characters.

2. You may not use spaces.

3. Do not use the following extensions: ALL, AUX, BAT, CHM, COM, CRS, DRS, EXE, FIL, FRS, IRS, PRS, SET, TUT, WPK, WPM, VRS.

4. You may use all letters and numbers and any of the following characters: ! @ # $ % & ( ) - { } ' ' WordPerfect will refuse to accept any other characters.

5. You may use uppercase or lowercase letters when typing a filename. The following examples would be valid filenames: WATERGAT.ART, VACATION.MEM, and SMITH.LTR.

You cannot have more than one document with the same filename in a directory (see Chapter 8, *System and Document Management*, for a discussion on directories). This means that if you edit a document that has already been saved, the new version automatically overwrites the old version when it is saved again. When you overwrite the old version of the document with the newly edited version, the original version will no longer be stored on the hard drive or floppy disk. If you want to retain the original version of the document you must use the Save As command (explained later), and save the document with a different filename.

Once you have given your document a filename, the new filename (including the drive and directory of the file) replaces the Document# designation in the title bar.

It is important to be consistent and logical when naming documents. Eventually you will have hundreds of documents stored on your computer, and locating files will be very difficult if you do not use an organized naming system.

Using the Save Command (Shft+F3)

The Save command is used to save a document to the current directory. If the document has been saved previously, the Save command automatically overwrites the old version of the document with the new version. Let's save a document using the Save command.

1. Type the following letter.

   October 15, 1991

   Ms. Tabitha Corn
   MountainView Inn
   Lookout Point Road
   Kennebunkport, Maine

   Dear Ms. Corn:

   Thank you very much for the colorful brochure containing information about your famous "Thanksgiving Weekend" at Mountainview Inn. Enclosed is the necessary deposit to confirm reservations for two adults for the entire weekend.

   We look forward to celebrating Thanksgiving at Mountainview Inn.

   Very truly yours,

   John and Jane Cobb

2. Click on File in the menu bar to open the menu seen in Figure 3.1.

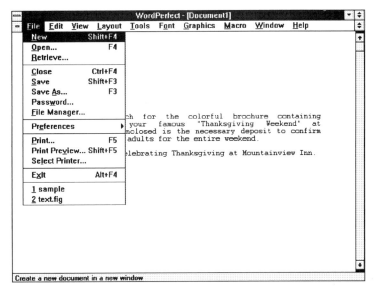

Figure 3.1—The File menu.

3. Click on Save to open the Save As dialog box, as shown in Figure 3.2. The insertion point is in the Save As text box.

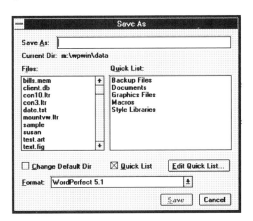

Figure 3.2—The Save As dialog box.

4. Type in the filename MOUNTVW.LTR.
5. Press Enter, or click on the Save command button. The letter has now been saved with the filename MOUNTVW.LTR.

Note that the letter is still in the window. It will remain there until you close the window or exit WordPerfect. If you decide to make any changes in the letter, you must save it again or you will lose your edits. Let's edit the letter and save it again.

1. Change the address to read "100 Lookout Point Road."
2. Save the letter again by clicking on File in the menu bar to open the File menu.
3. Click on Save.
4. Since the document already has a filename, it is not necessary to name it again. The new version of the letter is automatically saved to the same filename.
5. Close the window by clicking on File and then on Close. (The Close command is covered later in this chapter.)

Using the Save As Command (F3)

The Save command saves documents to the directory of origin, using the filename they were originally given. If you wish to give a document a new filename, or save it to a new directory, you must use the Save As command. Let's edit the file MOUNTVW.LTR and save it to a different name.

1. To open the file, click on File in the menu bar. When the menu is opened, click on Open to display the Open File dialog box. Double-click on the filename MOUNTVW.LTR in the File list box. The letter is in the window. (The Open command is covered later in this chapter.)
2. Edit the letter as follows:

    a. Change the name and address as follows:

    ```
    Mr. James Turkey
    Redwoods House
    200 Forest Road
    Forest, California
    ```

    b. Change the salutation to "Dear Mr. Turkey:"
    c. In the body of the letter, change Mountainview Inn to Redwoods House.
    d. Change the signature to Susan and Steven Leaf

3. Click on File in the menu bar to open the menu.

4. Click on Save As to display the Save As dialog box, as shown in Figure 3.2.

5. In the Save As text box, you will see the letter's current directory and filename.

6. Press the Bkspc key to delete the old name.

7. Type in the filename REDWOODS.LTR.

8. Press Enter, or click on the Save command button.

9. The letter is now saved with the new filename REDWOODS.LTR. The original letter is still saved with the filename MOUNTVW.LTR.

10. Close the window by clicking on File in the menu bar and then clicking on Close. (The Close command is discussed next.)

If you are using the Save As command and you try to save a file to a filename that already exists, a WordPerfect dialog box will appear, informing you that a file already exists with that name and asking if you want to replace the file. If you choose yes, the existing file will be overwritten. If you choose no, you will have to give the new file another name.

Using the Close Command (Ctrl+F4)

The Close command closes the window when you are finished working with a document. Unless you have a reason to work with more than one document at a time (see Chapter 6, *Advanced Editing Features*), you should close the window before you open another file. If you have modified the text in the window and not yet saved it, you will be asked if you want to save it before the window is closed. The Close command is a quick way to save a file and clear the window in one operation. Let's open the document MOUNTVW.LTR, edit it, save it, and close the window in one operation using the Close command.

1. To open the file click on File in the menu bar. When the menu is opened, click on Open to display the Open File dialog box. In the File list box, double-click on the filename MOUNTVW.LTR. The letter is in the window. (The Open command is covered later in this chapter.)

2. Edit the letter.

3. Click on File in the menu bar to open the menu.

4. Click on Close.

5. The WordPerfect dialog box appears, asking if you want to save your changes.

   a. Choose Yes to save the document and close the window.

   b. Choose No to close the window without saving the document.

   c. Choose Cancel to cancel the Close process.

6. If you choose Yes and the document has been saved previously, it will be saved again to the same filename.

7. If you choose Yes and the file has not been saved previously, the Save As dialog box appears, prompting you to name the file.

Using the Exit Command (Alt+F4)

The Exit command is used to exit from WordPerfect for Windows and return to the Windows program. It allows you to save any open modified files before exiting from the program. To exit from WordPerfect for Windows:

1. Click on File in the menu bar to open the File menu.

2. Click on Exit. If there are no unsaved open files, you will exit from the program.

3. If you have any modified open files, the WordPerfect dialog box appears. You will be prompted with the name of each open modified file and asked if you want to save it.
   New documents that have never been saved are identified as Document1, Document2, and so on.

4. If you choose Yes, the document(s) will be saved and you will exit from the program.

5. If you choose No, the document(s) will not be saved and you will exit from the program.

Saving a Block of Text to a New Filename

You can save a block of text from an existing document to a different filename so the text can be used over and over. This is particularly useful with text targeted for **boilerplating**, where you use a block of text as a template for new documents (see Chapter 12). When you save text in this manner, you create a new document out of the blocked segment. Let's try it with the document we saved as SAMPLE.

1. To open the file, click on File in the menu bar. When the menu is opened, click on Open. The Open File dialog box appears. Double-click on the filename SAMPLE in the File list box. The three-paragraph document on the Constitution is now in the window.

2. Using the mouse or the Select key (F8), select the third paragraph.

3. Press the Save key (Shft+F3). The Save Selected Text dialog box opens, as shown in Figure 3.3.

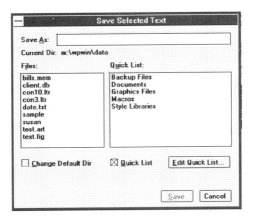

Figure 3.3—The Save Selected Text dialog box.

4. Type the filename BLOCK in the Save As text box.

5. Press Enter or click on the Save command button.

6. The selected text has been saved to the new filename BLOCK.

Using Original and Timed Backup

WordPerfect has some features that help protect against user error and system malfunction. Original and Timed Backup fall into this category.

Original Backup

As discussed above, when you replace a document with another document of the same name, the original document is overwritten. The Original Backup option allows you to save both the original document and the new document with the same name. It does this by renaming the original document to the same filename with a BK! extension (for example, SAMPLE.BK!). Each time you replace the document, the BK! file is replaced with the new original file. This means that if you are using the Original Backup option and you accidentally overwrite a file, you will be able to restore the original version by retrieving the file with the BK! extension.

Files with the same filename but different extensions use the same Original Backup. If you have a file named SAMPLE.LTR and a file named SAMPLE.MEM, they will both use the Original Backup filename SAMPLE.BK!. Therefore, only one of the files (the last one you saved) would have an Original Backup. If you use the Original Backup feature, be sure that all of your files have different filenames (not just different extensions).

To recover an Original Backup file, open the file and save it again (using the Save As command) with a filename that does not have a BK! extension.

A disadvantage of using the Original Backup option is that it doubles the amount of space required to store your documents, since each document is saved twice. If you wish to use the Original Backup option, be sure that you have enough storage space on your hard drive and that you periodically delete unneeded BK! files (see Chapter 8 for a discussion on how to delete files).

If you turn off the Original Backup feature, the next time you save a document, the Original Backup of that file is deleted. Before you turn off Original Backup, be sure to retrieve and save all backup files you wish to keep.

Timed Backup

As we discussed earlier, your work is not written to a storage device until it is saved. In the event of a keyboard lockup, system crash, or power failure, your work is lost if it has not been saved. The only way to prevent this catastrophe is to save your work periodically. WordPerfect can do this for you using Timed Backup.

When you use the Timed Backup feature, your open documents are saved at regular intervals to a temporary backup file. You determine the amount of time between backups when you configure the program during the installation procedure (see Appendix A). The files are saved to a specified directory (also determined when you configure the program) with a BK# extension (where # = the Document#).

WordPerfect makes a timed backup for each open document. However, it saves timed backups only for the documents modified since the last backup was made. For example, if you have a document in window #1 (Document #1) and a document in window #2 (Document #2), WordPerfect will not save a backup of both documents unless they have both been modified since the last backup interval. The BK# extension will correspond to the window number you are working in when the document is backed up. The next time a file backs up in the active window, the previous backup is replaced.

Let's assume you are working with a document named SAMPLE, and you configured WordPerfect to backup to the C:\WPWIN directory. If your document is lost before you save, the only stored version you have is the timed backup. To recover the timed backup:

1. Start up WordPerfect. A Timed Backup dialog box will appear informing you that a backup file exists (see Figure 3.4). You will be asked if you want to Rename, Open, or Delete the backup file. If you had more than one open file, there will be a timed backup of every open file that was changed in the last backup interval. Succeeding dialog boxes will appear for each backed up file.

Figure 3.4—A Timed Backup dialog box.

2. Click on Open to open the backed up document(s). Each open document is backed up to a separate window.
3. The documents are located in the directory specified for Timed Backups, with the filename plus a BK# extension. (For example, C:\WPWIN\SAMPLE.BK1.)

If the file does not have a filename when it is backed up, WordPerfect will designate the filename WP{WP}.BK# (where # = the Document#). On a network the filename will be USERNAME{WP}.BK# (where USERNAME = WP sign-in name).

4. Using the Save As command, save each document to the appropriate directory. Be sure to give the document a filename with a different extension (see Chapter 8, *System and Document Management*).
5. You may continue to work with the newly saved file.

If you choose to Rename the timed backup, a Rename dialog box appears. Give the file a new name and retrieve the file.

 Warning: If you choose to Delete the timed backup, the backup file is lost. There is no way to recover your work, unless you have a special disk utility program that recovers lost files.

When you exit WordPerfect properly, all timed backups are deleted. When you reboot the system after a system or power failure, only the work backed up in the last timed backup interval can be recovered. Therefore, it is advisable to set WordPerfect to back up as often as possible. When you back up, a Timed Backup message appears in the status bar. If you have a fast system, this is hardly noticeable. If you have a slower system and you are backing up long documents, this process is more noticeable, and you may have to interrupt your work while the backup is occurring. This should be taken into consideration when determining the intervals to set for the Timed Backup feature.

Retrieving Your Documents

Once you save your documents, they are permanently stored on your hard drive or floppy disk. If you want to edit the document, you must retrieve it to a window by opening the file.

This chapter will teach you how to retrieve files in the current directory only. For information on how to retrieve work stored on other directories or on floppy disks, see Chapter 8, *System and Document Management*.

When you retrieve a file to a window, the document remains stored on the hard drive or floppy disk, but is also loaded into RAM. Any changes made to the document are held in RAM only. If you want to store the edits, you must save the document before clearing it from the window.

Using the Open Command (F4)

The Open command is used to open an existing file to a new window. If you have a document already opened in one window, and you use the Open command to open another document, it will be opened to a new window. You can have nine documents opened in WordPerfect for Windows. See Chapter 6, *Advanced Editing Features*, for information on working with multiple documents. To open an existing document in the current directory:

1. Click on File in the menu bar to open the File menu.
2. Click on Open to display the Open File dialog box, as shown in Figure 3.5. The files located in the current directory are listed in the Files list box. If you cannot view all of the files at once, you can use the scroll buttons on the right side of the list box to scroll through the filenames.

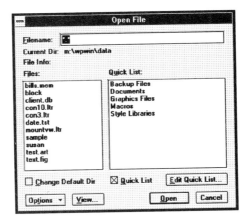

Figure 3.5—The Open File dialog box.

3. There are three ways you can open a file:

- Type the filename in the Filename text box and click on the Open command button; or
- Click on the filename in the File list box (the filename will appear in the Filename text box) and click on the Open command button; or
- Double-click on the filename in the File list box.

Viewing a Document

You can view a document before opening it. This is useful if you are not sure which document you want to open. To view a document:

1. Click on File in the menu bar to open the File menu.
2. Click on Open to display the Open File dialog box.
3. Click on the file you want to view in the Files file box.
4. Click on the View command button. A View window opens, containing the text of the document (see Figure 3.6). You may scroll through the document using the scroll buttons, but you cannot edit the document in this window.

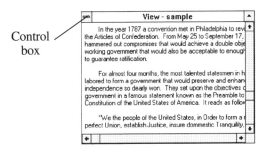

Figure 3.6—A View window.

5. To close the View window, open the Control menu by clicking on the Control box (see Figure 3.6) and then clicking on Close; or press the Exit key (Alt+F4).

Using the Retrieve Command

The Retrieve command is used to retrieve an existing file into the active window. See the section on boilerplating in Chapter 12 for some examples of when the Retrieve command is useful.

When you use the Retrieve command, the retrieved document is inserted at the insertion point. The retrieved file remains stored on the hard drive or floppy disk, and the new file in the active window is saved to a different name.

When you retrieve text in a new window, the Retrieve command works the same way as the Open command. The filename of the retrieved document appears in the title bar. If you use the Save command to save the document, the original file will be overwritten. If you do not want to overwrite the original file, use the Save As command when you save the document.

Let's use the Retrieve command to retrieve a file into the active window.

1. In a new window type, "Let me begin this document by quoting the Preamble to the Constitution of the United States of America." Then press Enter twice.
2. Bring the insertion point to the end of the document.
3. Click on File in the menu bar to open the File menu.
4. Click on Retrieve to display the Retrieve File dialog box, as shown in Figure 3.7.

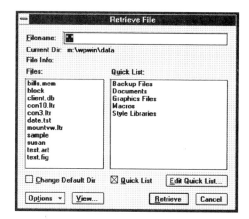

Figure 3.7—The Retrieve File dialog box.

5. There are three ways to retrieve the file BLOCK:

- Type BLOCK in the Filename text box and click on the Retrieve command button; or
- Click on the Filename BLOCK in the File list box (the filename BLOCK will appear in the Filename text box) and click on the Retrieve command button; or
- Double-click on the filename BLOCK in the File list box.

6. A WordPerfect dialog box appears asking if you want to insert the file into the current document (see Figure 3.8).

Figure 3.8—The Insert File dialog box.

7. Choose Yes. The file BLOCK is now inserted into the current document.

You can also use the View command before retrieving a file. Follow the instructions listed above in the section entitled "How to View a Document."

Using the New Command (Shft+F4)

The New command is used to create a new document in a new window. You should use this command when you have a document in the current window and you want to create a new document in another window.

To use this command:

1. Start WordPerfect and open a file or type a new file in the active window.
2. Click on File in the menu bar to open the File menu.
3. Click on New. You are now in a new window with Document2 in the title bar.
4. You can switch back and forth between Document1 and Document2 by clicking on Window in the menu bar to open the Window menu. All of the opened documents will be listed. The active document has a checkmark next to it. To switch documents, click on the document# you want to switch to.
5. Remember to close every open document before you exit WordPerfect.

The New command will be covered in greater detail in Chapter 6, *Advanced Editing Features*.

Printing Your Documents

Once you have typed a document, you will probably want to print it. The process of printing a job involves transmitting the file(s) to be printed, along with the necessary printer codes, to your printer. Different printers require different codes or instructions. These instructions are contained in the part of the WordPerfect program called **printer drivers**. Fortunately, WordPerfect makes the process of transmitting printer instructions very easy. When you install WordPerfect, you tell the program what types of printer(s) you will be using (see Appendix A). WordPerfect then selects the correct printer driver(s) to work with your printer.

WordPerfect for Windows also allows you to print documents

using the Windows printer drivers. Unless you are very knowledgeable about Windows, we do not recommend that you use the Windows drivers. For information about using Windows printer drivers, refer to your Windows manual.

Whether you use WordPerfect printer drivers or Windows printer drivers, if you have enabled the **Print Manager**, which handles all communications with the printer, all of the printer instructions are sent through it. This frees up WordPerfect and allows you to continue to work with the program. See Chapter 16 for more information on how Print Manager works.

If you are working on a network, you might want to bypass the Print Manager. Refer to your WordPerfect for Windows manual for information on how to print through a network.

This chapter will cover only the basic elements involved in printing a file. For information on how to use advanced printing enhancements, see Chapter 16.

Using the Print Command (F5)

The Print command opens a dialog box that controls most of the features involved in printing a document. Let's use this command to print the file named SAMPLE.

1. Open the document named SAMPLE. The document is in the active window.

2. Click on File in the menu bar to open the File menu.

3. Click on Print to open the Print dialog box, as shown in Figure 3.9.

4. Choose Print. The Current Print Job dialog box appears. This box informs you of the status of your print job (while this dialog box is on the screen you cannot edit a WordPerfect document or send another print job). If WordPerfect is properly configured to work with your printer, there should be no problems. If a problem occurs, choose Cancel Print Job and correct the problem (see Chapter 16 for suggestions on how to deal with the most common print problems).

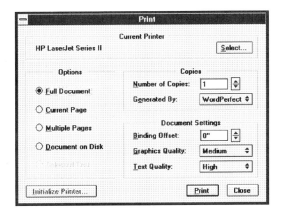

Figure 3.9—The Print dialog box.

The WordPerfect Print dialog box automatically defaults to the Full Document Option button. There are several other options.

Printing a Page

To print one page:

1. The document should be in the active window.
2. Bring your insertion point to the page you want to print.
3. Click on File in the menu bar to open the File menu.
4. Click on Print to open the Print dialog box, shown in Figure 3.9.
5. Choose the Current Page option.
6. Choose Print. The current page will print.

Printing Multiple Pages

You may want to print individual pages or groups of pages, rather than a whole document. To print multiple pages:

1. The document should be in the active window.
2. Click on File in the menu bar to open the File menu.
3. Click on Print to open the Print dialog box (see Figure 3.9).
4. Choose the Multiple Pages option.
5. Choose Print to display the Multiple Pages dialog box, as shown in Figure 3.10.

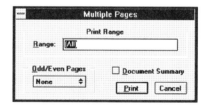

Figure 3.10—The Multiple Pages dialog box.

6. Fill in the Range text box using the following parameters:

Range	To Print
n	Page n
n,m,o	Pages n, m, and o
n m	Pages n and m
n-	Page n through end of document
-m	Beginning of document through page m
n-m	Pages n through m

Page numbers are represented by *n*, *m*, and *o*.

8. Choose Print. The specified range will print.

Printing a Document from Disk

You can print a document not in the active window by choosing the Document on Disk option. To do this:

1. The file you want to print should *not* be in the active window (if it is, you should use one of the above options).
2. Click on File in the menu bar to open the File menu.
3. Click on Print to open the Print dialog box (see Figure 3.9).
4. Choose the Document on Disk option.
5. Choose Print to display the Document on Disk dialog box, as shown in Figure 3.11.

Figure 3.11—The Document on Disk dialog box.

6. Type in the name of the document you want to print in the Filename text box; or click on the List button at the right of the Filename text box and select the filename from the Select File dialog box.

7. Fill in the Range text box using the parameters listed above in the section entitled "How to Print Multiple Pages."

8. Choose Print to print the document.

Printing Multiple Copies

WordPerfect automatically prints one copy of a document unless you instruct it otherwise. To print multiple copies of a document:

1. Select an option from the option list (Full Document, Current Page, Multiple Pages, or Document on Disk).

2. Click on the Number of Copies text box and type in the number of copies you want to print; or use the scroll buttons to select a number.

3. Choose Print to print the specified number of copies.

Selecting a Different Printer

If you have more than one printer, and you want to print to a printer other than the one currently selected, you will have to select a printer. You do this in the Select Printer dialog box. The Select Printer dialog box can be accessed in two ways:

1. If you are already in the Print dialog box, choose Select. The Select Printer dialog box appears, as shown in Figure 3.12; or open the File menu and choose Select Printer to open the Select Printer dialog box.

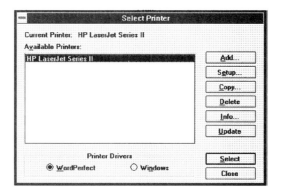

Figure 3.12—The Select Printer dialog box.

2. Highlight the printer you want to select.
3. Choose Select to make the highlighted printer your current printer.
4. Print the document using the new printer selection.

Shortcut: If you want to print the current document to the current printer without making any changes to the Print dialog box, you can use the Quick key Ctrl+P. The active document will be sent to the printer.

Review Exercises for Chapter 3

◆ Type a brief document and save it using the Save command.

◆ Save the same document to a different name using the Save As command.

◆ Close the file.

◆ Open a file from the Files list box.

◆ Edit the file and save it again.

◆ Block part of the file and save the block to a new Filename.

◆ Close the file.

◆ In a new window, type a short paragraph.

◆ At the end of the paragraph, retrieve the selected block of text you saved to a new filename.

◆ Print two copies of the file.

◆ Using the Exit command, save the document and exit from WordPerfect for Windows.

Before You Go On...

Before you continue on to the next chapter, you should feel comfortable saving, retrieving, and printing a document. You should know what constitutes a valid filename, and understand how Original and Timed Backup work.

Chapter 4

Basic Text Formatting and Typing Enhancements

What You Will Learn in this Chapter

- ◆ How to change left and right margins
- ◆ How to change line spacing
- ◆ How to work with tabs
- ◆ How to use the indent features
- ◆ How to align text
- ◆ How to justify text
- ◆ How to use bold, italics, and underline
- ◆ How to convert uppercase and lowercase text
- ◆ How to use the Date and Time feature
- ◆ How to use hyphenation
- ◆ How the Auto Code Placement feature works
- ◆ How to use the WordPerfect ruler

In the previous chapters, we focused on some important basics. While is necessary to master these features, they are rather dull compared to the really exciting things you can accomplish in WordPerfect. In this chapter, you are going to learn to use WordPerfect to produce documents that allow you to express your imagination and personality. After all, that is what WordPerfect is really all about.

The documents you have created so far use the WordPerfect system default settings. The programmers at WordPerfect made certain decisions regarding the generic formatting of documents. These decisions determine how your text appears when a document is printed. You will be happy to learn that you are not forced to use these settings; you can change some or all of them at any point in a document. By changing margins, tabs, line spacing, and other formatting features, you can change the entire appearance of a document. Simple typing enhancements, such as bold or underline, can also change the impact of your words. Even these most basic of WordPerfect text enhancements will allow you to create polished and attractive documents.

Many of the features we will be working with are affected by Auto Code Placement. This feature is explained later in the chapter.

Changing Left and Right Margins (Ctrl+F8)

Left and right margin settings determine the distance between the text and the left and right edges of the page. For example, let's assume an 8.5" page width and left and right margins of 1"—that is, the left edge of the text is 1" from the left edge of the page and the right edge of the text is 1" from the right edge of the page. Margins remain constant unless you change them, regardless of the font or paper size you are using.

Figure 4.1 shows how left and right margins affect the appearance of text on a page. If the margins are both set at 1", then the left and right edges of the text are 1" from the left and right edges of the page.

WordPerfect offers an array of settings to accommodate all of your formatting needs. You can change left, right, top and bottom margins; choose several styles of tabs; choose between several forms of text alignment using the **1"** justification feature; use the **1"** Special Codes feature to insert ↔ unusual formatting codes into your document; and use the indent codes to indent text.

Advance formatting features allow you to set up complex text columns; automatically number your paragraphs and create special desktop effects. Page numbering and headers and footers are easy to master and make your projects look professional.

Figure 4.1—Text with 1" left and right margins.

The WordPerfect default setting for left and right margins is 1". Let's change the margins in the document named SAMPLE.

1. Open the file named SAMPLE.
2. Bring the insertion point to the beginning of the document.
3. Click on Layout in the menu bar to open the Layout menu.
4. Click on Margins to open the Margins dialog box, as shown in Figure 4.2.

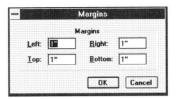

Figure 4.2—The Margins dialog box.

5. Change the left and right margins to 1.5".
6. Choose OK.

When you change your left and right margins, if Auto Code Placement is turned on, the new margins will take effect at the beginning of the paragraph where your insertion point was located when you entered them. If you turn on Reveal Codes, you will see a [L/R Mar:] code. If Auto Code Placement is turned on, and you place the codes in the middle of a line or paragraph, the codes will automatically move to the beginning of the paragraph.

If Auto Code Placement is turned off when you set new margins, WordPerfect will place the set margin codes at the location of the insertion point, but will include a hard return [HRt] after the codes.

When you set a new left or right margin, the new margin is effective from the point of the code to the end of the document, or until a new margin code is encountered.

You can also change margins by selecting paragraphs and then changing the margins for the selected text. Using the document on the screen (SAMPLE), let's change the margins for the last two paragraphs.

1. Using the mouse or the keyboard, select the last two paragraphs in the document SAMPLE.
2. Click on Layout in the menu bar to open the Layout menu.
3. Click on Margins to open the Margins dialog box, as shown in Figure 4.2.
4. Change the left and right margins to 1.5".
6. Choose OK. The margins are changed only for the selected paragraphs. The succeeding text returns to the previous margins.

Use this method only to indent several paragraphs. If you only want to indent one paragraph, instead of changing your margins, you might prefer to use the Indent command covered later in this chapter.

Different printers have different limitations regarding minimum margins. If you select a margin setting that is invalid for your printer, WordPerfect will refuse to accept the setting and will prompt you with the minimum valid setting.

You can also change your left and right margins using the WordPerfect ruler. We'll cover using the ruler later in this chapter.

Changing Line Spacing

Line spacing is the amount of space between the lines in your text. You can set line spacing in WordPerfect in increments of hundredths, from .5 to 160. In single-spaced text, the distance from the bottom of one line to the bottom of the next line is based on the line height of the font you are using. When you change line spacing to a new number, the space from the bottom of one line to the bottom of the next line is multiplied by the new line spacing number. The default line spacing in WordPerfect is 1. Let's change the line spacing in the document SAMPLE:

1. If the document is not in a window, open it.
2. Bring your insertion point to the beginning of the document.
2. Click on Layout in the Menu bar to open the Layout menu.
3. Click on Line (Shift + F9) to open the Line cascading menu.
4. Click on Spacing to display the Line Spacing dialog box, as shown in Figure 4.3.

Figure 4.3—The Line Spacing dialog box.

5. Set the line spacing to 2, either by using the scroll buttons or by typing the figure into the text box.
6. Choose OK.

When you change your line spacing, if Auto Code Placement is turned on, the new spacing will take effect in the beginning of the paragraph where your insertion point was when you entered the new line spacing. If you turn on Reveal Codes, you will see a [Ln Spacing:#] code.

If Auto Code Placement is turned on, and you place the code in the middle of a line or paragraph, the code will automatically move to the beginning of the paragraph.

If Auto Code Placement is turned off when you set new line spacing, WordPerfect will place the line spacing code at the location of the insertion point.

When you set new line spacing, the line spacing is effective from the point of the code to the end of the document, or until a new line spacing code is encountered.

You can also select paragraphs and then change the line spacing for the selected text. Using the document on the screen (SAMPLE), let's change the line spacing for the second paragraph.

1. If the document is not in a window, open it.
2. Bring your insertion point to the beginning of the second paragraph and select the entire paragraph.
3. Click on Layout in the menu bar to open the Layout menu.
4. Click on Line to open the Line cascading menu.
5. Click on Spacing to display the Line Spacing dialog box, as shown in Figure 4.3.
6. Set the line spacing to 2, either by using the scroll buttons or by typing the figure into the text box.
7. Choose OK.

You can also change your line spacing using the WordPerfect ruler. Instructions on how to use the ruler are set out later in this chapter.

Working with Tabs

Tabs align text at a precise location. You should never use the Spacebar to accomplish this. If you do, depending upon the font you are using, you will probably find that your text will not align properly.

You must have a distance of at least one character width between the insertion point and the next tab. If you do not, your insertion point will skip to the next tab. If you press tab and your insertion point does not move, you probably do not have any more tabs set from the insertion point to the end of the line.

There are four different types of tabs in WordPerfect. Each one aligns text in a different way. You can set tabs at any interval from

0 through 54.5". The default setting in WordPerfect is for Left Align tabs set every .5".

When you change your tab set, if Auto Code Placement is turned on, the new tab set will take effect in the beginning of the paragraph where your insertion point is located. If you turn on Reveal Codes you will see a [Tab Set:type#] code. "Type" indicates a left edge or left margin position (see below), and "#" indicates the position on the line of the tab settings.

If Auto Code Placement is turned on, and you place the code in the middle of a line or paragraph, the code will automatically move to the beginning of the paragraph.

If Auto Code Placement is turned off when you change a tab setting, WordPerfect will place the new tab set at the location of the insertion point.

When you set new tabs, the tab setting is effective from the point of the code to the end of the document, or until a new tab setting is encountered.

Position from Left Edge or Left Margin

You can set WordPerfect to position tabs from the left edge of the page (absolute) or the left margin of your text (relative). The system default in WordPerfect is for left margin tabs.

When you set tabs to position from the left margin, they are measured relative to the left margin. If you adjust your left margin, the tabs will automatically adjust accordingly. The left margin is set at 0, and tabs are measured from that point. For example, let's assume you have a left margin setting of 1"—which reads 0 on your tab line—your first tab is set at .5" (.5" from the left margin), and you have typed in a page of text. If you change the left margin at the beginning of the text to 1.5", your text will automatically adjust to a tab setting of 1". Both the left margin and the tab have adjusted a distance of .5". When you set your position from the left margin, you will notice that there are negative numbers to the left of the 0 setting. This allows you to use the **Margin Release** key (see below) to tab to the left of the left margin.

When you set tabs to position from the left edge of the page, they will remain the same even if you change your margin. This is because they are being measured from the left edge of the paper, which remains constant, and not from the left margin, which can be adjusted. The left edge of the page is set at 0 and tabs are measured from that point.

Types of Tab Settings

WordPerfect offers four types of tab settings.

Left Align Tabs

The Left Align tab is the standard system tab, which left-aligns text at the tab setting. Left Align tabs are represented in Reveal Codes as [Tab]. An example of a Left Align tab appears as follows:

```
        While   learning   how   to   use   the   Tab
feature in WordPerfect might seem confusing
at first, once you master the intricacies
of this feature, you will be pleased at the
formatting sophistication it offers you.
```

WordPerfect defaults to Left Align tabs.

Center Tabs

Center tabs center text over the tab setting. Center tabs are represented in Reveal Codes as [Cntr Tab]. They are usually used to center headings over columns. For example, the Headings (1975, 1976, and so forth) in the following example are centered over the columns using Center tabs:

```
    1975            1976            1977            1978
$ 30,500.50  $   25,250.00  $   50,500.00  $   45,900.25
    65,000.00       75,901.00       85,300.90         450.00
```

Center tabs and their uses will be discussed further in Chapter 11.

Right Align Tabs

Right Align tabs right-align text at the tab setting. Right Align tabs are represented in Reveal Codes as [Rgt Tab]. Columns of text using Right Align tabs appear as follows:

```
Jan, 1985    Feb, 1986    Mar, 1987    Apr, 1988
May, 1985    June, 1986   July, 1987   Aug, 1988
Sept, 1985   Oct, 1986    Nov, 1987    Dec, 1988
```

Decimal Align Tabs

Decimal Align tabs align text at the **align character**, which need not be a decimal. Decimal Align tabs are represented in Reveal Codes as [Dec Tab]. Columns of figures using Decimal Align tabs with a decimal for the align character appear as follows:

```
2,500.00      1,000.25    3,500.50    4,750.95
8,000.25(1)     600.00    7,000.00      25.85
  900.75        600.25          50     100.00
```

When you use Decimal Align tabs, text or numbers align to the left and right of the align character. Chapter 11 contains more information on how to use the Decimal Align tab, as well as instructions on how to change the Decimal Align character.

Dot Leaders

When you set a tab with leader dots, a string of dots appears between where you pressed the Tab key and the next tab setting. A Right Align tab with leader dots appears as follows:

```
Chapter 5  . . . . . .Page 10
Chapter 6  . . . . . .Page 50
Chapter 8  . . . . . Page 100
```

Chapter 11 contains more information on how to use leader dots.

Setting Tabs

To set new tabs:

1. Place the insertion point at the beginning of the paragraph where you want to change the tabs.
2. Click on Layout in the menu bar.

3. Click on the Line (Shift+F9) command.

4. Click on Tab Set to open the Tab Set dialog box, as shown in Figure 4.4. The Tab Set dialog box displays all of the current tab settings.

   a. To clear all of these tabs, click on Clear Tabs.

   b. To clear some of these tabs, position the highlight on the tab(s) you want to clear and click on Clear Tab.

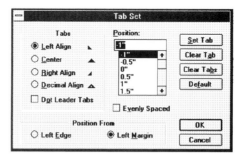

Figure 4.4—The Tab Set dialog box.

5. To set a new tab, type the tab setting in the Position text box, or select a tab in the list box.

6. Select the type of tab from the options listed in the Tabs Group box.

7. Click on Set Tab.

8. Repeat steps 5 through 7 for each tab you want to select.

9. Choose OK to save the settings.

Clear All Tabs

You can clear all tabs by clicking on Clear Tabs in the Tab Set dialog box.

Set Default Tabs

You can set tabs back to the system default by bringing the insertion point to where you want the default tabs to take effect and clicking on Default in the Tab Set dialog box.

Evenly Spaced Tabs

You can set tabs to space evenly at certain intervals. To set evenly spaced tabs:

1. Bring the insertion point to where you want the new tab settings to take effect.
2. Click on Layout in the menu bar.
3. Click on Line.
4. Click on Tab Set to open the Tab Set dialog box.
5. Click on Clear Tabs to clear all of the tabs.
6. Select Evenly Spaced Tabs.
7. In the Position text box, type a number for the first tab setting.
8. In the Repeat Every text box, type a number for the space you want between tabs.
9. Select the type of tabs you want.
10. Choose Set Tab.
11. Choose OK.

Using Hard Tabs

Use Hard Tabs when you want to set a tab for use on one line only. The next tab setting will change to the Hard Tab setting, but the rest of the document will not be affected. To insert a Hard Tab, move the insertion point to the location in the line where you want to set the Hard Tab. Then:

1. Click on Layout in the menu bar.
2. Click on Line.
3. Click on Special Codes to display the Special Codes dialog box, as shown in Figure 4.5.

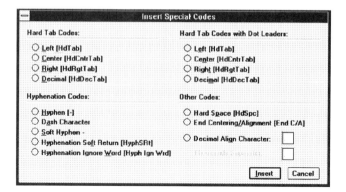

Figure 4.5—The Special Codes dialog box.

4. Select a Hard Tab.
5. Click on Insert.

When you press the Tab key, the Hard Tab you have selected will be the next tab. The rest of the document will revert back to the tab settings that were in effect before you selected the Hard Tab. The following table shows the types of Hard Tabs available, and their codes as they will appear in Reveal Codes.

Type of Hard Tab	Code
Hard Left Align	[HdTab]
Hard Left Align with Dot Leader	[HdTab]
Hard Center Align	[HdCntrTab]
Hard Center Align with Dot Leader	[HdCntrTab]
Hard Right Align	[HdRgtTab]
Hard Right Align with Dot Leader	[HdRgtTab]
Hard Decimal Align	[HdDecTab]
Hard Decimal Align with Dot Leader	[HdDecTab]

Shortcut: One of the most commonly used Hard Tabs is the Hard Decimal Align key. You can insert this code by pressing the Decimal Tab shortcut key (Alt+Shift+F7).

Using the Margin Release Key (Shift+Tab)

You can use the Margin Release key to tab backward, or left on the line instead of right. This key is usually used to tab into the margin.

Try this example:

1. If you have any documents in the window, close them.
2. In a new window, press the Margin Release key (Shift+Tab). Notice that you have tabbed backward into the margin.
3. Type "#1" and press Tab once. You are now back to the left margin.
4. Type "Open your Test Booklet and fill in the information requested in Sections 1, 2, and 3." Notice that the #1 is in the left margin, and the sentence following it starts at the left margin and continues to wrap to the left margin.
5. Close the window without saving the document.

Using the Indent Keys

You can use the Indent keys to indent a paragraph without having to change the margin settings. The Indent keys work on the current tab settings. However, while pressing the Tab key indents only on one line, using an Indent key will indent an entire paragraph. There are three types of Indent keys you can use in WordPerfect.

Left Indent (F7)

Using the Left Indent (F7) key will indent the text in the paragraph one tab space on the left (using the current tab settings) every time you press it. The text will continue to indent until you end the paragraph by pressing Enter. Let's try using the Left Indent key.

1. In a new window, press the Left Indent (F7) key. You have indented one tab space.
2. Press the Tab key to tab the first line of the paragraph.
3. Type the following paragraph:

```
     Using the Indent feature can enhance
text by setting if off from the rest of
the text in the document.  This is a very
good way to catch the reader's eye and set
off quotes and other special text.
```

4. At the end of the paragraph, press Enter. Notice that your insertion point is now back to the left margin.

Let's try another example.

At the left margin of a new paragraph, type "1." Press the Left Indent (F7) key, then type the following text. Your paragraph should look like this:

```
1. This is the first of many steps that will assist
   you in turning out an exciting document.
```

Double Indent (Ctrl+Shift+F7)

The Double Indent key (Ctrl+Shift+F7) works the same as the Indent key, except that it indents a paragraph one tab space on the left and one tab space on the right (using the current tab settings) every time you press it. The text will continue to indent until you end the paragraph by pressing the Enter key.

Press the Left Indent key twice and type the following paragraph:

```
Using the Indent feature can enhance text by
setting it off from the rest of the text in
the document. This is a very good way to catch
the reader's eye and set off quotes and other
special text.
```

Notice that the text is indented two tab spaces (1" if your tabs are set for .5" intervals) on both the left and the right margins.

Hanging Indent (Ctrl+F7)

A Hanging Indent keeps the first line of the paragraph flush with the left margin (or wherever the insertion point is when you press the command) and indents the remaining lines. The insertion point can be at the left margin or after a tab when you press the Hanging Indent key.

Press the Hanging Indent key and type the following text:

```
Using the Indent feature can enhance text
   by setting it off from the rest of the
   text in the document. This is a very
   good way to catch the reader's eye and
   set off quotes and other special text.
```

You can use the Indent keys to indent text that is already typed by selecting a paragraph and then pressing the Indent key, or you can go to the beginning of a paragraph and press the Indent key.

You can also indent text by selecting it and then:

1. Clicking on Layout in the menu bar to open the Layout menu.
2. Clicking on Paragraph.
3. Choosing an indent.

Centering Lines of Text

You can center text between the left and right margins or at a specific location on a line. You can also center several lines of text.

Centering Text Between the Left and Right Margins

To center text between the left and right margins:

1. Bring the insertion point to the left margin.
2. Click on Layout in the menu bar.
3. Click on Line.
4. Click on Center.
5. Type the text you want centered. The text will be centered between the left and right margins.
6. Press Enter to end the centering.

Centering Text at a Specific Location on a Line

To center text at a specific location on a line, either tab or space to where you want to begin centering and:

1. At the location of the insertion point, click on Layout in the menu bar.
3. Click on Line.
4. Click on Center.

5. Type the text you want centered. The text will be centered over the location of the insertion point.

6. Press Enter to end the centering, or Tab or space further on the line to a new insertion point and follow steps 2 through 5 to center text over the insertion point.

7. When you are finished centering on the line, press Enter.

When you center text at a position on the line, the position must be preceded by at least a space or a tab. You may center more than one segment of text on a line, but if you do, be sure that there is enough space between segments. Otherwise, they may overlap.

 Shortcut: You can center text on a line by positioning the insertion point at the left margin or at a location on the line and pressing the Center key (Shift+F7). Type the text you want centered.

Ending a Center Code

When you choose Center you insert a Center code [Center] into your document. The following codes or keystrokes end the centering: Enter, Tab, Soft Return, Flush Right, End Centering/Alignment.

Centering Text With Leader Dots

When centering text, you can insert leader dots from the left margin to the beginning of the centered text. To do this:

1. Press the Center key (Shift+F7) twice.
2. Type the centered text.

To continue the leader dots from the centered text to the end of the line, continue as follows:

3. Press the Flush Right key (Alt+F7) twice.
4. Press Enter. The text is centered with leader dots on both sides.

End Centering in the Middle of a Line

You can end centering in the middle of a line by using the End Centering/Alignment feature. When you use this code, the text following the Center code will remain centered and the text following the End Centering/Alignment code will continue along the line without being centered. Let's try an example.

1. At the left margin, press the Center Key (Ctrl+F7).
2. Type your name.
3. Click on Layout in the menu bar.
4. Click on Line.
5. Click on Special Codes.
6. Choose End Centering/Alignment.
7. Choose Insert.
8. Continue typing on the line. The text is no longer centering.

Centering Existing Text

You can center existing text by moving the insertion point to the beginning of the text and choosing Center, or by selecting the existing text and choosing Center.

Centering Multiple Lines of Text

You can center several lines of text by selecting the lines and choosing Center, or by using the Justification feature explained later in this chapter.

Using Flush Right

The Flush Right feature aligns text with the right margin. You can begin flush right alignment anywhere on the line. When you choose Flush Right, as you type, the text is pushed to the left of the insertion point. When you press Enter, flush right alignment ends. Let's try an example of flush right text.

1. At the left margin click on Layout.
2. Click on Line.
3. Click on Flush Right. The insertion point moves to the right margin.
4. Type a few words of text.

5. Press Enter. Flush right alignment ends and the insertion point moves to the left margin of the next line.

Shortcut: You can flush right text on a line by positioning the insertion point at the location where you want flush right alignment to begin and pressing the Flush Right key (Alt+F7). Type the text you want to be flush right. Press Enter to end the flush right alignment and return the insertion point to the left margin of the next line.

Using Flush Right with Leader Dots

To insert leader dots before flush right text, press the Flush Right key (Alt+F7) twice and then type in the text.

Flush Right Aligning Existing Text

You can flush right existing text by moving the insertion point to the beginning of the text and choosing Flush Right or by selecting existing text and choosing Flush Right. Be sure that there is a hard return after the line before you choose Flush Right.

Flush Right Aligning Several Lines of Text

You can flush right several lines of text by selecting the lines and choosing Flush Right (be sure that there is a hard return after each line), or by using the Justification feature explained later in this chapter.

You can use more than one alignment code (such as, Tab, Flush Right, Center) on a line. Be sure that the aligned text does not overlap.

Aligning Text with Justification

When you justify text, you align it at a particular location. Contrary to its common usage, the word "justification" does not refer only to a flush right margin. WordPerfect allows you to justify (align) text at four locations: Left, Center, Right, and Full. Justification is usually used to align blocks of text. Single lines of text can be aligned using the align codes covered earlier in this chapter. Figure 4.6 shows examples of each type of justification on a page.

Thank you for your assistance at the last parent meeting. Without your help, we could not have done such a wonderful job planning the bake sale. We look forward to seeing you at the sale with more of your fabulous cookies.

Ms. Amy Jones
150 Elm Street
Mainville, NY 11111

Thank you for your assistance at the last parent meeting. Without your help, we could not have done such a wonderful job planning the bake sale. We look forward to seeing you at the sale with more of your fabulous cookies.

Ms. Amy Jones
150 Elm Street
Mainville, NY 11111

Figure 4.6—Examples of justified text.

Left Justification

The first paragraph in Figure 4.6 is an example of **left justification**. The text is aligned at the left margin of the page. This produces a ragged right margin.

Right Justification

The second segment of text in Figure 4.6 is an example of **right justification**. Each line is aligned at the right margin of the page. This produces a ragged left margin.

When Right Justification is active, you cannot use Center, Flush Right, or any of the Tab Align features. You also cannot use hyphenation.

Full Justification

The third paragraph in Figure 4.6 is an example of **full justification**. Text is aligned at both the right and left margins. The spacing between words and letters may expand or compress as necessary to force the text to align at both margins. You might want to hyphenate long words at the end of a line to prevent text from "stringing out" to align at the right margin.

You can also change the Word Spacing Justification Limits in the Typesetting dialog box to set the minimum and maximum limits that words can be compressed or spread apart. This feature is covered in Chapter 16.

Center Justification

The last segment of text in Figure 4.6 is an example of **center justification**. Each line of text is centered between the left and right margins.

When Center Justification is active, you cannot use Center, Flush Right, or any of the Tab Align features. You also cannot use hyphenation.

Setting Justification

To set justification:

1. Bring the insertion point to the beginning of a paragraph.
2. Click on Layout in the menu bar.
3. Click on Justification to display the Justification cascading menu.
4. Choose the Justification menu item you want.

You can also set justification by selecting text and applying justification to the selected text.

1. Bring the insertion point to the beginning of the first paragraph you want to select.
2. Select all of the text you want to justify.
3. Follow steps 2 through 4 above. Only the text you have selected is changed.

When you set justification, WordPerfect inserts a justification code in the document [Just:Full]. This code remains in effect until WordPerfect encounters a different justification code.

When you select text to justify, WordPerfect inserts a new justification code at the beginning of the selected text. After the selected text, WordPerfect inserts the justification code you were using before the text was selected and changed. Type the following example using Full Justification:

```
Thank you for offering to bake something for
the Junior High School Bake Sale. We are
thrilled to report that this year's effort
should top all previous sales.  Please bake
anything included in the following list:

Cookies
Cakes
Brownies
Donuts
Muffins
Fudge

We know with your assistance, this year's
Bake Sale will top all others.
```

Now:

1. Using the mouse or keyboard, select the items in the list.
2. Click on Layout in the menu bar.
3. Click on Justification.
4. Choose Center Justification. The list is now centered between the margins.
5. Look in Reveal Codes. Note that WordPerfect has inserted a [Just:Center] code at the beginning of the selected text and has inserted a [Just:Full] code at the beginning of the last paragraph.

If Auto Code Placement is turned on, and you place justification codes in the middle of a line or paragraph, the codes will automatically move to the beginning of the paragraph.

If Auto Code Placement is turned off when you insert justification codes, WordPerfect will place the codes at the location of the insertion point.

Justification changes can also be made using the ruler, which is covered later in this chapter.

Enhancing Words with Bold, Italics, and Underline

You can really add pizazz to your text by using some simple typing enhancements to emphasize your words. Features such as **Bold**, *Italics*, and Underline help you to get your meaning across in an attractive and professional way. These enhancements are easy to achieve in WordPerfect.

Please note that all typing enhancements depend upon the ability of your printer to support them.

Bolding Your Words

You can either bold text as you type, or you can select text that is already typed and make it bold. To bold as you type:

1. Type to the point where you want to begin bolding.
2. Press Ctrl+B to begin bolding.
3. Type the word(s) you want to bold.
4. Press Ctrl+B again to stop bolding.

To bold selected text:

1. Select the word or words you want to bold.
2. Press Ctrl+B to bold the selected text.
3. Press F8 or click the mouse to end select mode.

You can also use the Bold command in the Font menu:

1. Select the word or words you want to bold.
2. Click on Font in the menu bar to open the Font menu.
3. Click on Bold. The selected text is bolded.

Deleting Bold Codes

Bolded text is surrounded by [Bold On] and [Bold Off] codes. You can unbold the text by locating either of these codes in Reveal Codes and deleting them.

Italicizing Your Words

You can either italicize text as you type, or you can select text and italicize it. To italicize as you type:

1. Type to the point where you want to begin italics.
2. Press Ctrl+I to begin italics.
3. Type the word(s) you want to italicize.
4. Press Ctrl+I again to stop italics.

To italicize selected text:

1. Select the word or words you want to italicize.
2. Press Ctrl+I to italicize the selected text.
3. Press F8 or click the mouse to end select mode.

You can also use the Italic command in the Font menu:

1. Select the word or words you want to italicize.
2. Click on Font in the menu bar to open the Font menu.
3. Click on Italic. The selected text is italicized.

Deleting Italic Codes

Italicized text is surrounded by [Italc On] and [Italc Off] codes. You can unitalicize the text by locating either of these codes in Reveal Codes and deleting them.

Underlining Your Words

You can either underline text as you type, or you can select text and underline it. To underline as you type:

1. Type to the point where you want to begin underlining.
2. Press Ctrl+U to begin underlining.
3. Type the word(s) you want to underline.
4. Press Ctrl+U again to stop underlining.

To underline selected text:

1. Select the word or words you want to underline.
2. Press Ctrl+U to underline the selected text.
3. Press F8 or click the mouse to end select mode.

You can also use the Underline command in the Font menu:

1. Select the word or words you want to underline.
2. Click on Font in the menu bar to open the Font menu.
3. Click on Underline. The selected text is underlined.

Deleting Underline Codes

Underlined text is surrounded by [Und On] and [Und Off] codes. You can remove underlining by locating either of these codes in Reveal Codes and deleting them.

Double Underlining Your Words

You can also double underline text:

1. Select the word or words you want to double underline.
2. Click on Font in the menu bar to open the Font menu.
3. Click on Double Underline. The selected text is double underlined.

Deleting Double Underline Codes

Double Underlined text is surrounded by [Dbl Und On] and [Dbl Und Off] codes. You can remove double underlining by locating either of these codes in Reveal Codes and deleting them.

Underlining Spaces and Tabs

When you underline more than one word in WordPerfect, the spaces between the words are automatically underlined. However, when you underline text and then press the Tab key, the tabbed space is not underlined. You can instruct WordPerfect not to underline spaces between words. You can also instruct WordPerfect to underline between tabs.

To change the Underline Space or Underline Tab settings:

1. Click on Layout in the menu bar to open the Layout menu.
2. Click on Typesetting to open the Typesetting dialog box, as shown in Figure 4.7.

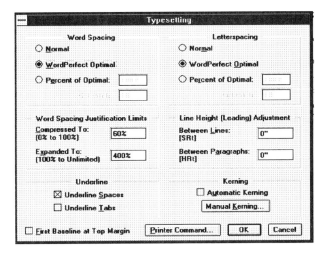

Figure 4.7—The Typesetting dialog box.

3. To underline spaces, choose Underline Spaces in the Underline options.

4. To underline tabs, choose Underline Tabs in the Underline options.

5. When an option is chosen, an X appears in the box. To deselect, click on the box again and the X is removed.

6. Choose OK.

When you change the Underline Space or Underline Tab option, the change takes effect at the insertion point. It will remain in effect until you change it again.

Converting Case

You can select text and instruct WordPerfect to convert it to uppercase or lowercase. This is particularly useful if you have accidentally typed a large segment of text with the CapsLock key on.

To convert text to uppercase or lowercase:

1. Select the text you want to change.

2. Click on Edit in the menu bar to open the Edit menu.

3. Click on Convert Case to open the Convert Case menu.

4. Choose Uppercase or Lowercase.

Using the Date and Time Feature

You can use WordPerfect to insert the date and/or time into your document in a number of different formats. WordPerfect uses the date and time set on your computer. This means that your computer must be set to the correct date and time for this code to work properly. Consult your computer manual to set the date and time.

WordPerfect uses the date and time when you first started the program as the current date and time. If you have been working in WordPerfect for several hours without exiting, the time (and the date, if you have worked past midnight) will not be current.

Inserting Date Text

When you insert a date using the Date Text code, WordPerfect inserts the current date as text, which means it will not change if you retrieve or print the document thereafter. The WordPerfect default inserts the date only at the insertion point. To insert the date:

1. Bring the insertion point to where you want the date inserted.
2. Press Ctrl+F5. The current date is inserted into your document at the insertion point. The default date format reads as follows:

```
November 10, 1991
```

You can also insert the date by using the Date command in the Tools menu:

1. Place the insertion point where you want the date inserted.
2. Click on Tools in the menu bar to open the Tools menu.
3. Click on Date. The Date cascading menu opens.
4. Choose Date Text. The current date is inserted into your document at the insertion point.

Inserting a Date Code

When you insert a date using Date Code, WordPerfect inserts the current date as a code that is updated to the current date if you retrieve or print the document thereafter. The WordPerfect default inserts the date only at the insertion point. To insert a date code:

1. Bring the insertion point to where you want the date code inserted.
2. Press Ctrl+Shift+F5. The current date and a [Date] code are inserted into your document at the insertion point. The default date format reads as follows:

```
November 10, 1991
```

If you retrieve or print the document at a later date, the date code will update it.

You can also insert a date code by using the Date command from the Tools menu:

1. Bring the insertion point to where you want the date code inserted.
2. Click on Tools in the menu bar to open the Tools menu.
3. Click on Date to open the Date cascading menu.
4. Choose Date Code. The current date and a date code are inserted into your document at the insertion point.

Changing the Date Format

The default date format prints only the date (not the time) and prints the month first, followed by a comma, a space, and the year. You can change the default format by using the Format option. To do this:

1. Bring the insertion point to where you want to insert a new format.
2. Click on Tools in the menu bar to open the Tools menu.
3. Click on Date to open the Date cascading menu.
4. Click on Format to display the Document Date/Time Format dialog box, as shown in Figure 4.8.

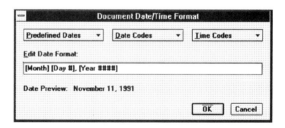

Figure 4.8—The Document Date/Time Format dialog box.

You can choose from a predefined format or you can design your own. To select a predefined format, follow these steps:

1. Follow steps 1 through 4 above.
2. Select one of the formats in the Predefined Dates drop-down list box.
3. The new format appears in the Edit Date Format text box.
4. Date Preview shows how the date will appear in your document.

To design your own format:

1. Bring the insertion point to where you want to insert a new format.
2. Click on Tools in the menu bar to open the Tools menu.
3. Click on Date to open the Date cascading menu.
4. Click on Format to display the Document Date/Time Format dialog box, as shown in Figure 4.8.
5. Combine codes from the Date Codes and Date Times drop-down list boxes to define your own format. Make changes in the Edit Date Format text box.
6. Date Preview shows how the date will appear in your document.

When you change the format for date and time, the new format becomes effective at the insertion point. It remains effective until a new format is encountered. To change the system Date and Time default, see Appendix A.

Using Hyphenation

As you type in WordPerfect, the text automatically wraps at the end of the line when you reach the **hyphenation zone**. If you prefer, you can set WordPerfect so that it will hyphenate words that are too long to fit on a line.

To turn hyphenation on:

1. Bring the insertion point to where you want hyphenation to begin.
2. Click on Layout in the menu bar to open the Layout menu.
3. Click on Line.
4. Click on Hyphenation to display the Line Hyphenation dialog box, as shown in Figure 4.9.

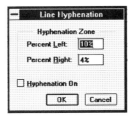

Figure 4.9—The Line Hyphenation dialog box.

5. Select Hyphenation On.
6. Choose OK. Hyphenation is now turned on.

What WordPerfect does when it reaches a word that needs to be hyphenated depends on how the Prompt for Hyphenation options are set. To set the Prompt for Hyphenation options:

1. Click on File in the menu bar to open the File menu.
2. Click on Preferences to open the Preferences cascading menu.
3. Click on Environment to display the Environment Settings dialog box, as shown in Figure 4.10.

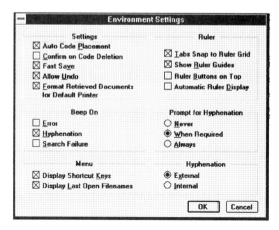

Figure 4.10—The Environment Settings dialog box.

4. Select one of the Prompt for Hyphenations options (explained below).
5. Click OK.

Never tells WordPerfect to hyphenate the word according to the instructions in the hyphenation dictionary. If the word cannot be found in the dictionary, WordPerfect will wrap it to the next line.

When Required tells WordPerfect to hyphenate the word according to the instructions in the hyphenation dictionary. If the word cannot be found in the dictionary, a Position Hyphen dialog box appears prompting you to position the hyphen. Use the left or right arrow keys or click where you want to place the hyphen. Then choose Insert Hyphen. This is the WordPerfect default.

Always tells WordPerfect to stop at each word requiring hyphenation. The Position Hyphen dialog box appears, prompting you to position the hyphen.

Inserting Soft Hyphens

You can manually hyphenate a word, even if the hyphenation feature is turned off by using Soft Hyphens and Hyphenation Soft Returns. To manually hyphenate a word using a Soft Hyphen:

1. Bring the insertion point to the location in the word where you want to insert the hyphen.
2. Press Ctrl+Shift+ – (minus sign). A soft hyphen appears

in Reveal Codes and the word is hyphenated. If you edit the text later and the word no longer falls in the hyphenation zone, the soft hyphen disappears.

Hyphenation Soft Returns are used to break up a long word when it falls in the hyphenation zone. A hyphen is not inserted in the printed text; the word is simply broken up. This is useful for words separated by slashes (such as January/February/March). To insert a Hyphenation Soft Return:

1. Bring the insertion point to the location in the word where you want to insert a hyphen.
2. Click on Layout in the menu bar to open the Layout menu.
3. Click on Line.
4. Click on Special Codes to display the Insert Special Codes dialog box.
5. Select Hyphenation Soft Return.
6. Choose Insert.

If Auto Code Placement is turned on, and you turn hyphenation codes on in the middle of a line or paragraph, the codes will automatically move to the beginning of the paragraph.

If Auto Code Placement is turned off when you set hyphenation codes, WordPerfect will place the hyphenation codes at the location of the insertion point.

Hyphenation Zone

When Hyphenation is turned on, the Hyphenation Zone determines which words will be hyphenated. Increasing the size of the zone *decreases* the number of words that need to be hyphenated, while decreasing the size of the zone *increases* the number of words that need to be hyphenated. To set the hyphenation zone:

1. Bring the insertion point to where you want the hyphenation zone to begin.
2. Click on Layout in the menu bar to open the Layout menu.
3. Click on Line.
4. Click on Hyphenation to display the Line Hyphenation dialog box, as shown in Figure 4.9.

5. Type the hyphenation zone settings in the Percent Left and Percent Right text boxes.
6. Choose OK.

Auto Code Placement

Certain WordPerfect codes are designed to be placed at the beginning of a paragraph or a page. If Auto Code Placement is turned on when you insert these codes into a document, the codes are automatically moved to the correct location, no matter where the insertion point was when the code was inserted.

The default setting for Auto Code Placement is On. To change the default setting, see Appendix A.

The following table shows where codes are moved when Auto Code Placement is turned on.

Code	Beginning of Paragraph	Beginning of Page
Hyphenation Zone	X	
Letterspacing	X	
Justification	X	
Line Numbering	X	
Line Height	X	
Line Spacing	X	
Margins, Left and Right	X	
Margins, Top and Bottom		X
Page, Center		X
Page Numbering		X
Page, Size		X
Paragraph Numbering	X	
Suppress		X
Tab Set	X	
Word Spacing	X	
Justification Limits	X	

The WordPerfect Ruler

The ruler is one of the exciting new features found in WordPerfect for Windows. When it is displayed, you can use it to make quick formatting changes, bypassing the Layout and Font menus. The ruler always appears at the top of the document window, although you can use it to make changes anywhere in the document. Any changes you make in the ruler will be inserted into the document at the insertion point (unless they are affected by Auto Code Placement). You can use the ruler to define tables and columns, set margins and tabs, change fonts and line spacing, create styles, and turn on justification.

Let's type a new document and make changes in formatting using the ruler. In a new window, type the following document. Tab once after each colon:

```
                    MEMO TO STAFF
        To: All Staff

        From:    The Managing Partners

        Re: Vacations Memos for 1992

        Please be advised that all Vacation Memos
        for the year 1992 must be submitted to the
        Managing Partners no later than March 30,
        1992.
```

Your window should look like Figure 4.11.

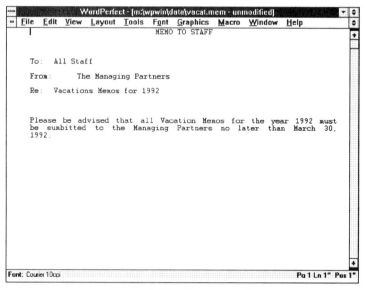

Figure 4.11—Memo to staff.

To turn the ruler on:

1. Click on View in the menu bar to open the View menu.
2. Click on Ruler (Alt+Shift+F3). The ruler is displayed at the top of the document window, as shown in Figure 4.12.

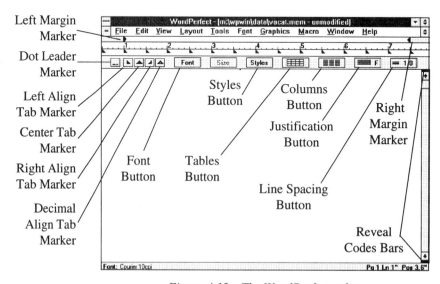

Figure 4.12—The WordPerfect ruler.

Setting New Left and Right Margins

You can change left and right margins in the ruler by dragging the left and right margin markers. If you double-click on either margin marker, the margins dialog box will appear. You can also make changes in the dialog box.

When you drag a margin or tab marker, a vertical line appears, helping you to mark the setting.

Let's change the margins in our vacation memo using the ruler.

1. Position the insertion point at the beginning of the memo. Remember, even though the ruler is at the top of the window, changes become effective at the insertion point.

2. Drag the left margin marker from 1" to 2". The right margin now begins 2" from the left edge of the page.

3. Drag the right margin marker from 7.5" to 6.5". The right margin now ends 2" from the right edge of the page. Your memo should now look like Figure 4.13.

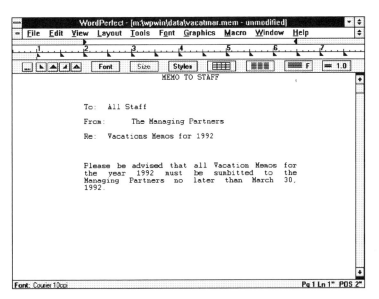

Figure 4.13—Using the ruler to change margins.

Deleting and Setting Tabs

WordPerfect defaults to Left Align tabs set for every .5". You can change these settings in the ruler.

Deleting Tabs

To delete tabs in the ruler, bring the insertion point to the tab(s) you want to delete and drag it off the ruler. Let's delete a tab in our memo.

1. Bring the insertion point to the beginning of the memo.
2. Point to the tab located at 2.5" and drag it off the ruler. Notice that the text after the colons now lines up, as shown in Figure 4.14.

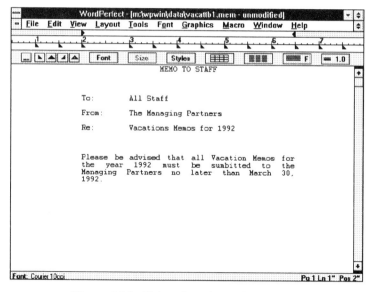

Figure 4.14—Using the ruler to delete a tab.

Inserting Tabs

There are five tab markers that are used to set tabs in the ruler, as shown in Figure 4.14. You can set a tab on the ruler by dragging one of the tab markers to a position on the ruler line. If you double-click on any of the tab markers, the Tab Set dialog box appears. You can also make changes in the dialog box.

As you drag along the ruler line, the position prompt in the status bar keeps you informed of your position. This makes it easier to locate a position on the ruler.

Let's insert a tab in our memo.

1. Bring the insertion point to the first paragraph in the body of the memo (right before the word "Please").
2. Drag the Left Align tab marker to 2.5".
3. Press the Tab key before the word "Please." Your memo should now look like Figure 4.15.

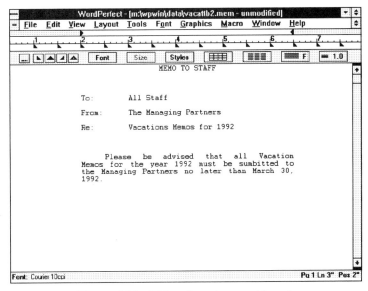

Figure 4.15—Using the ruler to add a tab.

You can insert any type of tab by dragging the appropriate tab marker to a position on the ruler. If you click on the Dot Leader tab marker, all of the tab markers have leader dots.

Changing Line Spacing

To change the line spacing using the ruler, point to the Line Spacing button, press the mouse, and hold. A Line Spacing pop-up list appears with 1.0, 1.5, and 2.0 line spacing choices. You can select one of these choices or double-click on the Line Spacing button to bring up the Line Spacing dialog box. To change the line spacing in your vacation memo:

1. Bring the insertion point to the beginning of the body of the memo (right before the word "Please").
2. Choose 2.0 Spacing from the Line Spacing pop-up list. The body of the memo is now double-spaced.

Changing Justification

The Justification feature is explained earlier in this chapter. To change justification using the ruler:

1. Bring the insertion point to where you want to change justification.
2. Make a choice from the Justification pop-up list.

Using Reveal Codes

Chapter 3 explains how Reveal Codes is used. You can use the Reveal Codes bar right under the ruler (see Figure 4.11) to split the screen for Reveal Codes:

1. Position the insertion point over the Reveal Codes bar.
2. When the insertion point changes to a double arrow, drag the bar as far up or down as you want to split the window for Reveal Codes. You can make the Reveal Codes screen larger or smaller, depending upon where you position the bar.

To turn Reveal Codes off:

1. Click on View in the menu bar to open the View menu.
2. Click on Reveal Codes; or
3. Drag the Reveal codes bar back to its original position.

Using the Ruler with Fonts

You can assign fonts to the ruler and then select assigned fonts. This feature is covered in Chapter 16.

Using the Ruler with Styles

You can select styles in the ruler. This feature is covered in Chapter 15.

Using the Ruler with Tables

You can define tables with the ruler. This feature is covered in Chapter 11.

Hiding the Ruler

To hide the ruler:

1. Click on View in the menu bar to open the View menu.
2. Click on Ruler (Alt+Shift+F3). The ruler is now hidden.

Review Exercises for Chapter 4

◆ Type a short document.
◆ Change the left and right margins, first using the menu and then using the ruler.
◆ Double space one paragraph only.
◆ Clear the tabs using the menu, then, using the ruler, insert Left Align tabs at 1" intervals.
◆ Add a paragraph with a hanging indent at the end of the document.
◆ At the beginning of the document, center a title.
◆ Change the justification in the entire document to left. Change it back to full.
◆ Bold two words in the document. Underline two words. Double underline two words.
◆ Convert one sentence to uppercase. Convert it back to lowercase.
◆ Insert the date at the end of the document, using the Date Text feature.
◆ Turn Hyphenation on at the beginning of the document. Hyphenate words that fall into the hyphenation zone.

Before You Go On...

Before you go on, you should be comfortable with all of the basic formatting codes, including margin changes, line spacing, tab sets, and justification. You should be able to use the menus and the ruler to accomplish formatting changes. You should know how to use bold, italics, and underline, and how the Date and Time feature works. You should know how to hyphenate words and you should understand how the Auto Code Placement Feature affects the placement of codes.

Chapter 5

Working with Multiple Page Documents

What You Will Learn in this Chapter

- ◆ How to use headers and footers
- ◆ How to use page numbering
- ◆ How to change top and bottom margins
- ◆ How to center text vertically on a page
- ◆ How to work with page breaks
- ◆ How to scroll through long documents

So far we have only worked with documents that are less than one page in length. However, most documents are longer. In this chapter you are going to create multiple-page documents and learn how to work with the formatting codes that relate to them.

Creating a Two-Page Letter

In a new window, type the following letter. Press Enter five times after the first address, four times after the date, and three times before and after the Re: line.

```
                              General Beetle Bailey
                              The Pentagon
                              Washington, DC



                              November 1, 1991


His Excellency, George Bush
The White House
1600 Pennsylvania Avenue
Washington, DC


         Re:  Intergalactic Defense System


Dear Mr. President:

     In  response  to  your  urgent  request
concerning  our  ability  to  defend  this  Planet
against  an  attack  from  outer  space,  we  are
honored  to  submit  the  following  proposed defense
plan  which  has  been  developed  by  our  topmost
defense  expert  to  deal  with  this  predicament.

     For  your  convenience,  we  have  organized
this  proposed  plan  into  300  major  chapters,
including  4,000  subchapters,  complete  with
footnotes  and  summaries.  We  trust  that  you  will
```

appreciate our efforts to summarize this material and present it in an orderly and logical sequence.

Also enclosed with this letter, as exhibits, are summaries of total costs for the plan, and a chart listing our major areas of vulnerability in the event of such a dastardly attack.

Unfortunately, since our exploration of outer space has been somewhat limited, we have been unable to develop the necessary contacts to provide us with useful allies on other planets. We also lack information regarding possible enemy life forms and weaponry. Therefore, we have developed an alternative plan which will deprive any attacking party from enjoying the fruits of his victory in the event that the attached plan is unsuccessful. We have strategically placed nuclear nodes in key locations all over the planet and, if necessary, we will detonate them and destroy the entire Earth. For further information concerning this plan, please contact our public relations department. Your request, however, should be labeled "TOP SECRET."

If you have any further questions concerning the enclosed plan, please do not hesitate to contact the undersigned. We at the Pentagon are always pleased to be of service to our revered national leader and Armed Forces Chief of Staff.

Very truly yours,

THE PENTAGON

General Beetle Bailey
Chief, Department of
Outer Space Defense

/Enclosures

You should now have a document that extends beyond the window. Notice that there is a line across the window representing a page break at the end of page 1. WordPerfect automatically breaks your document into pages. The location of the page break is determined by your fonts and top and bottom margin settings. You will find out later that you can control where WordPerfect breaks up pages.

Working with Headers and Footers

Headers are text and/or numbers that print on the top of every page. Footers are text and/or numbers that print on the bottom of every page. You can have up to two headers and/or two footers on each page; there is no limit to the number of headers or footers you can have in a document.

Headers and footers are considered part of the text. Headers start printing at the top margin and footers end at the bottom margin. Headers and footers never print inside the top or bottom margin. If you feel that your headers are starting too low or your footers are ending too high, adjust your top and bottom margins (see "Top and Bottom Margins" later in this chapter).

The best place to put header and footer codes is at the top of your document or after a hard page break (hard page breaks are explained later in this chapter). This way they are not moved around when you insert or delete text.

If Auto Code Placement is turned on, WordPerfect automatically places the header or footer code at the beginning of a page. The new header or footer affects the page that contains the insertion point and all subsequent pages until the header or footer is discontinued or replaced.

If Auto Code Placement is turned off, be sure that header and footer codes are placed at the beginning of the page. Headers and footers that are inserted after text will not appear until the next page ("text" means any character at all, even a space). A header or footer will continue to appear on each specified page (every page, odd pages, or even pages) until you replace it with a new header or footer or discontinue it.

You can have two headers (Header A and Header B) and two footers (Footer A and Footer B) on each page. While you can define headers and footers in any order, it is easier to keep track of them if you define Header A and Footer A before Header B and Footer B. Header A can be replaced only by a new Header A, Header B can be replaced only by a new Header B, and so on.

To delete a header or footer code, locate it in Reveal Codes and delete it. If you accidentally delete a header or footer code, you can use the Undelete or Undo feature to restore it.

You can use most formatting codes in headers or footers, including fonts, columns, line spacing, left and right margins, and so forth. The codes will not affect the rest of your document. You cannot change top or bottom margins.

A single header or footer can contain up to one page of text as defined by the current format. If you attempt to put more than one page of text in a header or footer, you will get an error code.

WordPerfect inserts one blank line between a header or a footer and the text. If you want additional lines, add them in the Header or Footer window when you type in the text for the header or footer.

Creating a Header or Footer

To create a header or footer:

1. Position the insertion point on the page where you want the header or footer to start (preferably at the beginning of a page; if Auto Code Placement is turned off, your insertion point must be at the top of the page).

2. Click on Layout in the menu bar to open the Layout menu.

3. Click on Page (Alt+F9).

4. Choose either Headers or Footers. Depending upon your choice, the Headers or Footers dialog box will open (see Figure 5.1).

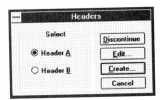

Figure 5.1—The Headers dialog box.

5. Select either Header A or B or Footer A or B.

6. Choose Create. The Header or Footer window appears with the prompt Header A or Header B or Footer A or Footer B in the status bar.

7. Type the text of the header or footer. You can edit as you would a normal document. You can also change formatting codes if desired. Any features that are not available when formatting headers and footers are dimmed in the menus.

8. Choose Placement to specify on which pages you want the header or footer to appear.

    a. Every Page—WordPerfect places the header or footer on every page.

    b. Odd Pages—WordPerfect places the header or footer on odd pages only.

    c. Even Pages—WordPerfect placed the header or footer on even pages only.

9. Choose Page Number to place a page number in your header or footer. WordPerfect will insert ^B at the insertion point. This instructs WordPerfect to begin numbering on the current page and to consecutively number every page thereafter.

10. Choose Close to save the header or footer and return to the document window.

You will not see the header or footer in the document window. To view your header or footer without printing it, you must use the Print Preview command (see Chapter 16).

Odd and Even Pages

You may want headers or footers to print on odd or even pages. An example would be setting Header A to print text and page numbers at the left margin on odd pages, and setting Header B to print text and page numbers at the right margin on even pages (see Figure 5.2). To specify odd or even pages, choose Placement in the Header or Footer dialog box.

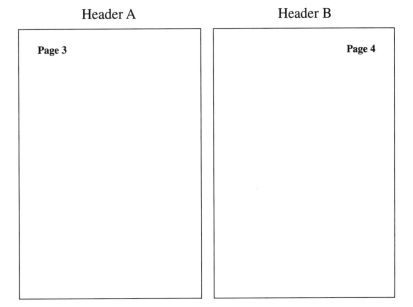

Figure 5.2—Odd and even headers.

Editing a Header or Footer

You can edit a header or footer once it has been saved. To do this:

1. If you have more than one header or footer in the document, bring the insertion point to the page containing the Header or Footer code you want to edit.
2. Click on Layout in the menu bar to open the Layout menu.
3. Click on Page.
4. Click on Headers or Footers to display the Headers or Footers dialog box.

5. Select the header or footer you would like to edit (A or B).
6. Choose Edit to display the Header or Footer window.
7. Edit the header or footer.
8. Choose Close to confirm your changes.

Discontinuing a Header or Footer

When you discontinue a header or a footer, it stops printing from the point where it was discontinued until the end of the document. To discontinue headers or footers:

1. Place your insertion point where you want to discontinue the header or footer.
2. Click on Layout in the menu bar to open the Layout menu.
3. Click on Page.
4. Click on Headers or Footers to display the Headers or Footers dialog box.
5. Choose Discontinue. The header or footer is discontinued for the rest of the document. If you want to turn it back on for a subsequent page, you must recreate it or copy it. If you change your mind about discontinuing a header or footer, you can delete the Discontinue code in Reveal Codes.

Suppressing a Header or Footer

You can suppress a header or footer for a specific page. This option is usually used on page 1 when you want the text and/or numbering to begin on page 2. To suppress a header or footer for one page:

1. Place the insertion point where you want to suppress the header or footer. If Auto Code Placement is turned on, the code will be moved to the top of the page. If Auto Code Placement is turned off, place the code after the header or footer code or after a hard page break (hard page breaks are explained later in this chapter).
2. Click on Layout in the menu bar.

3. Click on Page.

4. Choose Suppress to display the Suppress dialog box, as shown in Figure 5.3.

Figure 5.3—The Suppress dialog box.

5. Choose the item(s) you want to suppress.

6. Choose OK to return to the document window.

The Suppress feature suppresses the header or footer for one page only. If you want to discontinue the header or footer for the rest of the document use Discontinue (see above).

Now that we know how headers and footers work, let's put a header on our letter to George Bush.

1. Bring the insertion point to the beginning of the letter.

2. Click on Layout in the menu bar to open the Layout menu.

3. Click on Page.

4. Click on Headers to display the Headers dialog box.

5. Select Header A and choose Create. The Header window opens.

6. Click on Placement and choose Every Page.

7. At the margin, type:

```
His Excellency, George Bush
November 1, 1991
Page
```

8. Type a space after the word "Page" and click on Page Number. A ^B code will appear. This code tells WordPerfect to start numbering on the current page, and consecutively numbers every page thereafter.

9. Choose Close to save the header and return to the document window.

We have placed the header code for our letter at the beginning of the first page, but we do not want the header to print on the first page. Therefore, we must suppress the header on the first page, so that it begins printing on the second page. To suppress the Header:

1. Place the insertion point right after the header code on the first page.
2. Click on Layout in the menu bar to open the Layout menu.
3. Click on Page.
4. Click on Suppress to display the Suppress dialog box.
5. Select Header A.
6. Choose OK to return to the document window. Header A has now been suppressed on the first page.

Using Page Numbering

If you have several lines of text that you want to print at the top or bottom of every page, you should use headers or footers. If you want to use page numbers with a limited amount of text and limited placement options, you should use the Page Numbering feature.

You can also use the Page Numbering feature to insert a page number in text at a specific location on current page (see "Insert Page Number" below).

The best place to put a Page Numbering code is at the top of your document or after a hard page break. This way they are not moved around when you insert or delete text.

If Auto Code Placement is turned on, the Page Numbering code is automatically placed at the beginning of the page. If Auto Code Placement is turned off, WordPerfect inserts the Page Numbering code at the insertion point, and numbering begins on the next page. In both cases, the Page Numbering code will remain in effect until the end of the document, or until it is turned off.

To delete a Page Numbering code, locate it in Reveal Codes and delete it. If you accidentally delete a Page Numbering code, you can use the Undelete or Undo feature to restore it.

To use the Page Numbering feature:

1. Place the insertion point where you want Page Numbering to begin.
2. Click on Layout in the menu bar to open the Layout menu.
3. Click on Page.
4. Click on Numbering to display the Page Numbering dialog box, as shown in Figure 5.4.

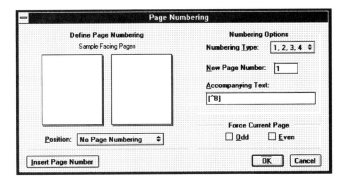

Figure 5.4—The Page Numbering dialog box.

5. Fill in the information requested by the dialog box.
6. Choose OK.

Page Numbering Position

You may select any of the following positions for your page numbers (if you do not select a position, WordPerfect defaults to No Page Numbering, and page numbers will not appear in the document):

- No Page Numbering
- Top Left
- Top Center
- Top Right
- Alternating Top (top-left corner for even pages, top-right corner for odd pages)

- Bottom Left
- Bottom Center
- Bottom Right
- Alternating (bottom-left corner for even pages, bottom-right corner for odd pages)

Use the Position drop-down list to make your selection. The location you have selected is displayed on the sample facing pages (see Figure 5.4).

Page Numbering Styles

Page Numbering allows you to select from the three different types of numbering systems listed below. Use the Numbering Type drop-down list to make your selection.

- Arabic numerals (1, 2, 3)
- Lowercase Roman numerals (i, ii, iii); and
- Uppercase Roman numerals (I, II, III).

You can use this feature to change the numbering style in headers and footers as well. Before you define your header or footer, select the numbering type in the Page Numbering dialog box. Page Numbering Position should be set to No Page Numbering. Click on OK. Then define your header or footer. The Page Numbering code *must* precede the header or footer code in Reveal Codes for the new numbering type to be reflected in your header or footer.

New Page Number

When you insert a Page Numbering code, WordPerfect assumes that you want page numbering to begin with the page number that contains the insertion point. This is not always the case. For example, you might have a document that begins with a cover page. The next page is the first page of the actual text, but because it follows the cover page, WordPerfect thinks it is page 2 of the document. You can renumber this page using New Page Number. You can use this option to begin renumbering pages at any point in your document.

To insert a New Page Number:

1. Place the insertion point on the beginning of the page where you want to begin renumbering.
2. Open the Page Numbering dialog box.
3. Type the new number in the New Page Number text box. Use arabic numerals (1, 2, 3...) to change the page number. Do not use roman numerals, even if you have selected a roman numerals numbering type. The new number is displayed in the status bar. The pages that follow are numbered consecutively, starting with that number.

You can change the page number in headers and footers as well, by using this feature. Before you define your header or footer, type a new page number in the Page Numbering dialog box. Page numbering position should be set to No Page Numbering. Click on OK. Then define your header or footer. The Page Numbering code *must* precede the header or footer code in Reveal Codes for the new page number to be reflected in your header or footer.

Accompanying Text

You can use a limited amount of text with the Page Numbering feature (if you require a lot of text, you should be using headers or footers). The text is typed in the Accompanying Text text box.

The page number code [^B] is already in the box. You should position this code where you want it to appear in the text. For example, if you want the text to read "Chapter 1 -- Page 1," the Accompanying Text text box should contain the following information: Chapter 1 -- Page [^B]. If you forget to include the page number code [^B], WordPerfect inserts it at the end of the text in the Accompanying Text text box.

Forcing Current Page Number

You can force WordPerfect to assign an odd or even number to a page. For example, you might want the first pages of all the chapters in a manual to begin on an odd page. If you want to force an odd or even page number, insert the Page Number code at the beginning of the page and choose Odd or Even in the Force Current Page box.

Inserting Page Numbering

You can insert page numbers in text anywhere on a page. For example, in a will there is usually an attestation clause that reads in part: "The foregoing instrument, consisting of # pages, including this page ..." The # represents the number of pages. If you insert a page number using the Insert Page Numbering code, the page number will increase or decrease as you add or delete pages.

To insert a page number:

1. Place the insertion point where you want to insert a page number.
2. Open the Page Numbering dialog box.
3. Specify the Numbering Type.
4. If you want any text to accompany the page number, type it in the Accompanying Text text box. If you want a page number only, be sure there is no text in this box.
5. Choose Insert Page Number. The page number code [^B] is inserted into the text at the insertion point, along with any text that accompanies it.

If you make any changes to the Page Numbering dialog box while inserting a page number, these changes affect all subsequent page numbers in the document.

Discontinuing Page Numbering

When you discontinue Page Numbering, it stops printing from the point where it was discontinued until the end of the document. To discontinue Page Numbering:

1. Place your insertion point where you want to discontinue Page Numbering. The same Auto Code Placement rules apply as for headers and footers.
2. Click on Layout in the menu bar to open the Layout menu.
3. Click on Page.
4. Click on Numbering to open the Page Numbering dialog box.
5. Select No Page Numbering from the Position drop-down list.
6. Choose OK. Page Numbering is discontinued for the rest of the document, or until you turn it back on.

Suppressing Page Numbering

You can suppress Page Numbering for a specific page. This option is usually used on page 1 when you want numbering to begin on page 2. To suppress Page Numbering for one page:

1. Place the insertion point where you want to suppress Page Numbering. The same Auto Code Placement rules apply as for headers and footers.
2. Click on Layout in the menu bar.
3. Click on Page.
4. Choose Suppress to display the Suppress dialog box, as shown in Figure 5.3.
5. Select Page Numbers.
6. Choose OK to return to the document window.

The Suppress feature suppresses page numbering for one page only. If you want to discontinue page numbering for the rest of the document, use Discontinue (see above).

Changing Top and Bottom Margins (Ctrl+F8)

Top and bottom margin settings determine the distance between the text and the top and bottom edges of the page. For example, let's assume an 11" page length, and top and bottom margins of 1". The top edge of the text is 1" from the top edge of the page, and the bottom edge of the text is 1" from the bottom edge of the page. Margins remain constant unless you change them, regardless of the font or paper size you are using.

The WordPerfect default setting for top and bottom margins is 1". Let's change the top and bottom margins in the George Bush letter.

1. If the document is not in the window, open it.
2. Place the insertion point at the beginning of the document.
3. Click on Layout in the menu bar to open the Layout menu.
4. Click on Margins to display the Margins dialog box, as shown in Figure 5.5.

Figure 5.5—The Margins dialog box.

5. Change the top and bottom margins to 1.5".
6. Choose OK.

When you change your top and bottom margins, and Auto Code Placement is turned on, the new margins take effect at the beginning of the page that contains the insertion point. If you turn on Reveal Codes, you will see [T/B Mar:].

If Auto Code Placement is turned on, and you place the code in the middle of the page, the codes will automatically move to the top of the page.

If Auto Code Placement is turned off when you set new margins, WordPerfect will place the set margin codes at the location of the insertion point, but will include a hard return [HRt] after the codes.

When you set a new top or bottom margin, it is effective from the point of the code to the end of the document, or until a new margin code is encountered.

Different printers have different limitations regarding minimum margins. If you select a margin setting that is invalid for your printer, WordPerfect will refuse to accept the setting and will prompt you with the minimum valid setting.

Centering Text Between Top and Bottom Margins

You can use the Center Page feature to center text vertically on the page. For example, on a cover page you might want the heading centered between the top and bottom margins, as shown in Figure 5.6.

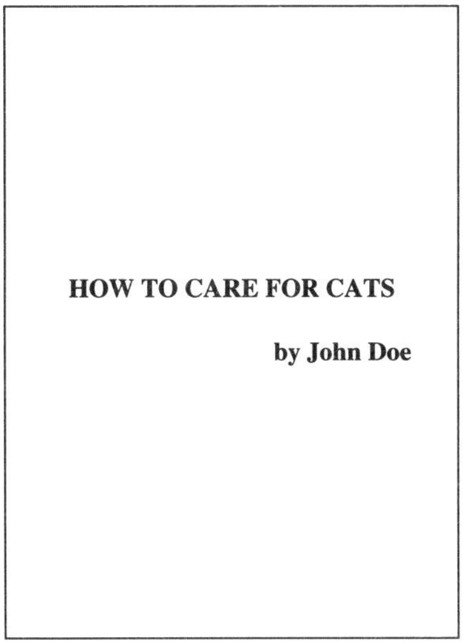

HOW TO CARE FOR CATS

by John Doe

Figure 5.6—Text centered using the Center Page feature.

To center text between the top and bottom margins using Center Page:

1. Place the insertion point at the beginning of a page. (If Auto Code Placement is turned on, the code will move to the beginning of the page, regardless of where the insertion point is.)
2. Click on Layout in the menu bar to open the Layout menu.
3. Click on Page.
4. Click on Center Page.

Center Page does not affect the way text appears in your window. However, when you print the page, the text will be vertically centered between the top and bottom margins.

When you select Center Page, a checkmark appears next to the item in the menu. If a checkmark appears next to the Center Page menu item, it means that the current page is already vertically centered.

Choosing Center Page inserts a Center Page code [Center Pg]. The code affects only the current page.

Hard and Soft Page Breaks

WordPerfect uses two types of page breaks: soft page breaks and hard page breaks. Soft page breaks [SPg] are automatically inserted by WordPerfect when no more text can fit on a page. WordPerfect makes this decision based on the margins and font being used. A soft page break is represented by a line extending across the document window. Soft page breaks automatically change location as you add or delete text from the document.

Hard page breaks [HPg] are manually inserted by you to force a new page. The location of a hard page break in the text always remains the same. It cannot be deleted, except by you. A hard page break is represented by a double line extending across the window.

To insert a hard page break:

1. Place the insertion point where you want to insert a hard page break.
2. Press Ctrl+Enter.

Hard page breaks should be used only when it is necessary to start a new page. They should not be used to force a page break because you do not like where the soft page break has occurred. To correct awkward page breaks, use the Conditional End of Page or Block Protect feature.

Using Conditional End of Page and Block Protect

Conditional End of Page and Block Protect are used to keep a specified amount of text together. This allows you to avoid awkward soft page breaks.

Conditional End of Page

Conditional End of Page keeps a certain number of lines together. A common use of this feature is to prevent titles from appearing at the bottom of a page with subsequent paragraphs on the next. For example, you might have a heading, followed by several paragraphs. WordPerfect may insert a soft page break after the heading, but before the first paragraph. This creates an awkward page break. By using Conditional End of Page, you can instruct WordPerfect to keep together the heading and a certain number of lines in the paragraph. To use Conditional End of Page:

1. Move the insertion point to the line immediately *above* the lines you want to keep together (even if there is text on that line).

2. Count the number of lines you want to keep together, starting from the insertion point. If the document is double spaced, count the blank lines.

3. Click on Layout in the menu bar to open the Layout menu.

4. Click on Page.

5. Click on Conditional End of Page to display the Conditional End of Page dialog box, as shown in Figure 5.7.

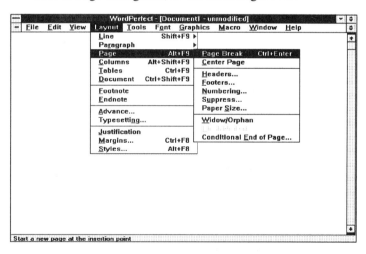

Figure 5.7—The Conditional End of Page dialog box.

6. Enter the number of lines you want to keep together.

7. Choose OK.

When you use Conditional End of Page, all of the lines being kept together move to the next page.

If your soft page break does not adjust, try increasing the number of lines in the Conditional End of Page dialog box.

Block Protect

Block Protect is used to keep together a block of text, even if the number of lines in the block increases or decreases. This feature is usually used to prevent tables and charts from being broken up by soft page breaks. When you choose Block Protect, protect codes [Block Pro] are placed at the beginning and end of the block. Any text between those codes will be kept together. This means that if you add or delete text within the block, the block still will not break.

To protect a block of text:

1. Select the block of text you want to protect.
2. Click on Layout in the menu bar to open the Layout menu.
3. Click on Page.
4. Click on Block Protect.

When you use Block Protect, if the protected block of text cannot fit on a page, the entire block is moved to the next page.

You cannot use Block Protect to protect text longer than a page in length.

Widows and Orphans

Widows and orphans are awkward page breaks that occur when one line of a paragraph appears alone on a page. This is considered poor syntax and should be avoided.

Widows occur when the last line of a paragraph is carried over to the next page. **Orphans** occur when the first line of a paragraph appears at the bottom of a page and the rest of the paragraph is carried to the next page. WordPerfect's Widow/Orphan protection feature prevents widows and orphans.

To turn on Widow/Orphan protection:

1. Place the insertion point where you want Widow/Orphan protection to begin.
2. Click on Layout in the menu bar to open the Layout menu.
3. Click on Page.
4. Click on Widow/Orphan. Widow/Orphan protection is turned on.

When Widow/Orphan protection is on, a checkmark is displayed next to this item in the menu. Choose Widow/Orphan again to turn it off (the checkmark disappears).

You can also turn Widow/Orphan protection off by deleting the code in Reveal Codes.

Getting Around in Multiple Page Documents

When you are working with multiple-page documents, you must to be able to scroll through the document and locate pages quickly. In addition to the movement keys listed below, you can use your window scroll bar and the Go To feature to move around in your document.

Using Movement Keys

The movement keys are found on the right side of the keyboard. You can use these keys to get to different locations in your document. The following table lists the movement keys available with the CUA keyboard.

Keystroke	Result
↑	Moves up one line
↓	Moves down one line
→	Moves one character to the right
←	Moves one character to the left
Ctrl + →	Moves one word to the right
Ctrl + ←	Moves one word to the left
End	Moves to end of line
Home	Moves to beginning of line
Ctrl + ↑	Moves to beginning of previous paragraph
Ctrl + ↓	Moves to beginning of next paragraph
Ctrl + Home	Moves to beginning of document
Ctrl + End	Moves to end of document
PgUp	Moves to beginning of window
PgDn	Moves to end of window
Alt + PgUp	First line of previous page
Alt + PgDn	First line of next page

If you are using an enhanced keyboard, be sure the NumLock key is turned off if you plan to use the keys in the numeric keypad as movement keys rather than as numeric keys.

Using the Scroll Bar

Scroll bars, scroll buttons, and scroll boxes allow you to scroll up and down in windows. This allows you to see information that cannot fit into the window. If you click on the scroll button with the up arrow (at the top of the scroll bar), the text will move down in the window, allowing you to view text further up in the document. If you click on the scroll button with the down arrow (at the bottom of the scroll bar), the text will move up in the window, allowing you to view text further down in the document. If you hold the mouse button down on either of these buttons, the text will scroll continuously.

The scroll box is the little empty box in the scroll bar. It is sometimes called an elevator, because it travels up and down the scroll bar as the text scrolls up and down. You can use the scroll box to scroll text quickly in the window. To move the scroll box, drag it up or down with the mouse. If you drag the scroll box up, text will move down in the window; if you drag it down, text will move up. You can scroll through your document a screen at a time by clicking on the gray area above or below the scroll bar.

Open the George Bush letter and practice using the scroll buttons and scroll box to move up and down the text.

Using Go To

Use the Go To feature to move quickly to the top or bottom of a specific page. To use Go To:

1. Press Ctrl+G; or click on Edit in the menu bar, then choose Go To. The Go To dialog box is displayed, as shown in Figure 5.8.

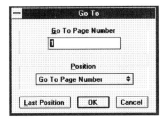

Figure 5.8—The Go To dialog box.

2. Type the page number you want to go to; or select the desired position from the Position drop-down list; or choose Last Position.
3. Choose OK

Position

In normal text (not columns or tables), you can choose the following options in the Position drop-down list:

- Go To Page Number
- Top of Current Page
- Bottom of Current Page

If text is selected, you have two additional options:

- Beginning of Selection (moves the insertion point to the beginning of the selected text)
- Reselect Text (restores previous selection if you have already selected Beginning of Selection)

Last Position

You can choose Last Position to return to the previous location of the insertion point. This option is useful if you have used such movement keys as Page Up and Page Down, or if you have used the Go To feature to move to another part of the document.

Review Exercises for Chapter 5

◆ In a new window, type a three-page document. The first page should be a cover page with text centered between the top and bottom margins. Use a hard page break between the cover page and the rest of the document.

◆ Change the page numbering so that the page following the cover page is page 1.

◆ Insert a footer that will print two lines of text at the left margin on the bottom of every page, and a page number in the center.

◆ Suppress the footer for the first page of the document (the page after the cover page).

◆ Use Conditional End of Page to correct any awkward page breaks.

◆ Practice scrolling around in the document. Use Go To to go to the second page. Use the scroll bar to move up and down in the text.

Before You Go On...

Before you continue to the next chapter, you should feel comfortable working with multiple-page documents. You should know how to use headers and footers and page numbering. You should understand how top and bottom margins work, and how to center text vertically. You should know how to work with page breaks, and be able to scroll around in multiple-page documents.

Chapter 6

Advanced Editing Features

What You Will Learn in this Chapter

- ◆ How to cut, paste, and copy blocks of text
- ◆ How to select more than one window of text
- ◆ How to work with multiple documents
- ◆ How to copy or move text between documents
- ◆ How to append selected text to a file
- ◆ How to search and replace
- ◆ How to use draft mode
- ◆ How to use document comments
- ◆ How to set a document's initial settings
- ◆ How to use the Help feature

The ability to perform complex editing tasks is one of the main reasons for the existence of word-processing packages. A beautiful result is very nice, but it is not cost efficient if, in order to achieve it, you have to type a document over and over. In this chapter we are going to master the advanced editing features that make WordPerfect such a time saver.

Cutting, Pasting, and Copying Blocks of Text

In Chapter 2 you learned how to select and delete small blocks of text. We are now going to learn how to select and manipulate large blocks of text. For purposes of simplicity, we will refer to selected information as text. However, you can cut, paste, or move any text, codes, or graphics in your document.

Selecting More than One Window of Text

So far, we have used the mouse to select small blocks of text that fall within one window. In this chapter, we are going to learn how to work with larger blocks of text. To select large blocks of text with the keyboard, press the Select command (F8) and use the movement keys. To select text that goes beyond one window using the mouse, place the insertion point where you want to begin selecting, and press Select (F8). Then, while holding down the Shift key, scroll to the end of the text you want to select, and click. You can also select more than one window of text by placing the insertion point where you want to start selecting and dragging the mouse to the end of the window. Keep dragging while the insertion point is in the status bar; the window will move up and continue to select text.

Cutting Text (Shft+Del)

When you cut text, you delete it from the document. It can be permanently deleted, or it can be pasted into another location in the document, or even into another document.

When text is cut from a document, it is placed in the **Windows Clipboard**. This is a special holding pen in Windows for text that will be used again. When you cut or copy text again, the new selection replaces the old one in the Windows Clipboard. To cut text:

1. Using the mouse or the keyboard, select the text you want to cut. Be sure to select any codes that should go with the text.
2. Click on Edit in the menu bar to open the Edit menu.
3. Click on Cut. The text is cut from the document and placed in the Windows Clipboard.

Shortcut: You can also use the WordPerfect Quick key Ctrl+X to cut selected text.

Pasting Text (Shft+Ins)

When you paste, you are retrieving text that has been cut and placed in the Clipboard. Text—including headers, footers, columns, graphics, and so on—can be pasted anywhere in a document. The Paste command inserts into your document the last block of text you cut. (See Chapter 2 for information on how to use the Undelete command to retrieve a previous deletion.) To paste:

1. Place the insertion point where you want to paste the contents of the Clipboard. Be sure to take into consideration any codes at the insertion point.
2. Click on Edit in the menu bar to open the Edit menu.
3. Click on Paste. The contents of the Clipboard are inserted into the document at the insertion point.

Shortcut: You can also use the WordPerfect Quick key Ctrl+V to paste text.

Because contents remain in the Clipboard until you exit Windows or until you cut or copy another segment of text, you can paste the same selection into the document in many locations.

Copying Text (Ctrl+Ins)

When you copy text, it is copied into the Clipboard without removing it from its original location in the document. You can then paste it anywhere in the document. The text remains in the Clipboard until you cut or copy again. To copy text:

1. Select the text you want to copy. Be sure to select any codes that should remain with the text.

2. Click on Edit in the menu bar to open the Edit menu.

3. Click on Copy to place the text in the Clipboard.

4. Place the insertion point where you want the text to be copied.

5. Paste the text following the instructions above in "How to Paste."

Shortcut: You can use the WordPerfect Quick key Ctrl+C to copy selected text.

Cutting, Pasting, and Copying a Rectangle

In addition to regular text, you can also cut, paste, or copy rectangles of text or tabular columns. Cutting, pasting, and copying tabular columns is covered in Chapter 11. To cut, paste, or copy a rectangle:

1. Position your insertion point on the upper-left corner of the rectangle you want to select. Drag the mouse down and over to the lower-right corner of the rectangle; or press Select (F8) and, while holding the Shift key, click on the lower-right corner of the rectangle; or use the keyboard to select it. The whole line of text is selected.

2. Click on Edit in the menu bar to open the Edit menu.

3. Click on Select to display the Select cascading menu.

4. Click on Rectangle to select the rectangle of text.

5. Follow the instructions above on how to cut, paste, and copy text.

Working with Multiple Documents

You can work with up to nine open documents at one time in WordPerfect. When you open a new document it is placed in its own document window. The window you are currently working in is called the **active window**.

Document windows that cover the entire screen are **maximized**. If you are working with more than one open document, you might want to be able to see more than one document on the screen. This is done by arranging document windows. To arrange windows:

1. Open several documents.
2. Click on Window in the menu bar to open the Window menu.
3. If you click on Cascade, the windows are arranged so that they overlap one another, with the Title bar of each window visible.
4. If you click on Tile, each window takes up a portion of the screen, with no windows overlapping.

You can switch between windows by clicking on the title bar of the window in which you want to work. You can also click on the document name in the Window menu. (Each time you open a new document window, the document name is added to the Window menu.)

You can also switch windows using the Previous Document key (Ctrl+Shift+F6) or the Next Document key (Ctrl+F6) to cycle through the windows.

If you have several documents in the screen, you can select one and maximize it by clicking on the Maximize button (see Figure 6.1).

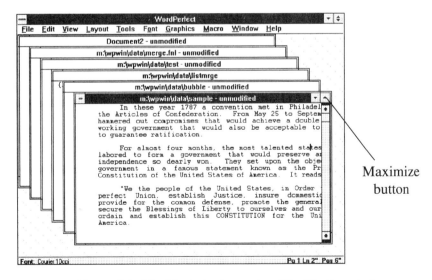

Figure 6.1—The Maximize button in a WordPerfect window.

Close windows one at a time before you exit WordPerfect. Chapter 19 explains in more detail how to work with windows.

Copying or Moving Text Between Documents

To copy or move text from one document to another:

1. Open the documents.
2. Select the text and cut or copy it.
3. Switch document windows to the document into which you want to paste the text.
4. Place the insertion point where you want to paste the text.
5. Paste the text in the document.

 Lo**Ok**   Don't forget to close both windows before you exit WordPerfect.

Appending to File

This feature allows you to append selected text to the end of a file without using the Clipboard. To append to file:

1. Select the text you want to append to another file.
2. Click on File in the menu bar to open the File menu.
3. Click on Save (Shift+F3) to open the Save Selected Text dialog box.
4. Type or select the name of the file you want to append to in the Save As text box.
5. Choose Save to display the Overwrite/Append dialog box, as shown in Figure 6.2.

Figure 6.2—The Overwrite/Append File dialog box.

6. Choose Append. The text is appended to the end of the file.

 Do not choose Overwrite. If you do, the selected text will overwrite the entire existing file.

See Chapter 8 for more information on working with multiple-page documents.

Using Search (F2)

The Search feature lets you search through a document for text or codes. For example, you might want to find the name of an individual in a document. Instead of scrolling through the whole document looking for the name, you can let Search find the name for you.

Searching for Text

To search for a word or string of words:

1. You can search forward or backward from the insertion point. If you want to search forward through the whole document, be sure the insertion point is at the beginning of the document.

2. Click on Edit in the menu bar to open the Edit menu.

3. Click on Search to open the Search dialog box, as shown in Figure 6.3.

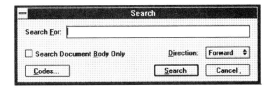

Figure 6.3—The Search dialog box.

4. In the Search For text box, type in the word or string of words you are searching for. The text in the text box must appear exactly as it does in the document. If you use lowercase characters in the text box, WordPerfect will search for both uppercase and lowercase occurrences of the text. If you use uppercase characters in the text box, WordPerfect will search only for uppercase occurrences of the text.

5. Use the Direction pop-up list to select the direction in which

you want to search. WordPerfect will search from the insertion point to the beginning of the document or the end of the document, depending upon the direction you choose.

6. Select Search. A Please Wait message appears in the status bar, and WordPerfect begins the search.

7. WordPerfect locates the first occurrence of the text you typed in the Search For text box. If you want to look for the next occurrence, click on Search Next in the Edit menu or press Shift+F2. WordPerfect will search for the next occurrence of the text in the document.

8. If you want to search for the previous occurrence of the text, click on Search Previous in the Edit menu or press Alt+F2. WordPerfect will search for the previous occurrence of the text in the document.

Searching for Codes

You can also use the Search feature to search for codes in the document. To search for a code:

1. Place your insertion point where you want to begin searching.

2. Click on Edit in the menu bar to open the Edit menu.

3. Click on Search to open the Search dialog box (see Figure 6.3).

4. Choose Codes to display the Codes dialog box, as shown in Figure 6.4.

Figure 6.4—The Codes dialog box.

5. Select the code you want to search for from the Search Codes list, then choose Insert to insert the code in the Search For text box.

6. Choose Close to close the Codes dialog box. You are back in the Search dialog box.

7. Select a direction in the Direction pop-up list.

8. Select Search. WordPerfect will search for the first occurrence of the code in the document.

9. Use Search Next and Search Previous to search for next and previous occurrences of the codes in the document.

The default is to search the body of the document, as well as headers, footers, footnotes, and so on. If you select Search Document Body Only in the Search dialog box, WordPerfect will search only the body of the document.

Using Search and Replace (Ctrl+F2)

You can use the Replace command to search for text or codes and replace them with different text or codes. For example, if you misspelled a name in a document, you can search for each occurrence of the name and replace it with the correct spelling. To search and replace:

1. Place your insertion point where you want to begin the search.

2. Click on Edit in the menu bar to open the Edit menu.

3. Click on Replace to open the Search and Replace dialog box, as shown in Figure 6.5.

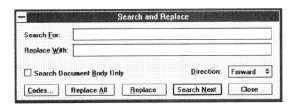

Figure 6.5—The Search and Replace dialog box.

4. Type the text that you want to search for in the Search For text box. The same rules apply as in the Search feature. (If you are replacing a code, follow the steps above, in "How to Search For Codes," to insert a code from the Code dialog box.)

5. Type the text that you want to replace the original text. (If you are replacing a code, insert a code from the Code dialog box.) If you want to replace the text or code with nothing (for example, if you want to delete a code every time it occurs), leave this text box empty.

6. Select the direction in which you want to search.

7. Choose Find Next. WordPerfect finds the first occurrence of the text or code you are replacing.

8. If you want to replace the text or code, select Replace. The insertion point moves to the next occurrence of the text or code.

9. Repeat step 8 until all replacements have been made.

10. If you are sure that you want to replace every occurrence of text or code in the document (without viewing them first), you can use Replace All. WordPerfect will automatically search for and replace every occurrence of the search string in the document. This is much faster, but it gives you no control over each replacement. You will not see the replacements occurring, but the changes will be made.

11. When you are finished, choose Close to return to the document.

WordPerfect will find parts of words and replace them, so when you search for and replace a word, be sure to put a space before and after the word in the Search For text box. For example, if you search for the word "numbers," WordPerfect will also find the word "number" every time it occurs. If you put spaces around the word, WordPerfect will not have a problem identifying the exact word. You should also put spaces around the word you replace it with.

Draft Mode (Ctrl+Shft+F3)

Draft mode allows you to work faster in documents with complex formatting. However, the display is more like the screen in WordPerfect 5.1. You will not see changes in fonts, and graphics will not display. You can use Print Preview to see what the document will look like when it prints out. To switch to Draft mode:

1. Click on View in the menu bar to open the View menu.
2. Click on Draft Mode.
3. To turn Draft mode off, click on it again.

Document Comments

This feature allows you to write helpful little notes and insert them in the document. The comments will display, but not print as part of the document (see Figure 6.6). This is particularly useful if more than one person is working with a document.

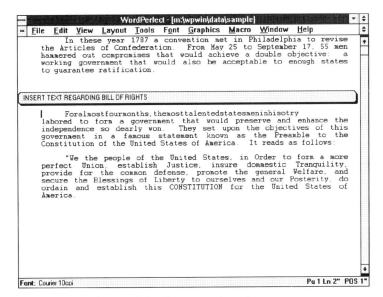

Figure 6.6—Comments in a document.

Creating Comments

To create a document comment:

1. Place the insertion point where you want the comment to appear in the document.
2. Click on Tools in the menu bar to open the Tools menu.
3. Click on Comment.
4. Click on Create to open the Create Comment dialog box, as shown in Figure 6.7.

Figure 6.7—The Create Comment dialog box.

5. Type the text of your comment. You can use bold, italic, or underline by selecting the Attribute button, typing the text, then selecting the Attribute button again to turn off the attribute. You can also use WordPerfect characters in a comment (see Chapter 16).
6. When you have finished typing your comment, choose OK to return to the document window.

The comment will appear as a shaded bar in the document.

 Some people find comments distracting when they edit a document. You can hide comments by clicking on Comments in the View menu. To redisplay the comments, click on Comments again. Comments do not display in columns.

Converting Text to Comments

You can convert existing text to a comment.

1. Select the text you want to turn into a comment.
2. Click on Tools in the menu bar to open the Tools menu.

3. Click on Comment.
4. Click on Create. The selected text becomes a comment.

Converting Comments to Text

You can convert comments to text, which then becomes a part of your document.

1. Place the insertion point directly after the comment you want to convert into text.
2. Click on Tools in the menu bar to open the Tools menu.
3. Click on Comment.
4. Click on Convert to Text. The comment is converted to regular text in your document. You may have to add spaces and punctuation to the text of the comment, so that it blends in with the rest of the text. Comments converted to text print just like normal text when you print the document.

Editing a Comment

You can edit an existing comment:

1. Place your insertion point immediately after the comment.
2. Click on Tools in the menu bar to open the Tools menu.
3. Click on Comment.
4. Click on Edit to open the Edit Comment dialog box.
5. Edit the comment. When you are finished, choose OK to save your edits.

Document Initial Settings (Ctrl+Shft+F9)

When you begin typing a new document, your document is formatted using the WordPerfect default settings. You can change these system settings using the Preferences command in the File menu (see Appendix A). You can also change the settings for the current document only by changing the Document Initial Settings.

When you change the Document Initial Settings, the new settings override the system settings for the current document. This feature is useful, because some features in WordPerfect default to the system settings even if you have changed the setting in the document window. For example, let's assume you are working on a document with footnotes, and the system default setting is for a 1" left margin, but you want the left margin in this document to be 1.5". You can change the left margin at the beginning of the document in the document window, and the text in the document will print using a 1.5" margin. However, since footnotes do not recognize formatting changes made in the document window, the footnotes will not reflect the margin change. They will still default to the system setting of a 1" left margin. If you change the margin in the Initial Document Settings, the new left margin will be recognized by the text *and* the footnotes.

You can change the Document Initial Settings for codes, fonts, redline method, and display pitch. The entire document will be affected by the changes, no matter where the insertion point is when you make the changes. To make the changes:

1. Click on Layout in the menu bar to open the Layout menu.
2. Click on Document to open the Document cascading menu.
3. Select the setting you want to change.
4. An appropriate window or dialog box will appear reflecting the current system settings.
5. Make your changes and save them.

When you change the initial font, a font dialog box appears with the current system font selected. Select the new font and choose OK.

When you change the initial codes, a Document Initial Codes window appears. Any changes made to the system initial codes using Preferences (see Appendix A) will be reflected in the window. Use the menu bar or keyboard commands to make any formatting changes you want for the current document. When you are finished, choose Close.

When you change redline method, a dialog box appears with Redline Options. These affect the way redline appears on the page when you print the document. Select an option and choose OK.

When you change the display pitch, a dialog box appears with Display Pitch Options. When you are working with features that require a great deal of screen space (columns, for example), the text can overlap on the screen. You can change your display pitch to adjust the position of absolute measurement codes (indents, tabs, table margins, and column margins), so that the text displays properly on the screen. You can change the display pitch for normal or Draft mode. Be sure you are in the correct mode before you change the pitch. You may have to experiment to get the best results. Changing display pitch affects only the screen display. It does not affect the way the document prints.

You can use Summary to create a document summary for the current document. This feature summarizes information about the document. Refer to Chapter 8 for information on how to use Document Summary.

Remember that changes made to Document Initial Settings affect only the current document. No other documents will be affected.

Using the Help Feature (F1)

The WordPerfect Help feature is the last item on your menu bar. When you click on Help in the menu bar, you have immediate on-screen answers to your WordPerfect questions. This means that if you are in a document and you hit a snag, you can access the Help feature without having to leave your document. When you select Help from the WordPerfect menu bar, you access the Help menu, which lists all of the Help options, as shown in Figure 6.8.

Figure 6.8—The Help menu.

When you press F1 in a document window, the Help index is displayed on your screen. Press F1 while you are in a WordPerfect function and Help will display context-sensitive information in the Help window. For example, click on View in your menu bar. Now press F1. The Help window contains information pertinent to View.

The Help menu has five commands: Index, Keyboard, How Do I, Glossary, Using Help, What Is, and About WordPerfect.

Index

The Index is an alphabetical listing of all of the topics covered by WordPerfect in Help. When you select Index from the Help menu, the Help Index window is displayed. If you select a topic in the Help Index list, an explanation of that topic appears in the window.

The Help Index window has four menu bar items and five command buttons, as shown in Figure 6.9. These menu bar items and command buttons appear in every menu command except About WordPerfect.

Figure 6.9—The Help Index window.

The Command Buttons

The command buttons, Index, Back, Browse ►►, Browse ◄◄, and Search, all provide ways to access topics in Help.

Index

If you access Help while you are performing a function in WordPerfect, the Help window contains topics about that feature. To access the complete Index list, select the Index command button.

Back

The Back command button brings you back a topic at a time through all of the topics you have viewed in Help during the current help session.

Browse ▶▶ and Browse ◀◀

Choosing Browse command buttons will bring you to the next sequence of the topic you are in. WordPerfect determines the sequence of related topics. To see how Browse works:

1. Select Absolute Tab Settings from the list of topics in the Help Index. You are in the Absolute Tab Settings Help window.
2. Select Browse ▶▶. You have accessed the next related sequence in the Tab Help topic. You can view as many related sequences in a particular topic as you wish until you reach the one that answers your questions. When you reach the last related sequence in a topic, the Browse ▶▶ command button will be dimmed.
3. Select Browse ◀◀. You have been moved back one sequence on the topic you have chosen. When you reach the first sequence in the topic, the Browse ◀◀ command button will be dimmed.

Search

The Search command button allows you to search through Help to find the topic you are interested in. To use the Search feature:

1. Select the Search command button to open the Search dialog box.
2. Type the feature you want to access in Help in the Search For text box.
3. Select Search.
4. A list of related topics appears in a list box. The first topic in the list is highlighted, and the topic appears in the bottom half of the dialog box. Select the topic you want.

5. Select Go To and the topic you selected is displayed in the Help window.

To exit the Help window and return to your document, move your insertion point outside of the Help window and click once.

The Help Index window menu bar has four menu choices: File, Edit, Bookmark, and Help. The menu choices are available in every Help command except About WordPerfect.

File

The File menu choice allows you to:

1. Choose Open to open any Help file from any directory.
2. Print the current Help topic by choosing Print Topic.
3. Choose Printer Setup to select and configure the printer you want to use in Help.
4. Choose Exit to exit the Help feature.

Edit

The Help window Edit command has two choices:

1. Choose Copy to copy the current Help topic to the Clipboard. You can then retrieve the topic into a document or document window by choosing Paste in the Edit menu in your document window.
2. Choose Annotate to add comments of your own to any topic that is displayed in the Help window. When you choose Annotate, the Help Annotation dialog box appears. Type in your comments and choose OK. The next time you choose this topic in Help, a paper clip will be displayed next to the topic title. To see your annotation, choose the Paper clip (see Figure 6.10).

Figure 6.10—The paper clip is displayed in the Tab Set Help window.

Bookmark

The Bookmark command allows you to create a list of topics that can be quickly accessed. To use the Bookmark command:

1. Select the Help topic you want to add to the Bookmark list.
2. Select Bookmark.
3. Select Define to display the Bookmark Define dialog box, as shown in Figure 6.11.

Figure 6.11—The Bookmark Define dialog box.

4. The name of the current topic is displayed in the Bookmark Name text box. You can accept the name or type in a name of your choosing.
5. Choose OK.
6. Return to the Help Index list by clicking on the Index command button.

7. Select Bookmark. The topic you entered is displayed in a list.

8. Select that topic. You are in the Help window for that topic.

Help

The Help command accesses the Microsoft Windows Help feature. For answers to Windows questions, select this command.

To exit Help, move your insertion point outside of the Help window and click once.

Keyboard

The next Help menu bar command is Keyboard (see Figure 6.8). Keyboard displays the templates and keystrokes of the CUA and WordPerfect 5.1 keyboards. To use the Keyboard command:

1. From your WordPerfect document window, click on Help in the menu bar.

2. Click on Keyboard to display the Keyboard Help window.

3. Scroll down through the Keyboard explanation. At the bottom of the explanation you will see a list of Related Topics.

4. Select CUA Keyboard and a Help window appears with the CUA Keyboard displayed in it.

All of the menu and command button features are available in the Keyboard Help window.

How Do I

How Do I lists the most common tasks about which WordPerfect users have questions. Select a task from the list to view the Help information window about it. All of the menu and command button features are available in the How Do I Help window.

Glossary

The Glossary contains an alphabetical listing of WordPerfect and Windows terms and their definitions. To use the Glossary:

1. Choose Glossary.
2. Put your insertion point on the term.
3. Press and hold down the mouse button to read the definition.

All of the menu and command button features are available in the Glossary Help window.

Using Help

Select Using Help for an explanation of the WordPerfect Help command. All of the menu and command button features are available in the Using Help window.

What Is

What Is can be accessed only if you are using a mouse. The What Is command allows you to access context-sensitive help. To use this command:

1. Select What Is. A mouse pointer with a question mark is displayed on your screen.
2. Click your mouse pointer on the item for which you need help. A Help screen appears containing information about the topic.

All of the menu and command button features are available in the What Is Help window.

About WordPerfect

The About WordPerfect Help window displays your WordPerfect license number and information about your version of WordPerfect.

To exit the Help feature, place your insertion point outside of the Help window and click once.

Review Exercises for Chapter 6

◆ Open the George Bush letter.
◆ Select a paragraph and cut it.
◆ Paste it into another location.
◆ Select another paragraph and copy it to a third location.
◆ Leave the Bush letter in the window, and open another document in a new window.
◆ Use the Tile command so that you can see both documents in one window.
◆ Copy a block of text from the Bush letter into the second document.
◆ Close the second document without saving it.
◆ Bring your insertion point to the beginning of the Bush letter.
◆ Replace the word "plan" with the word "thesis" throughout the document.
◆ Close the document without saving it.

Before You Go On...

Before you continue to the next chapter, you should be able to cut, paste, and copy text and codes within a document and between documents. You should be able to work with several open documents and know how to manipulate windows. You should know how to search for text and codes, and how to search and replace text and codes. You should know how to work in Draft mode, and how to use the Comment and Help features.

Chapter 7

Using the Speller and the Thesaurus

What You Will Learn in this Chapter

- ◆ How to use the speller
- ◆ How to spellcheck a document
- ◆ How to spellcheck a word
- ◆ How to spellcheck a page
- ◆ How to manually edit a word in spellcheck
- ◆ Spellcheck command buttons
- ◆ How to look up a word phonetically
- ◆ Speller menu bar selections
- ◆ How to use the thesaurus
- ◆ How to look up and replace a word
- ◆ How the thesaurus is organized
- ◆ Finding additional alternatives
- ◆ Thesaurus menu bar selections

Once you have typed a document in WordPerfect you should use the Speller to check for misspelled words, for more than one occurrence of the same word in a row, and for some types of capitalization errors. The WordPerfect Speller feature allows you to check a single word, a single page, a portion of a document, or the entire document. Speller also permits you to type a word phonetically or to display all of the words in the Speller dictionary that match the pattern of the letters you have entered. The Speller Utility can be accessed without entering WordPerfect. You can access Speller by clicking on the Speller icon in Windows.

Using the Speller (Ctrl+F1)

Type the following letter, including all misspelled words:

```
November 9, 1991

Mr. and Mrs. John Smith
1 Main Street
Anywhere, USA

Dear Mr. and Mrs. Smith:

Congradulations!!  You have just wone a terrrific
vacation for two in the sunny Carribbean.  To claim
your prize, mail in the enclossed claim check and
ninty-three Wonderful Bubble Gum wrappers within
three days of reciept of this letter.  We hope
you will enjoy your Wonderrful vacation.

Very truly yours,


John Doe
Public Relations Manager
Wonderful Bubble Gum Company
```

Now, to check the spelling:

1. Click on Tools in the menu bar.
2. Click on Speller to open the Speller dialog box, as shown in Figure 7.1. The Speller default is to spellcheck the entire document, which is what we want to do.

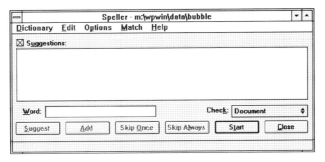

Figure 7.1—The Speller dialog box.

3. Click on Start. The word "Congradulations" is highlighted in the text of the letter and the highlighted word "Congratulations" appears in the Suggestion box.
4. Click on Replace. "Congradulations" is replaced with "Congratulations" and "wone" is now highlighted. The Speller Suggestion box has a list of possible replacements for the highlighted "wone," as shown in Figure 7.2.

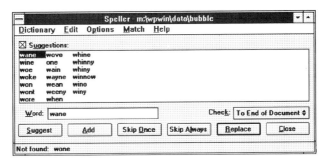

Figure 7.2—The Speller Suggestion box.

5. Click on the word "won" and click on Replace. Continue until you have spellchecked the entire document.

Notice that when the Speller identifies words that start with a capital letter (such as "Carribbean"), it replaces them with the same format.

If you have made any changes to your document during spell-check—such as replacing incorrect words with correct ones from the dictionary, you should save it again.

To spellcheck one word, click on the Check list box and select Word. The Speller will check the word directly following the insertion point.

To spellcheck one page, click on the Check list box and select Page. The Speller will check the page that is currently on the screen.

If you are in the middle of a document and want to spellcheck only from that point on, click on the Check list box and select either To End of Document or To End of Page. The Speller will spellcheck from the insertion point to either the end of the document or the end of the page, depending on your choice.

To spellcheck a selected portion of text in a document:

1. Select the text you wish to spellcheck.
2. Click on Speller.
3. Click on the Check list box and select Selected Text.

If you select To End of Selection, the Speller will spellcheck the document from the insertion point to the end of the selected text.

Manually Editing a Word During Spellcheck

During the spellcheck process, if you wish to manually retype a word rather than have it replaced by the Speller:

1. Click on the highlighted word in the text of the document.
2. Retype or edit the word.
3. Click on the Resume command button in the Speller.

When you first enter the Speller, the command buttons below the Word text box are dimmed (see Figure 7.1). When you select Start, these command buttons become available to you. When a misspelled word is highlighted in the text of your document and the Suggestion list box contains possible replacement words, you may select any of the command buttons instead of Replace.

Suggest

If you click on Suggest, the Speller will expand the list of possible replacement words in the Suggestion list box to include a larger selection of possibilities. These possible replacement words will be more far-fetched as replacements than the original set of replacement words.

Add

If you click on Add, the Speller will add the word to a supplemental dictionary created by WordPerfect. The Speller checks this dictionary as well as the WordPerfect main dictionary when you spellcheck a document.

Skip Once

If you click on Skip Once, the Speller will skip past the word that is currently highlighted in your document and continue to the next misspelled word it finds. Thereafter, it will stop at every occurrence of the word you instructed it to skip.

Skip Always

If you click on Skip Always, the Speller will skip past the word that is currently highlighted in your document and will skip that word for the rest of the spellcheck process.

Looking Up a Word Phonetically

If you are typing a document and do not know the spelling of a word:

1. Click on Tools in the menu bar.
2. Click on Speller.
3. In the Word text box, type the word you wish to look up phonetically.
4. Click on Suggest.

WordPerfect will search its main dictionary for a list of words that most closely resemble the word you have phonetically typed in. A list of these words will appear in the Suggestion list box.

Speller Menu Bar Selections

The Speller menu bar provides you with numerous possibilities to customize the spellchecking of your document.

Dictionary

The Speller automatically checks the WordPerfect main dictionary and the WordPerfect supplemental dictionary created when you added new words. In addition, you can edit the main and supplementary dictionaries, and create and edit supplemental dictionaries of your own using the Speller utility (this is an advanced feature and will not be covered in this book). If an advanced user has created another dictionary for you, you can access it by:

1. Click on Dictionary.
2. Click on Main or Supplementary to open a dialog box, as shown in Figure 7.3.

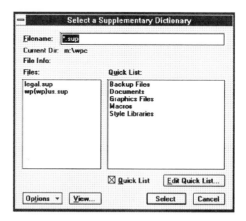

Figure 7.3—The Supplementary Dictionary menu.

3. Click on the dictionary you wish to use.
4. Click on Select.

Edit

This feature interfaces with the Clipboard, and will be covered in Chapter 8.

Options

The Options feature of the Speller allows you to choose to spellcheck words with numbers in them and check for duplicate words and for certain capitalization errors.

Click on Options in the Speller menu bar to access the menu shown in Figure 7.4. The first three options listed in the Options menu are toggles. To select one of these options, click on it and a checkmark appears. To deselect an option, click on it again and the checkmark disappears.

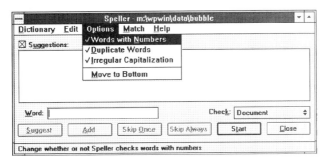

Figure 7.4—The Speller Options menu.

Words with Numbers

If this option is toggled on, the Speller spellchecks all words with numbers in them exactly as it spellchecks any other word. If this option is toggled off, the Speller will ignore all words with numbers in them.

Duplicate Words

If this option is toggled on, the Speller searches for all instances of identical words appearing in a row (such as "the the") and highlights the second word. The dialog box shown in Figure 7.5 appears.

Figure 7.5—The Speller Duplicate Words dialog box.

Continue

If you click on Continue, the Speller will continue to spellcheck the document, leaving both words intact.

Delete 2nd

If you click on Delete 2nd, the second (or highlighted) word is deleted. To spellcheck the rest of the document, click on Continue.

Disable Checking Duplicate

If you click on Disable Checking and then click on Continue, the Speller skips all instances of duplicate words for the rest of the document.

Irregular Capitalization

The Speller checks for five different kinds of errors in capitalization. Only the first three letters of the word are taken into account by Speller. When Irregular Capitalization is toggled on, the Speller stops when it encounters certain capitalization errors—for example, CLaim, cLaim, cLAim, clAim, and aN (the last error applies to two-letter words only)—and the dialog box shown in Figure 7.6 appears.

Figure 7.6—The Speller Irregular Capitalization dialog box.

Continue

If you click on Continue, the Speller does not change the currently highlighted word, and continues to spellcheck the rest of the document. It will not skip any subsequent occurrence of the error in the rest of the document, but will stop each time.

Replace

Click on Replace and the Speller replaces the highlighted word using the following formula:

1. CLaim becomes Claim
2. cLaim becomes Claim
3. cLAim becomes Claim
4. clAim becomes Claim
5. aN becomes An

Even if you click on Replace, the Speller does not automatically replace all identical capitalization errors that occur in the document. It stops and the Speller Irregular Capitalization Found dialog box appears each time the error occurs.

Disable Checking Capitalization

If you click on Disable Checking and then on Continue, the Speller ignores all capitalization errors for the rest of the document.

Match

Match in the Speller menu bar allows you to search for words in the Speller that fit a specified pattern. For example:

1. Type "psycho" in the Word text box.
2. Click on Match in the Speller menu bar.
3. Click on 1 Character in the Match dialog box.
4. Click on Suggest.
5. All of the words that match the pattern "psycho," or "psycho" plus one character, appear, as shown in Figure 7.7.

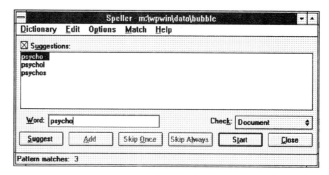

Figure 7.7—The Speller Suggestion box with one wildcard match.

You can also match a specified pattern plus multiple letters. For example:

1. Type "psycho" in the Word text box.
2. Click on Match in the Speller menu bar.
3. Click on Multiple Characters in the Match dialog box.
4. Click on Suggest.
5. All of the words that match the pattern "psycho" plus any subsequent letters appear in the Suggestion box, as shown in Figure 7.8. Scroll across the Suggestion box to see all the possibilities.

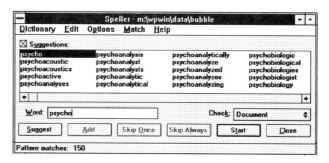

Figure 7.8—The Speller suggestion box with multiple wildcard match.

Using the Thesaurus (Alt+F1)

The Thesaurus enables you to look up synonyms and antonyms for a specified word. Imagine typing a document and being able to look up an entire series of words until you find one that has just the right shade of meaning, without ever having to leave WordPerfect. You can also access the Thesaurus without entering WordPerfect, by clicking on the Thesaurus icon in Windows.

Looking Up an Existing Document Word in the Thesaurus

1. Put the insertion point on the word "claim."
2. Click on Tools in the menu bar.
3. Click on Thesaurus in the Tool dialog box.
4. Click on Look Up in the Thesaurus dialog box, as shown in Figure 7.9.

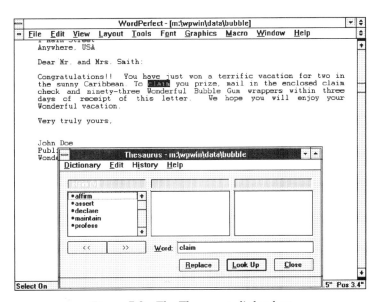

Figure 7.9—The Thesaurus dialog box.

5. Click on the word you want to use in the Synonym and Antonym display area.
6. Click on Replace.

The word on which you placed the insertion point has now been replaced. If you do not want to replace the word, click on Close.

Looking Up a Word Before You Type It

1. Click on Tools in the menu bar.
2. Click on Thesaurus in the Tool dialog box.
3. Type the word in the Word text box.
4. Click on Look Up in the Thesaurus dialog box.
5. A list of words appears in the Synonym and Antonym Display Area.
6. Click on the word you wish to use.
7. Click on Replace.

The word you select in the Synonym and Antonym Display Area appears in your text. If you do not want to choose any of the words displayed, click on Close.

How the Thesaurus is Organized

The Synonym and Antonym Display Area of the Thesaurus is divided into three columns (see Figure 7.9). To see how these columns work:

1. Click on Tools in the menu bar.
2. Click on Thesaurus.
3. Type the word "claim" in the Word text box.
4. Click on Look Up.

Finding Additional Alternatives

Scroll down through the list of words in the Synonym and Antonym Display Area. Notice that the words are arranged in a certain order. The first word in each group is the **headword**, or the word you

looked up. It is followed by an indication of its part of speech—
that is, noun (n), adjective (a), and so on—and a listing of its
antonyms (ant). The words in each grouping under the headword
are known as **references**. References that are preceding by a bullet
can also be looked up in the Thesaurus. Double-click on the word
"assert" in the Synonym and Antonym Display Area, and a listing
in the second column appears with the headword "assert" followed
by its own list of references. (See Figure 7.10.) Double-click on
the word "avow" in the second column, and a listing in the third
column appears with the headword "avow" followed by its own
list of references. (See Figure 7.11.)

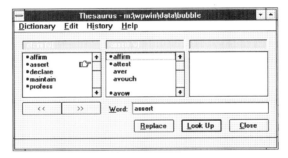

Figure 7.10—The Thesaurus dialog box with two headword columns.

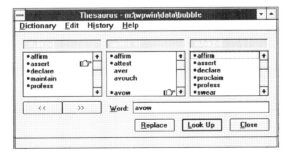

Figure 7.11—The Thesaurus dialog box with three headword columns.

Although the Synonym and Antonym Display Area has only
three columns, you are not limited to a choice of three headwords
in the Thesaurus. You can continue to choose more headwords and
use the Arrow command buttons to move among the columns.

The Thesaurus Menu Bar

Dictionary

The Dictionary option in the Thesaurus menu bar allows you to chose a dictionary other than the WordPerfect main dictionary to look up synonyms and antonyms. Creating a new dictionary is an advanced feature that will not be covered in this book. If another user has created a dictionary for you, to access it:

1. Click on Dictionary in the Thesaurus menu bar.
2. Click on Change Dictionary in the Dictionary dialog box.
3. Click on the dictionary you want to use in the Select a WordPerfect Thesaurus dialog box.
4. Click on Select.

Edit

The options in the Edit dialog box interface with the Clipboard and will be covered in Chapter 8.

History

The History dialog box contains a list of all of the words you looked up during the current session in the Thesaurus. If you click on one of the words in the History dialog box, it will become the next headword in the Synonym and Antonym Display Area.

Review Exercises for Chapter 7

- ◆ Type a two-page document. Include misspelled words.
- ◆ Spellcheck a word.
- ◆ Spellcheck a page.
- ◆ Spellcheck the entire document.
- ◆ Do not accept the Speller possibilities for one of your misspelled words. Go into the text of the document and edit the word manually.
- ◆ Look up a word phonetically in the Speller.
- ◆ Access the Thesaurus. Look up and replace a word in your document.
- ◆ Look up a word. Find additional alternatives to the original suggestions in the Thesaurus.

Before You Go On...

Before you go on to the next chapter, you should feel comfortable with spellchecking a document, a word, a page, and selected sections of a document. You should also know how to look up ad replace a word in the Thesaurus.

Chapter 8

System and Document Management

What You Will Learn in this Chapter

- ◆ How to create directories
- ◆ How to change directories
- ◆ How to delete files
- ◆ How to copy files
- ◆ How to move/rename files
- ◆ How to print a list of files
- ◆ How to copy to the Windows Clipboard
- ◆ How to append to the Windows Clipboard
- ◆ How to access other Windows applications
- ◆ How search for a document when you know a word in the document
- ◆ How to search for documents by file patterns
- ◆ How to use other File Manager features
- ◆ How to change your default directory
- ◆ How to save and retrieve documents from floppy disks

175

This chapter is concerned with system and disk management; that is, organizing your hard drive. Consider a file cabinet. If you take all of your files and dump them in a drawer without subdividing them, the next time you need a file from that drawer you are going to have to sift through the entire mess. Your hard drive is the equivalent of that file cabinet.

Directories are the equivalent of the divisions in your file cabinet; the root directory is the equivalent of the entire file cabinet. You already have several directories on your hard drive. If you followed the automatic installation of WordPerfect for Windows, you have a directory called WPWIN in your root directory. On most computers, C is the root directory of the hard drive. Therefore, WordPerfect for Windows is located in C:\WPWIN. The C: represents the root directory, the \ is a separator, and WPWIN is a **drive,** or a directory located within the root directory, where your WordPerfect program files are located. C:\WPWIN is known as a **path.** It indicates the location of a directory on your hard drive. If you followed the automatic installation of WordPerfect, you also have a subdirectory that can be found in this path: C:\WPWIN\LEARN. This path designation means that all of the WordPerfect Learn files are located in a subdirectory called LEARN, which is a subdivision of the directory WPWIN.

First-level divisions on your hard drive, such as WPWIN, are known as **directories**; second-level divisions, such as LEARN, are known as **subdirectories**. Even though LEARN is a subdirectory of WPWIN, the accepted convention is to refer to it as a directory when it is referred to alone. For example, "the WPWIN subdirectory LEARN" or "the LEARN directory." We will follow this convention in this chapter.

WordPerfect has a feature called the File Manager, which you can access either as an icon in the WordPerfect Group window in Windows, or through WordPerfect in the Document window. The File Manager allows you to list all of your directories and subdirectories, list files in a specified directory, delete files, copy files, move or rename files, create directories, and change directories. File Manager also allows you to open files in the WordPerfect document window, search one or more directories for files that contain specified words or phrases, and print or view files.

Using File Manager

To access File Manager from your WordPerfect Document window:

1. Click on File.
2. Click on File Manager. You are now in the File Manager (see Figure 8.1).

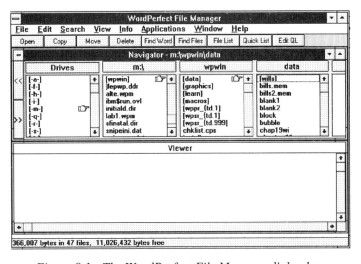

Figure 8.1—The WordPerfect File Manager dialog box.

If you have accessed File Manager through WordPerfect, you can use the Alt+Tab keys to go back and forth between the two.

Using the Navigator and the File Viewer

If the display default has not been changed, your window will display two of the five types of windows included with File Manager. You should be looking at the Navigator on the top half of your window, and the File Viewer on the bottom. At the very top of the Navigator, you will see your default directory displayed. If you accepted the WordPerfect installation defaults, your default directory is C:\WPWIN. The Navigator display will show the current drive and directories selected. The last list box will display all of the files in the selected directory. The WPWIN list box contains all of the files in the WPWIN directory. All subdirectories in the WPWIN directory are displayed before the files are listed. Subdirectories are enclosed by brackets, as shown in Figure 8.1.

To change to the LEARN subdirectory in the Navigator, double-click on LEARN in the WPWIN directory. The files and any subdirectories in LEARN are now displayed in the last list box, following the subdirectories and files listed in the WPWIN list box, as shown in see Figure 8.2.

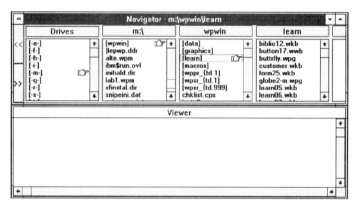

Figure 8.2—Directory and subdirectory listings in Navigator.

Click on BUTTRFLY.WPG. The WordPerfect Butterfly graphic is now displayed in the File Viewer, as shown in Figure 8.3.

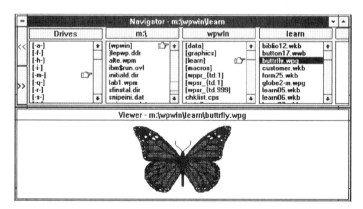

Figure 8.3—The File Viewer showing a WordPerfect graphic.

You can view both data files and graphics files in the File Viewer. If you are not sure which file you want to open, you can view files until you find the one you want. Each time you click on a file, File Viewer will clear the previous file from the window and display the new file. You cannot edit a document that is in the File Viewer, although you can select text and copy or append it to the Clipboard. To view a file in the WordPerfect Document window:

1. Click on File in the menu bar to open the File menu.
2. Click on Open or Retrieve to display the Open or Retrieve dialog box.
3. Select the file you want to review.
4. Click on Select.

If you double-click on a file in the Navigator list box, you will access the Open dialog box. The entire path of the file you select will be shown, and you will have a choice of Open or Cancel, as shown in Figure 8.4.

Figure 8.4—The Open dialog box.

If you select Open, File Manager will open the file in the WordPerfect document window. If you already have a file open, File Manager will open the selected file in a new window. You can also open a file by clicking on File, clicking on Open, and typing in the path and filename in the Open dialog box.

You can use the Navigator to quickly access any directory or subdirectory on your hard drive. If you want to change your directory from LEARN to GRAPHICS, bring your insertion point to the WPWIN list box and double-click on GRAPHICS. All of the files in the GRAPHICS directory are now listed.

To go back a directory, move your insertion point to where WPWIN is listed, and double-click. Now the last list box in the Navigator contains the subdirectories and files in the WPWIN directory.

Creating a Directory (Ctrl+T)

You will usually want to create more than one directory in order to organize your files in a logical fashion. Generally, file directories are located as subdirectories under the directory that contains the program files. The File Manager is currently in the GRAPHICS directory. You would not want to create a subdirectory to contain files in the GRAPHICS directory, since you would not logically expect to find a data directory in that location. Creating all of your data subdirectories in the same directory will save you the trouble of having to search for them. If you have been working your way through this book, you have created several documents, which are probably located in your WPWIN directory. Let's create a new subdirectory for them named DATA; later we will use File Manager to move them all to their new home. To create a new directory:

1. Click on File.
2. Click on Create Directory to display the Create Directory dialog box.
3. The current directory should be C:\WPWIN.
4. If the current directory is C:\WPWIN, all you have to do is type DATA in the New Directory text box. If the current directory is not C:\WPWIN, type C:\WPWIN\DATA in the New Directory text box.
5. Select Create.

Your new subdirectory should now be in the last list box in the Navigator.

Path and directory names are not case-sensitive. You can type them in either uppercase or lowercase, or in any combination of the two.

The usual method of naming directories is by category. For example, a student might create a directory called LETTERS and another called PAPERS. A secretary in a law firm might create several directories, such as TRUSTS, ESTATES, WILLS, and so on. When creating directories, there are several rules you must follow. You cannot create a directory that is more than eight characters long. You cannot include spaces in a directory name. You could not, for example, create a directory named REAL ESTATE. If you tried to do so, File Manager would inform you that it could not create an invalid directory in the path. If you tried to create a directory called LITIGATION, File Manager would inform you that the name you specified is too long.

Changing Directories (Ctrl+G)

File Manager has two windows, which allows you to change directories easily. You have already seen the first—the Navigator lets you change directories up and down the path. The other window is the File List window. To access it:

1. Click on View.
2. Click on File List to open the File List dialog box.

Unlike the Navigator, the File list has only one list box. It does not show you the entire path for the directory you are in. It does, however, list all of the subdirectories and files contained in the current directory. Access the File list now. Your current directory should be C:\WPWIN. To change directories to C:\WPWIN\DATA, click twice on DATA in your File list. To return to C:\WPWIN, click twice on the two dots enclosed in brackets [..] at the top of the directory contents in the File list. You can open or retrieve a document from the File list exactly the same way you did in the Navigator. Simply click twice on the file you want to open or retrieve, then choose Open in the Open File dialog box.

If you have gone into File Manager from the WordPerfect Group icon in Windows and have not started WordPerfect, when you double-click on a file, the File Manager will start WordPerfect for you and then open the file. To change directories in the WordPerfect Document window:

1. Click on File in the menu bar to open the File menu.
2. Click on Open or Retrieve to display the Open or Retrieve dialog box.
3. Click on the directory you wish to access in the Quick list. The files in the selected directory now appear in the File list.

When you save a file that has been opened in a changed directory, WordPerfect will automatically save it in the same directory, then return you to your default directory. The default directory is the directory you first access when you enter WordPerfect.

Deleting Files (Ctrl+D)

Eventually you will want to delete some files from your computer. It is amazing how quickly they can multiply, and how much space they can eventually take up. To delete a file from a directory:

1. Make sure you are in the correct directory. If you are not, change directories.
2. Select the file you want to delete in the list box in either the Navigator or the File list.
3. Click on File.
4. Click on Delete to open the Delete File(s) dialog box, as shown in Figure 8.5. The file you have selected will be listed in the File(s) to Delete text box. If the wrong filename is listed, either backspace to delete the name and type in the correct file name.
5. Choose Delete. The file has disappeared from the list box and has been deleted.

Figure 8.5—The Delete File(s) dialog box.

You can also delete a file in the WordPerfect document window. Follow these steps:

1. Click on File in the menu bar to open the File menu.
2. Click on either Retrieve or Open.
3. Highlight the file your want to delete.
4. Click on Options to display the Options drop-down list.
5. Select Delete.

Warning: You cannot undelete files, so be sure you are deleting the right one(s).

Deleting Several Files at Once

1. Select the files you want to delete in the list box in either the Navigator or the File list. You can select all of your files at once by using the Select All feature. To access this feature, click on Edit and select Select All. If you change your mind, click on Edit and select Unselect All. If the files you want to delete are not in consecutive order, you can highlight all the files, from the first one you want to delete to the last, including those you do not wish to delete.
2. Click on File.
3. Click on Delete to open the Delete File(s) dialog box (see Figure 8.5), which will contain a list of all of the files you selected.
4. Choose Delete to delete the first file. You are now positioned on the second file.
5. If you want to delete the second file, choose Delete. If you do not want to delete this file, choose Skip. You are now positioned on the third file in the list.
6. If you want to delete all of the files listed in the Delete File(s) dialog box, choose Delete All.
7. When you have gone through the entire list of files, the Delete File(s) dialog box will close.

Copying a File (Ctrl+C)

Before you can copy a file, you must know the path of the new location. If you are not certain of the path, use the Navigator. To copy a file to a floppy disk, you need to know only the drive designation, rather than the entire path. If you have only one floppy drive, the drive designation is A. If you have two floppy drives, the one on the top is probably called A, and the one on the bottom is probably called B. Floppy disks can be divided into directories just as your hard drive can, but because they hold so much less data, this is rarely done. When you copy a file, it exists in two places—the original location and the one to which it is copied. To copy one of the documents you have already created in the C:\WPWIN directory into your new DATA directory:

1. If you are not already in the C:\WPWIN directory, use the Navigator or the File list to change directories.
2. Select one of the documents you have typed.
3. Click on File.
4. Click on Copy to open the Copy File(s) dialog box. The File(s) to Copy text box should contain the correct path and filename of the file you want to copy.
5. In the To text box, type C:\WPWIN\DATA. You do not need to type in the name of the file. WordPerfect will copy the file into the DATA directory and give it exactly the same name. If the directory you are copying the file into already contains a file with that name, and you have enabled Replace Files with Same Name and Confirm Replace in the Copy File(s) dialog box, WordPerfect will prompt you before copying. You can copy a file and give it another name by typing the name you want it to have in the To text box. For instance, if you have a file named NEWS.JAN and want to copy it into your C:\WPWIN\DATA directory and call it NEWS91.JAN, you would type C:\WPWIN\DATA\NEWS91.JAN.
6. Choose Copy.

You have now copied a file into your DATA directory.

You can also copy a file in the WordPerfect document window if you follow these steps:

1. Click on File in the menu bar to open the File menu.
2. Click on either Retrieve or Open.
3. Highlight the file you want to copy.
4. Click on Options to display the Options drop-down list.
5. Select Copy to display the Copy File dialog box.
6. Fill in the Copy To text box with the complete path.
7. Select Copy.

Copying Several Files at Once

1. Select the files you want to copy in the list box in either the Navigator or the File list. You can select all of your files

at once by using the Select All feature. To access this feature, click on Edit and select Select All. If you change your mind, click on Edit and select Unselect All. If the files you want to copy are not in consecutive order, you can highlight all the files, from the first one you want to copy to the last, including those you do not wish to copy.

2. Click on File.

3. Click on Copy to open the Copy File(s) dialog box (see Figure 8.6), which will contain a list of all of the files you selected.

4. Choose Copy to copy the first file. You are now positioned on the second file.

5. If you want to copy the second file, choose Copy. If you do not want to copy this file, choose Skip. You are now positioned on the third file in the list.

6. If you want to copy all of the files listed in the Copy File(s) dialog box, choose Copy All.

7. When you have gone through the entire list of files, the Copy File(s) dialog box will close.

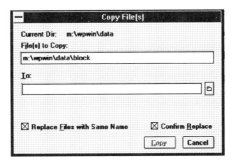

Figure 8.6—The Copy File(s) dialog box.

Moving/Renaming a File (Ctrl+R)

When you copy a file, you end up with two copies of it, each in a different location. When you move a file, you remove it from one location and place it in another. You may move a file when editing, when you have accidently saved it in the wrong directory, or when you have created a new directory and want to move a file or group of files into it. When you rename a file, it is still the same file, it just has a different name. But the Move/Rename feature lets you move a file, rename a file, or move and rename it simultaneously. Let's move one of the files we created in C:\WPWIN.

1. If you are not in the C:\WPWIN directory, use the Navigator or File List to change directories.

2. Select the file you want to move. **Warning:** If you move a WordPerfect program file, the program may not operate properly. Be sure to select a file you have typed in.
3. Click on File.
4. Click on Move/Rename to open the Move/Rename dialog box. The path and filename of the file you selected are in the File(s) to Move/Rename text box.
5. In the To text box, type C:\WPWIN\DATA.
6. Choose Move. If you have another file in the DATA directory with the same name, WordPerfect will not let you move the file; you will have to move and rename it. Type C:\WPWIN\DATA\FILENAME in the To text box to move and rename a file.

The file has now disappeared from the Navigator or File List list box. If you change your directory to C:\WPWIN\DATA, you will see it listed there.

You can also move a file in the WordPerfect document window if you follow these steps:

1. Click on File in the menu bar to open the File menu.
2. Click on either Retrieve or Open.
3. Highlight the file you want to move.
4. Click on Options to display the Options drop-down list.
5. Select Move to display the Move/Rename File dialog box.
6. Fill in the To text box with the complete path.
7. Select Move.

Moving Several Files At Once

1. Select the files you want to move in the list box in either the Navigator or the File list. You can select all of your files

at once by using the Select All feature. To access this feature, click on Edit and select Select All. If you change your mind, click on Edit and select Unselect All. If the files you want to move are not in consecutive order, you can highlight all the files, from the first one you want to move to the last, including those you do not wish to move.

2. Click on File.

3. Click on Move to open the Move/Rename File(s) dialog box (see Figure 8.7), which will contain a list of all of the files you selected.

4. Choose Move to move the first file. You are now positioned on the second file.

5. If you want to move the second file, choose Move. If you do not want to move this file, choose Skip. You are now positioned on the third file in the list.

6. If you want to move all of the files listed in the Move/Rename File(s) dialog box, choose Move All.

7. When you have gone through the entire list of files, the Move/Rename File(s) dialog box will close.

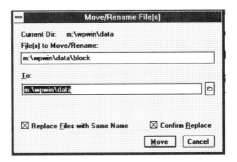

Figure 8.7—The Move/Rename File(s) dialog box.

Renaming a File Without Moving It

If you want to rename a file and have it remain in the same directory:

1. Select the file you want to rename in the Navigator or File List list box.

2. Click on File.

3. Click on Move/Rename to open the Move/Rename File(s) dialog box.

4. In the File(s) To Move text box, you will see the current path and filename.

5. In the To text box, repeat the path and type in a new filename (see Figure 8.8). Say, for instance, that you wanted to rename C:\WPWIN\TEST to C:\WPWIN\TEST1; you would type C:\WPWIN\TEST1 into the To text box.

6. Choose Move.

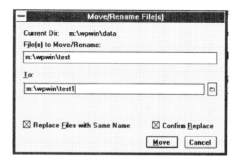

Figure 8.8—The Move/Rename File(s) dialog box with renamed file.

Printer Setup in File Manager

In order to print from File Manager, you must set up your printer defaults in Printer Setup. Unless you are going to use a different printer in File Manager than you are using in WordPerfect, your printer setup should match. If your printer is not set up in File Manager, you can copy the contents of the file to the Clipboard (covered later in this chapter) and paste them into a WordPerfect document window. You can then print the file in WordPerfect. (Printer installation is covered in Appendix A.)

Printing a File (Ctrl+P)

File Manager allows you to print the file you are currently viewing or, if you know the path and filename of the file you want to print, to print a file without opening it. To print a file currently in the File Viewer:

1. Click on File.
2. Click on Print to open the Print dialog box. The path and name of the file in the File Viewer is in the Files text box.
3. Choose Print.

To print a file that is not in the File Viewer:

1. Click on File.
2. Click on Print to open the Print dialog box.
3. Type in the path and filename of the file you want to print.
4. Choose Print.

Printing a List of Files

At times you will want a printed list of some or all of the files in a directory. The File Manager Print window allows you to do this. To print a list of files:

1. Click on File.
2. Click on Print Window. If you are using the Navigator, this will open the Print Navigator dialog box. If you are using File List, this will open the File List dialog box.
3. To print a list of only some of the files in the directory in your window, select the files you want on your printout.
4. To print a list of all of the files in the directory, do not select anything.
5. In the Navigator or File List dialog box, select either Print List of Selected Files or Print Entire List.
6. Choose OK.

You can select all of your files at once by using the Select All feature. To access this feature, click on Edit and select Select All. If you change your mind, click on Edit and select Unselect All.

Running Another Program from File Manager

The File Manager Run feature permits you to execute another program from within File Manager. When you exit the other program, you will be back in File Manager. For this feature to work, your computer must have enough memory to run both WordPerfect and the other program at once. To run another program from File Manager:

1. Click on File.
2. Click on Run to open the Run dialog box.
3. In the Filename text box, type in the full path and filename (including extension) of the execute file for the program you want to run. In Figure 8.9, the command to execute WordPerfect 5.1 was typed in the Filename text box.
4. Choose OK.

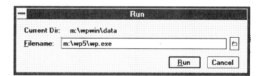

Figure 8.9—The Run dialog box.

Accessing the Windows Clipboard through File Manager

Copying to the Clipboard (Ctrl+Insert)

File Manager allows you copy selected text from a file in the File Viewer and place it in the Windows Clipboard. The text will remain in the Clipboard until you copy or cut another section of text (either in File Manager or in the WordPerfect document window). This allows you to have a document on the screen in the WordPerfect document window, click on File and then on File Manager to access the File Manager, view as many documents as necessary to find the one that contains the text you want to copy, place it in the Clipboard, then return to the WordPerfect document window and paste the text in your document.

1. Before you can copy text to the Clipboard, you must have a document in either the File Viewer window or the WordPerfect document window.
2. Select the text you want to copy.

3. Click on Edit.
4. Select Copy to Clipboard.

Appending to the Clipboard (Alt+Insert)

When you append text to the Windows Clipboard, the text remains there. Neither the Cut nor Copy commands will overwrite it. This means, however, that when you paste appended text into your document, you will have not only text you last cut or copied to the Clipboard, but all of the text you have ever appended to the Clipboard. You must then delete the unwanted text from your document. To append text to the Clipboard:

1. Select the text you want to append.
2. Click on Edit.
3. Select Append to Clipboard.

Cut, Copy, and Append all use the same Paste command. If the last time you used the Clipboard you copied text to it, the copied text will appear in your document when you paste. If you copy to the Clipboard and then append to it before you paste, you will get all of the text you ever appended to the Clipboard plus the text you copied to it.

Using the File Manager Search Feature

The File Manager Search feature allows you to search for documents in a drive, one or several directories, or a selected list. You can search by word, word patterns, or file patterns. This is extremely useful when you want to retrieve a document and you have forgotten what you named it, when you have several documents with almost exactly the same name and have forgotten which is which, or when you can't remember in what directory you saved a document. You can search from a list of directories or files in the Navigator, the File List, the Quick List, or from your Search Results.

Searching for a Document Containing a Word

If you want to search for a document or documents that contain a specific word in one of your WordPerfect directories:

1. Position the Navigator or File list in the C:\WPWIN directory.

2. If you know the directory the document is in, click once on the directory in either the Navigator, the File list, or the Quick list. (Listing your directories in the Quick list is covered later in this chapter.) If you are not certain where the document is, do not click on anything. Click on Search, then click on Find Words to access the Find Words dialog box.

3. In the Word Pattern text box, type the word or words that will identify the document you are searching for, as shown in Figure 8.10.

4. If you have selected a directory or a group of files in a directory, select Selected Items.

5. If you want to search through the current directory displayed as well as all subdirectories, select Current Window.

6. Choose Find.

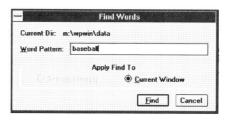

Figure 8.10—The Find Words text box.

WordPerfect will search through every file in the selected area. You will see a Performing Search status box on the screen. When WordPerfect has finished searching, the Search Results window will appear. It will list the filename, path, size, date, and time for each file that matches the search criteria, as shown in Figure 8.11. You could then search all of the files in the Search Results window for another word or word pattern until you locate the file you want.

Filename	Full Path	Size	Date	Time
bills.mem	m:\wpwin\data\	13,376	10/4/91	2:45PM
bills2.mem	m:\wpwin\data\	13,376	11/6/91	1:17PM
block	m:\wpwin\data\	995	11/5/91	9:39PM
client	m:\wpwin\data\	13,376	11/6/91	1:17PM
client.db	m:\wpwin\data\	13,376	10/4/91	2:45PM
con10.ltr	m:\wpwin\data\	3,170	10/4/91	3:10PM
con3.ltr	m:\wpwin\data\	3,170	10/4/91	3:07PM

Search Results - m:\wpwin\data*. *

Figure 8.11—The Search Results file list.

The Find Files feature in Search allows you to search all of your directories to locate a single file or a file that matches a specified file pattern. To locate a file:

1. Select Find Files to open the Find Files dialog box.
2. In the File Pattern text box, type in the name of the file you want to locate. If you are looking for a group of files, you can use a DOS wildcard to identify them. For information concerning DOS wildcards consult your DOS manual.
3. Selected Items will search only the specified directory; Subtree Directory will search the directory you are currently in and all of that directory's subdirectories; Directory will search only the directory you are in; and Drive will search the entire drive.
4. Choose Find.

When WordPerfect has completed its search, a Search Results window will be displayed on your screen listing all of the files found that match the search criteria.

Advanced Find lets you search for files that match either word or file patterns or both. You have a larger range of selection criteria. Once you have selected your search criteria, choose Find. Once again, a Search Results window will appear on your screen listing all of the files found that match the search criteria.

Adding a Directory to the Quick List

The Quick List is a short list that contains any directories or files you have added to it. For accessing your most commonly used directories and files, the Quick List is handier than using the Navigator or the File List. To add your DATA directory to the Quick List:

1. Click on View.
2. Click on Edit Quick List to open the Edit Quick List dialog box.
3. Select Add to open the Add Quick List Item dialog box.
4. Type the path of the directory (and filename if you are adding a file) you wish to add in the Directory/Filename text box. In this case, you would type C:\WPWIN\DATA.
5. Type the description of the item you have added in the Descriptive Name text box.

6. Choose OK to close the Add Quick List Item dialog box.
7. Choose OK to close the Edit Quick List dialog box.

Now access the Quick List from View in your menu bar. The DATA directory has been added to the list.

To add a directory to the Quick list in the WordPerfect document window:

1. Click on File in the menu bar to open the File menu.
2. Click on Open or Retrieve.
3. Click on Edit Quick List.
4. Select Add to display the Add Quick List Item dialog box.
5. Type the path of the directory you wish to add (and the filename if you are adding a file) in the Directory/Filename text box.
6. Type the description of the item you have added in the Descriptive Name text box.
7. Choose OK to close the Edit Quick List Item dialog box.

The File Manager View Feature

The View feature in File Manager permits you to access the Navigator, the File List, and the Quick List. You can have as many Navigator or File List windows open as you like. To return to the original File Manager window, simply close the extra windows you have opened.

View also allows you to change the layout of the File Manager window. Take a minute to select each of the choices you are offered and see which layout works best for you.

The button bar can be accessed through the View feature. Buttons can be added, deleted, and edited in View. Chapter 18 contains a complete explanation of button bars.

The Font feature in View permits you to decide which fonts will appear in any of the windows in File Manager.

The View Options dialog box allows you to decide the order in which files will be sorted in the Navigator and the File List, which criteria you want to sort them by, and whether you want to display files, directories, and/or hidden/system files in your list. You may also choose whether or not to include document summary information in the File Viewer. This information consists of a description of the document you typed in and a description of the type of file it is. The Document Summary can be accessed in WordPerfect by clicking on Layout. Click on Document and type in the information; you needn't fill the whole screen. To have WordPerfect automatically prompt you to fill in a Document Summary:

1. Click on File.
2. Click on Preferences.
3. Select Document Summary to open the Document Summary dialog box.
4. Enable Create Summary on Save/Exit.
5. Choose OK.

When you have made your choices in View Options, choose OK.

What the Info Windows Tell You

The Info feature in File Manager provides you with information concerning your system, windows, printer selection, and hard disk. The System window is useful for determining what DOS version you are using; it also tells you how may printer ports you have and whether they are parallel or serial. The Windows window provides you with information about the environment under which you are running Windows, which version of Windows you are running, and how much memory is still available in your system. The Printer window tells you what your default printer is, what printers are installed in Windows, and what printer port they are using. The Disk window tells you the name of the drive you are currently in, how much space is on your hard drive, how much space has been used, and how much space is still available. Any or all of these windows can be printed by clicking on Print Info Report and selecting the appropriate window.

The Applications Feature

The File Manager Applications feature allows to you access other applications within File Manager. When you install WordPerfect and enter File Manager, four applications will already be in the Applications menu: WordPerfect, Speller, Thesaurus, and WordPerfect Macro Facility. You can add more. In Figure 8.12, Clipboard and Solitaire have been added to the list of Applications.

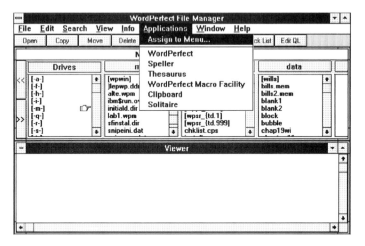

Figure 8.12—The Applications menu.

To add Solitaire to your list:

1. Click on Applications.
2. Click on Assign to Menu to open the Applications dialog box.
3. In the Descriptive Name text box, type Solitaire.
4. Type C:\WINDOWS\SOL.EXE in the Command Line text box. If Windows has been installed using the installation defaults, this is the correct path. If it has not, use the Navigator or File List to determine the correct path for Windows. Check to see if the file SOL.EXE, the execute file for Solitaire, is present. Then type in the correct path and the filename SOL.EXE.
5. Choose Add.

Now, when you click on Applications, Solitaire is on your list.

Setting Preferences in File Manager

You can set permanent preferences in File Manager. You can choose whether or not to confirm file deletes, moves, and copies; confirm on open or retrieve; whether or not to save the last layout in File Manager on exit and return to that screen when you re-enter; and so on. Figure 8.13 shows a complete list of all preferences.

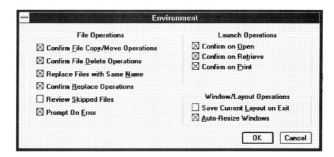

Figure 8.13—The Environment dialog box.

To make your choices:

1. Click on File.
2. Click on Preferences.
3. Select Environment to open the Environment dialog box.
4. Select the preferences you want to enable.
5. Choose OK.

Changing Your Default Directory

When you open WordPerfect, you will always default to the same directory. Sometimes you want to change that default. To do this:

1. Click on File.
2. Click on either Open or Retrieve to display the Open or Retrieve File dialog box.
3. In the Filename text box, type the path of the new default directory.
4. Enable Change Default Directory.
5. Double-click on the bar icon in the upper-left corner of the window to close it.

Your have changed your default directory.

Saving to Floppy Disks

1. Put the disk in the floppy drive.
2. Click on File.
3. Click on Save As to open the Save As dialog box.
4. Type A:FILENAME (such as, A:GEORGE.LTR) in the Save As text box. If you are saving to your second floppy drive, type B instead of A. Do not put a slash after the drive designation.
5. Choose Save.

Opening or Retrieving a Document from a Floppy Disk

To open or retrieve a document from a floppy disk:

1. Put the disk in the floppy drive.
2. Click on File.
3. Click on Open or Retrieve to display the Open or Retrieve File dialog box.
4. Type the drive letter (A or B) in the Filename text box and press Enter.
5. Select the document you want in the File list box.
6. Choose Open or Retrieve.

Setting Passwords for Your Documents

WordPerfect allows you to set passwords for your documents. Once you have decided on a password, it must be entered before the file can be opened. To set a password for a file:

1. Open the file.
2. Click on File.

3. Click on Password.
4. In the Password text box, type the password you have chosen. You will be asked to retype it.
5. Choose Set.

Once you have set a password, it can be removed only from within the document. If you forget your password, you are out of luck, so be careful.

Deleting a Password

To delete a password:

1. Open the document (which will require the password).
2. Click on File.
3. Click on Password.
4. Select Remove.

To set and remove passwords in the document window:

1. Click on File in the menu bar to open the File menu.
2. Click on Password to display the Password dialog box.
3. Type in the Password, and select Set or Remove.

Review Exercises for Chapter 8

◆ Access the File Manager from within WordPerfect.
◆ Using the Navigator or File List, list the files in the C:\WPWIN directory and the C:\WPWIN\DATA directory.
◆ If you have any duplicate files in these directories, delete them from one (but not both!).
◆ Rename a file.
◆ Copy a file.
◆ Locate a file using Word Search.
◆ Print a file from the File Viewer.
◆ Print a list of your files.
◆ Copy text from the File Viewer to the Clipboard and paste it into an existing WordPerfect document.
◆ Change your default directory and then change it back.
◆ Save a document to a floppy disk.
◆ Retrieve your document from the floppy disk.

Before You Go On...

Before you continue on to the next chapter, you should be familiar with the File Manager. You should understand directories and be able to work comfortably within their structure. You should be able to locate files using the Search feature. You should be able to save and retrieve documents on floppy disks.

Chapter 9

Outlining, Paragraph Numbering, and Footnoting

What You Will Learn in this Chapter

- ◆ How to define an outline numbering style
- ◆ How to create an outline
- ◆ How to define paragraph numbering style
- ◆ How to use paragraph numbering
- ◆ How to set options for footnotes and endnotes
- ◆ How to create and edit footnotes and endnotes
- ◆ How to move, copy, and delete footnotes and endnotes
- ◆ How to renumber footnotes and endnotes

Creating an outline in WordPerfect is simple. You do not have to track the numbering—WordPerfect does it for you.

Defining a Numbering Style

Before creating an outline or using paragraph numbering, you need to let WordPerfect know what numbering style you want to use. This is done in the following manner:

1. Click on Tools.
2. Click on Outline.
3. Click on Define to open the Define Paragraph Numbering dialog box, as shown in Figure 9.1.

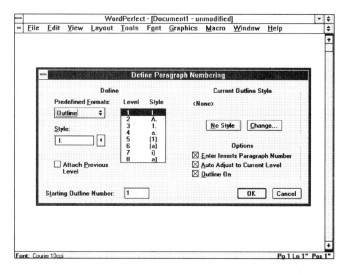

Figure 9.1—The Define Paragraph Numbering dialog box.

4. The Predefined Formats list box contains four pre-set numbering styles: Paragraph, Outline, Legal, and Bullets. There is a fifth choice, the User Defined format, which permits you to select your own numbering style.
5. The Style text box is used to create your own User Defined number format. If you have selected User Defined in the Predefined Formats list box, highlight the first level in the Level style box, select the Style text box, and choose a num-

ber style from the list. Move your cursor to highlight to the next level. The number format you have chosen appears in level 1. Continue until you have selected all the number formats for each level you need.

6. If you want the numbering style to reflect all of the numbers in the previous levels, use Attach Previous Level. For example, if you select Paragraph Numbering, the first three levels are 1, a, and i. If you want the second level to read "1.a" instead of "a," select level two in the Level style box, and select Attach Previous Level. When you are in level 2 in your outline, you will attach the previous level, level 1, and your numbering style will read "1.a."

7. The Current Outline style allows you to choose a style you have created for your outline. Styles are covered in Chapter 15.

8. All options will be enabled for outlining.

9. Starting Outline Number allows you to tell WordPerfect what number and what level you want to start your outline with. This option accepts only arabic numbers. Therefore, if you want your outline to start with V.C.iii, for instance, you would type 5,3,3 in the Starting Number text box. WordPerfect will pick up the numbering format from the Level style box.

10. Choose OK. Outline is turned on.

Creating and Turning On an Outline (Alt+Shft+5)

The Outline feature will automatically insert the next number after you press Enter. It will automatically bring you to the next level after you press Tab. In order to tab after each number, you must use Indent (F7). To get to the next level, after you press Enter, you must press Tab. To return to the previous level, press Shift+Tab.

Let's create an outline. To access the Define Paragraph Numbering dialog box, click on Tools, click on Outline, and then click on Define. Select Outline in Predefined Formats, choose OK, and:

1. Press Enter to activate outlining. The first level number appears.
2. Press F7 to indent and type "Things to do on Monday."
3. Press Enter, Tab, then F7 to go to the next number level. Type "Wake up."
4. Press Enter, then F7 and type "Feed cats."
5. Press Enter, then F7 and type "Drink coffee."
6. Press Enter, then F7 and type "Work."
7. Press Enter, then F7 and type "Drink more coffee."
8. Press Enter and then press Shift+Tab to return to the previous level. Press F7 and type "Things to do on Tuesday. Tuesday is a holiday and so the schedule is changed accordingly."
9. Press Enter and then press Tab+F7 and type "Wake up."
10. Press Enter, then F7 and type "Feed cats."
11. Press Enter, then F7 and type "Drink coffee."
12. Press Enter, then F7 and type "Do not work."
13. Press Enter, then F7 and type "Drink coffee."
14. Turn outlining off.

Your outline should look like this:

```
I.    Things to do on Monday.
      A.    Wake up.
      B.    Feed cats.
      C.    Drink coffee.
      D.    Work.
      E.    Drink more coffee.
II.   Thing to do on Tuesday. Tuesday is a holiday
      and so the schedule is changed accordingly.
      A.    Wake up.
      B.    Feed cats.
      C.    Drink coffee.
      D.    Do not work.
      E.    Drink coffee.
```

Now, go back to your outline, place your insertion point on the hard return after "D. Work," and press Enter. An "E" appears. Press F7 and type "Come home." Notice that all letters following the insertion have automatically adjusted to reflect the addition:

```
I.    Things to do on Monday.
      A.    Wake up.
      B.    Feed cats.
      C.    Drink coffee.
      D.    Work.
      E.    Come home.
      F.    Drink more coffee.
II.   Things to do on Tuesday. Tuesday is a holiday
      and so the schedule is changed accordingly.
      A.    Wake up.
      B.    Feed cats.
      C.    Drink coffee.
      D.    Do not work.
      E.    Drink coffee.
```

Now, change the order of your outline. Select all of the items in level 1. Be sure that you have selected all of the [HdTab] and [Par Num:Auto] codes with the text. Cut the level 1 items and paste them after level 2. Your outline now looks like this:

```
I.    Things to do on Tuesday. Tuesday is a holiday
      and so the schedule is changed accordingly.
      A.    Wake up.
      B.    Feed cats.
      C.    Drink coffee.
      D.    Do not work.
      E.    Drink coffee.
II.   Things to do on Monday.
      A.    Wake up.
      B.    Feed cats.
      C.    Drink coffee.
      D.    Work.
      E.    Come home.
      F.    Drink more coffee.
```

You have noticed that you are having trouble sleeping lately and have decided to cut down on your coffee consumption. Delete "C. Drink coffee" from the level 1 list. Be careful to include the [HdTab] and [Par Num:Auto] codes with the text you delete. Your outline now looks like this:

```
I.    Things to do on Tuesday. Tuesday is a holiday
      and so the schedule is changed accordingly.
      A.    Wake up.
```

```
     B.   Feed cats.
     C.   Do not work.
     D.   Drink coffee.
II.   Things to do on Monday.
     A.   Wake up.
     B.   Feed cats.
     C.   Drink coffee.
     D.   Work.
     E.   Come home.
     F.   Drink more coffee.
```

Using the examples listed above, you can create an outline of any length, move the text around, add and delete text, and edit it as you would any other document.

Turning Outline Off

1. Click on Tools.
2. Click on Outline.
3. Select Outline Off.

Using Paragraph Numbering (Alt+F5)

Paragraph numbering is very much like outlining. The main difference is that in outlining, a number is automatically inserted after every hard return; in paragraph numbering, you may choose whether or not the numbers will be inserted automatically. You do not have to turn Outline on or off. To use paragraph numbering:

1. Click on Tools.
2. Click on Outline.
3. In the Options section of the Define Paragraph Numbering dialog box, disable all options and choose OK.
4. Click on Define to open the Define Paragraph Numbering dialog box. Under Options, you can either enable or disable the hard return to automatically number your paragraphs. Disable the hard return automatic numbering

feature. The following instructions allow you to manually insert a number wherever you choose.

5. Press Alt+F5 and select Insert. Press Tab and then type "This is paragraph number 1. It will be followed by others." Press Enter.

6. Press Tab. Then press Alt+F5 and select Insert. Press Tab and type "This is another paragraph. There will be one more paragraph following this, then I am done." Press Enter.

7. Press Alt+F5 and select Insert. Press Tab, then type "This is the last paragraph. Eureka!"

Your paragraph should look like this:

```
I.   This is paragraph number 1. It will be fol-
lowed by others.
     A. This is another paragraph. There will be
one more paragraph following this, then I am
done.
II. This is the last paragraph. Eureka!
```

To change paragraph A to the first level of numbering, simply delete the Tab following the paragraph numbering code. To change paragraph II to B, simply insert a tab after the paragraph numbering code.

To change the numbering format for your paragraph numbering:

1. Click on Tools.

2. Click on Outline.

3. Click on Define to open the Define Paragraph Numbering dialog box.

4. Select the format you want.

5. In the Options section of the Define Paragraph Numbering dialog box, disable all of the options.

6. Choose OK.

7. Continue with your regular paragraph numbering routine (use Alt+F5).

Footnotes in WordPerfect

WordPerfect allows you to create, edit, and delete footnotes anywhere in your document except in table header rows. If you do not want to accept the WordPerfect default settings for footnotes, you should set the footnote options before you insert any footnotes. The default option starts numbering footnotes with a superscript 1, and continues consecutively throughout the document. Footnotes reflect the font you have selected for your document at the time they are inserted. All footnotes that follow the Footnote Options code will be in the font that is used where the code is inserted. If you want your footnotes to be in a different font, you must select the new font for each footnote.

Setting Footnote Options

All footnotes using the Footnote Options code will reflect the settings you make. To change Footnote Options:

1. Click on Layout.
2. Click on Footnote.
3. Click on Options to open the Footnote Options dialog box, as shown in Figure 9.2.

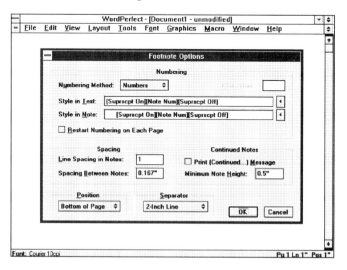

Figure 9.2—The Footnote Options dialog box.

4. To change your footnote numbering style, select Numbers, Letters, or Characters from the Numbering Method list box.

5. Type the character in the Characters text box. If you want to use characters that are not on the keyboard, place your insertion point in the Characters text box, press Ctrl+W, and select a character.

6. To change the appearance of the footnote number in the text of your document, change the codes in the Style in Text text box. You can add or delete spaces, enter characters, and change the size or appearance of the footnote number.

7. The Style in Note text box controls how the footnote number (or character) appears in the footnote. You can make the same changes as are available in the Style in Text text box.

8. To have your footnote numbering restart on each page, enable the option in the Footnote Options dialog box.

9. WordPerfect defaults to single spacing in footnotes with a .167" separation between footnotes. You can change these defaults in the Line Spacing text box and the Spacing Between Notes text box.

10. If you have a footnote that is too long to fit on a page, WordPerfect will continue it on the next page. The default is to keep at least a half inch of footnote text on one page. To change this default, enter a new setting in the Minimum Note Height text box.

11. If you want to print a message that says "(Continued)..." at the end of a footnote that is too long to fit on one page and at the beginning of the continuation on the next page, enable the Print (Continued)...Message.

12. If you want your footnote to print directly after the last line of text instead of at the bottom of the page, select After Text from the Position option.

13. To change the footnote separator (the line that divides the footnote from the text), select Separator. You may choose No Line, 2-Inch Line (the default), or Margin to Margin.

Creating a Footnote

Once you have set the options, you are ready to create footnotes. In your Footnote Options dialog box, set your options for an asterisk as your numbering method. Enable the Restart Numbering on Every Page option to have your asterisks start with one on each page. To create a footnote:

1. Type: "This is how a footnote option set for an asterisk looks."
2. After the period, click on Layout.
3. Click on Footnote.
4. Click on Create. The Footnote window appears with the number of the footnote displayed. Type in the text of your footnote. This is where you would put an Indent code or any font selections.
5. Choose Close.

Your text should look like this:

```
This is how a footnote option set for an
asterisk looks.*
```

You can see the footnote number in the text of your document. The footnote itself, however, does not appear in your window. To see how your footnote looks, you must either print your document, or use Print Preview. You can create a footnote anywhere in your document. If you add a footnote, all of the other footnotes in the document will renumber automatically to reflect the change.

Editing a Footnote

To edit a footnote:

1. Click on Layout.
2. Click on Footnote.
3. Click on Edit to open the Edit Footnote dialog box, as shown in Figure 9.3.
4. Type the number of the footnote you want to edit in the Footnote Number text box.

Figure 9.3—The Edit Footnote dialog box.

5. Choose OK. You are in the Footnote window. If WordPerfect cannot find the footnote, a "Not Found" message appears. Choosing OK will return you to your document.

6. Edit the footnote just as you would any other text in WordPerfect.

7. Choose Close.

If you have renumbered the footnotes in your document and have more than one footnote with the same number, you can use Search [F2] to locate the one you want to edit.

Deleting a Footnote

To delete a footnote, either position your insertion point on the footnote number in your text and press Delete, or delete the footnote code in Reveal Codes. The other footnotes in your document will automatically renumber to reflect the change. You can use Undelete or Undo to restore a footnote in the same way as any other text.

Copying or Moving a Footnote

Footnotes can be copied or moved anywhere in your document. To copy or move a footnote:

1. Select the footnote number in your text.

2. Click on Edit.

3. Click on Copy or Cut.

4. Place your insertion point where you want to put the footnote.

5. Paste the footnote. The footnotes in your document will automatically renumber to accommodate the change.

You can also copy or cut text in your document and move it to a footnote, or copy or cut text in a footnote and move it to your document.

Renumbering Footnotes

You can start renumbering footnotes anywhere in your document. Simply click on Layout, click on Footnote, and click on New Number. Type the new number you want in the Footnote Number text box. All of the footnotes in your document starting at that point will renumber consecutively.

Endnotes

The only difference between footnotes and endnotes is that endnotes are placed at the end of your document. Otherwise, they are created, edited, moved, copied, and deleted in exactly the same way as footnotes.

Review Exercises for Chapter 9

- ◆ Type a short outline.
- ◆ Change the numbering levels by adding and deleting tabs.
- ◆ Move text around (remember to include your codes) and watch your outline renumber.
- ◆ Type a paragraph. Create a footnote at the beginning and end of the paragraph.
- ◆ Change the numbering style of your footnotes.
- ◆ Copy one of the footnotes and create another in the middle of the paragraph.
- ◆ Delete a footnote.
- ◆ Edit a footnote.

Before You Go On...

Before you continue to the next chapter, you should be able to create and edit an outline and be able to use paragraph numbering in your documents. You should be familiar with footnotes and endnotes, how to set their options, edit them, move or copy them, and delete them.

Chapter 10

Creating Newspaper and Parallel Columns

What You Will Learn in this Chapter

- ◆ How to define newspaper columns
- ◆ How to define parallel columns
- ◆ How to enter text in columns
- ◆ How to edit columns
- ◆ How to copy, move, or delete column groups
- ◆ How to use the ruler with columns

Newspaper or parallel columns are used to align blocks of text into columns. Tab keys work well for simple tables and charts that have one-line entries. However, if an entry runs more than one line, the only feasible way to align the text is to use the **column** feature.

When you use the column feature in WordPerfect, text automatically wraps within the column. If you add or delete text within a column, it realigns automatically, without causing havoc in your other columns. In a sense, WordPerfect treats a column as it would a page. Most of the text-align features (center, flush right, justification, and so forth) can be used within a column.

There are three types of columns you can create in WordPerfect: Newspaper, Parallel, and Parallel with Block Protect. You can create from two to twenty-four columns, and you can adjust the **gutters**, or spaces between your columns. Your columns can be equal in width, or can be set to different widths.

By turning your columns on and off, you can easily switch back and forth between columns and regular text.

You can turn existing text into columns by placing your insertion point at the beginning of the text, defining the columns (see below), and turning them on.

You can also use the ruler to set columns. Setting columns with the ruler will be covered in a separate section of this chapter.

Working with Newspaper Columns

Newspaper columns start at the top-right corner of a page, continue down the page, and then wrap to the next column. They are called newspaper columns because they resemble a newspaper column format. Newsletters often use newspaper columns, which are shown in Figure 10.1.

DELICIOUS CATERING COMPANY

EMPLOYEE PERSONALS

We are pleased to announce that our employees have reported many exciting personal events over the past months.

MARRIAGES

Jamie Dough of the Bread Department was married on September 15th to Suzie Jones of Riverview City. Suzie is an accountant with the Numbers R Us Accounting Firm in Riverview. They have purchased a home here in Hightstown.

Jennifer Sweet of our Cake and Pies Department was married on October 5th to John Wood of Hightstown. John is a shipping clerk with the Willow Paper Company.

BIRTHS

Janis Pullet of our Poultry Department gave birth on September 8th to a 7 pound baby girl. She and her husband, Dan Horn, have announced that the baby has been named Katherine Jean. Janis has taken a three month leave of absence and will be returning to prepare her mouth watering poultry treats on December 10th.

Jerry Miller of our Booking Department has announced that he and his wife, Sally, are the proud new parents of an 8 pound baby boy, born on October 20th. Baby Miller hasn't been named yet because Jerry and Sally haven't been able to agree on a name. Hopefully, they will have decided on a name by our next issue!

APARTMENTS FOR SHARE

2 bedroom apartment in Elevator Building with 24 hour doorman. Looking for female roommate. Own bedroom w/bath. Rent $500 per month. Contact Denise Digit of the Accounting Department.

4 room apartment in Luxury Heights section of town. Seeking a third roommate, male or female. Own bedroom. Rent $700 per month. Contact Geraldine Gregg of the Secretarial Department.

1 Bedroom apartment, great part of town. Working fireplace in living room. Need female roommate. $300 per month. Call Rhonda, X286.

ITEMS FOR SALE

1989 Honda Civic. Excellent condition. Best offer. Contact Danielle, X315.

Steinway Baby Grand Piano. 5 years old. Superior Tone. Contact Steve, X382.

386/25 MHz computer. 52 MB Hard Drive, 4 MB in RAM, VGA Color Monitor. $1200. Contact John McCall, X351.

The Personal Section will be happy to print your news, ad, etc. The item must be submitted to us two weeks before publication. SHARE YOUR NEWS!

Figure 10.1—An example of newspaper columns.

Creating Newspaper Columns

The first step in creating columns is to define them. When you define columns, you determine the number of columns you are creating, their type, their margins or widths, and their gutter size.

Let's define two columns of equal width.

1. Bring your insertion point to the beginning of a new window.
2. Click on Layout in the menu bar to open the Layout menu.
3. Click on Columns (Alt+Shift+F9) to open the Define Columns dialog box, as shown in Figure 10.2.

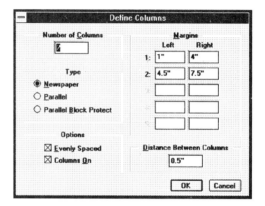

Figure 10.2—The Define Columns dialog box.

4. Enter "2" in the Number of Columns text box. (This is the default.)
5. Select the Newspaper option in the Type box.
6. Select Evenly Spaced in the Options box. Notice that two columns of equal width are defined in the Margins box.
7. Select Columns On in the Options box. This automatically turns the columns on so you can begin typing in them when you close the dialog box.
8. Set the Distance Between Columns text box at 0.5". This is the default, so unless you have changed it, this option should already be set.
9. Choose OK.

Since we selected the Columns On option, columns have automatically been turned on when we closed the Define Columns dialog box. If you turn on Reveal Codes, you will see a [Col Def:] code, followed by a [Col On] code. Whenever columns are turned on, the status bar displays the column number your insertion point is in. You are automatically placed in column 1 when columns are turned on.

You are now ready to begin typing text in your column. See if you can reproduce the columns in Figure 10.1. Do not type the heading. Begin typing with "We are pleased." To center the subheadings, just center as you normally do on a page.

Notice that when you reach the bottom of the page, the text automatically wraps to the next column. When you reach the end of the last column on a page, the text will wrap to the beginning of the first column on the next page.

If you do not want to fill an entire column (for example, you might want to start a new heading at the beginning of the next column), press hard page break [Ctrl+Enter] to move to the beginning of the next column. If you are working in the last column on a page, pressing hard page break will move you to the first column of the next page.

If you add or delete text in the columns, the text will automatically adjust and wrap within the column. Try it with the columns you have just created. Go to any paragraph and add several words to a line. Notice that the text automatically readjusts at the column's right margin, just as it would on a regular page of text. You can select text and move, copy, or cut it just as you would in any document.

Moving from Column to Column

The best way to move from one column to another is to move the insertion point to the column you want to be in and click. You can also use the Go To feature (see Chapter 5) to move to a specific location within a column. Pressing Alt+→ will move the insertion point to the corresponding line in the next column. Pressing Alt+← will move the insertion point to the corresponding line in the previous column.

Turning Columns Off

Frequently, columns are inserted between sections of regular text. This means that when you are finished typing your columns, you will want to turn them off and continue typing your regular text. To turn columns off:

1. Be sure that your insertion point is where you want to turn columns off and return to a regular text format.
2. Open the Define Columns dialog box. Select Columns Off.

Once columns have been defined, you can turn them on and off throughout the document. For example, after typing a segment of regular text, you might want to turn your columns back on. To do this, place the insertion point where you want columns to begin again and select Columns On in the Define Columns dialog box. When you are finished, turn them off again. When you turn columns on, WordPerfect inserts the last column definition. If you want a previous column definition, you must copy it and then turn columns on. You can turn columns on and off as frequently as you want in a document.

You cannot turn columns on unless you have defined them first.

If you change your mind and decide you do not want columns after all, you can delete the [Col Def:] code in Reveal Codes. Be sure to also delete the [Col On] code. The text will return to a normal format.

Working with Parallel Columns

Parallel columns keep related text together across columns in **column groups**. Special codes separate each column group so that you can edit the text in a column group without affecting the next column group. This is useful for such documents as charts or mailing lists. Figure 10.3 is an example of how parallel columns look.

Tables set up using the Tables feature can be turned into parallel columns. See Chapter 11 for information on how this is done.

PERSONNEL LIST

Jeremy Adams	Clerk Shipping Department 250 Main Street Hightstown, MA 11111	(413) 555-2111
Lynne Agars	Manager Accounting Department 450 River Road Riverview, MA 11211	(413) 544-3434
Marilyn Berman	Secretary Order Department Fairview Apartments 230 Fairview Road Hightstown, MA 11111	(413) 555-2167
John Calley	WordProcessor WordProcessing Department 120 Park Road South Hightstown, MA 11111	(413) 555-9087
Alan Demarest	Manager WordProcessing Department 25 Circle Drive Hightstown, MA 11111	(413) 555-4359
Elizabeth Farmer	Salesperson Sales Department 385 Elm Street Hightstown, MA 11111	(413) 555-6060
Sarah Grey	Manager Inventory Department 38 Hawthorne Lane Hightstown, MA 11111	(413) 555-8585

Figure 10.3—An example of parallel columns.

Creating Parallel Columns

Because of the way they are used, parallel columns often require columns of uneven widths. In Figure 10.3, the second column had to be wider to accommodate long addresses and department names. We are going to reproduce the figure to learn how to set up parallel columns with uneven margins.

We are using parallel columns as an example, but both newspaper and parallel columns can be defined with uneven margins.

To reproduce the columns in Figure 10.3:

1. Bring the insertion point to the beginning of a new page. Center the heading "Personnel List" at the top of the page and press Enter twice.
2. Click on Layout in the menu bar to open the Layout menu.
3. Click on Columns (Alt+Shift+F9) to open the Define Columns dialog box.
4. Enter "3" in the Number of Columns text box.
5. Select the Parallel option in the Type box.
6. Make sure that Select Evenly Spaced in the Options box is not selected.
7. Select Columns On in the Options box.
8. Set the Distance Between Columns text box at 0.5".
9. Do not close the Define Columns dialog box.

Now we are going to define the column widths by setting the margins. First, we must calculate the amount of space available for text in our columns. To do this, subtract all of the "white" space (margins, gutters, and so forth) from the total width of the page. We are working with a page that has a total width of 8.5". We have set our left and right margins for 1". That means that we must deduct 2" from the total width to accommodate our margins. That leaves us with 6.5" to work with (8.5" minus 2.0" = 6.5"). We also have two gutters; one between column 1 and column 2, and one between column 2 and column 3. Each gutter is .5", which means that together they will require a total of 1", which we must deduct from the available space. This leaves us 5.5" for our text (6.5" minus 1.0" = 5.5").

We now must decide how to apportion the available space (5.5") to accommodate our columns. For this exercise, columns 1 and 3 can be of equal width. Column 2 will have to be wider. The following widths should work well:

Column 1: 1.5"
Column 2: 2.5"
Column 3: 1.5"

To set the margins:

1. You should still be in the Define Columns dialog box.

2. Click on the Left Margin of column 1. This is set for 1". Column margins are measured from the left edge of the page. Since our document left margin is set for 1" (the system default), the left margin of the first column is automatically set for 1". If you want a different left margin for your first column, you can change the Left Margin setting in the Define Columns dialog box, or you can change the left margin in your document before you open the Define Columns dialog box. The new left margin will be reflected in the Define Columns dialog box.

3. Press the Tab key or use your mouse to get to the right margin of Column 2. To determine the right margin, add the column width to the left margin. The left margin is set at 1", and we have determined that the width of Column 1 should be 1.5". If we add the column width to the left margin, we arrive at a right margin of 2.5" (1.0" + 1.5" = 2.5"). Enter 2.5" in the Right Margin text box of column 1 (it is not necessary to type the" symbol; WordPerfect will automatically insert it).

4. Use the Tab key or your mouse to get to the left margin of column 2. To determine the left margin of a column, add the distance between columns (.5") to the right margin of the previous column. The right margin of column 1 is 2.5". If we add this to the distance between columns (.5"), we get a left margin for column 2 of 3". Enter 3 in the column 2 Left Margin text box (WordPerfect will add the .0" at the end of the 3).

5. Use the Tab key or your mouse to move the right margin of column 2. We have decided that column 2 should have a width of 2.5". Add the column width (2.5") to the left margin of column 2 (3.0") to get the right margin of column 2. The right margin will be 5.5" (3.0" plus 2.5" = 5.5"). Enter 5.5 in the column 2 Right Margin text box.

6. Use the Tab key or the mouse to move the left margin of column 3. To determine the left margin of column 3, we add the distance between columns (.5") to the right

margin of column 2 (5.5"). The left margin of column 3 should be set at 6" (.5" plus 5.5" = 6.0"). Enter 6 in the column 3 Left Margin text box.

7. Use the Tab key or your mouse to move to the right margin of column 3. We have decided that the column width of column 3 is to be 1.5". Add the column width (1.5") to the left margin of column 3 (6.0") to get the right margin of column 3. The right margin should be set at 7.5". Since our document right margin is set for 1", WordPerfect has already determined that the right margin of our last column should end at 7.5". This gives us a 1" distance between the right margin and the right edge of the page (remember that the total width of the page is 8.5"). You can extend the right margin in the Define Columns dialog box, or you can set a new right margin in the document before you open the Define Columns dialog box. The document right margin will be reflected in the Define Columns dialog box.

8. Choose OK. Since we selected Columns On, columns are automatically turned on when we close the dialog box. Your insertion point should be at the left margin of column 1.

 A much easier way to adjust the widths of columns is to use the ruler, which will be discussed later in this chapter.

Now let's type in the text for our columns.

1. Type the name Jeremy Adams. Press hard page break [Ctrl+Enter] to move to column 2.

2. In column 2, type:

   Clerk [Enter]

   Shipping Department [Enter]

   250 Main Street [Enter]

   Hightstown, MA 11111 [Enter]

   Press hard page break [Ctrl+Enter] to move to column 3.

3. In column 3, type (413) 555-2111. Press hard page break [Ctrl+Enter] to end the column group and move to column 1 to start the next column group. WordPerfect will automatically double-space between column groups.

4. Continue typing, following steps 1 to 3, until you have completed all of the column groups.

Redefining Columns

After you have typed in your columns, you might decide that you want to change the column widths, the number of columns, or the distance between columns. If Auto Code Placement is on, you can place your insertion point anywhere in the first column group. If Auto Code Placement is not on, place your insertion point immediately *after* the last column definition you want to change (do not delete the definition). Change the column definition, using either the Columns dialog box or the ruler. If Auto Code Placement is turned on, the new definition will replace the old one. The best way to redefine columns is to use the ruler.

Copying, Deleting, or Moving Column Groups

When you work with parallel columns, special codes are placed around column groups to keep the group together. These codes are visible in Reveal Codes. At the beginning of the first column group is a [Col On] code. At the end of the group, WordPerfect inserts [Col Off] [HRt] [Col On]. This turns columns off, inserts a hard return between the column groups, and turns columns on for the next column group. If you cut, copy, or move a column group, be sure to include the codes around it when you select the text. Be careful to include only the necessary codes, keeping in mind that when you cut, copy, or move a column group, the new insertion point will also contain column group codes.

Parallel with Block Protect

If your parallel columns are likely to run more than one page long, you should use Parallel with Block Protect. You must decide to do this when you define your columns; if you change your mind, you cannot automatically change your columns from Parallel to Parallel with Block Protect. When you use Parallel with Block Protect, WordPerfect places a Block Protect On code [Block Pro:On] and

Block Protect Off code [Block Pro:Off] around each column group. This prevents a column group from being broken up by a soft page break. If the group cannot fit at the bottom of the page, the entire group is moved to the beginning of the next page.

You cannot use Parallel with Block Protect if any of your column groups are more than a page long.

To use Parallel with Block Protect:

1. Open the Define Columns dialog box.
2. Select Parallel with Block Protect in the Type Options box.
3. Fill in the rest of the dialog box as instructed above.
4. Choose OK.

When using Parallel with Block Protect, you enter text and edit columns the same way as with Parallel columns.

Using the Ruler with Columns

GOOD IDEA

The best way to work with columns is to use the ruler, which can define columns, turn them on and off, and adjust the column widths and gutters. Double-clicking on the Column button in the ruler will bring up the Define Columns dialog box.

Defining Columns with the Ruler

You can define up to five newspaper columns with default settings using the ruler. To define columns using the ruler:

1. Place the insertion point where you want to define columns.
2. Click on the Ruler Column button. The Column drop-down list appears.
3. Select the number of columns you want to create. The columns are defined. You can enter text into them, or make adjustments using the Define Columns dialog box or the ruler.

Turning Columns On and Off with the Ruler

Once columns have been defined, you can turn them on and off using the ruler.

1. Place the insertion point where you want to turn the columns on or off.
2. Click on the Ruler Column button. The Column drop-down list appears.
3. Select Column On or Column Off.

Adjusting the Column Widths Using the Ruler

For those of you who are tired of using complex math formulas to constantly recalculate the margins of columns, this feature is a godsend. The best way to use it is to set your columns and type in the text, then, with the text visible on the screen, adjust the columns with the ruler until you are satisfied with the column widths. As you work, you will see the text automatically adjust to the new column widths.

To adjust column widths using the ruler, you must first define the columns using the ruler or the Define Columns dialog box. Then:

1. If the ruler is hidden, make it visible using the View menu on the menu bar.
2. If the columns are off, turn them on.
3. Now look at the margin markers on the ruler (see Figure 10.4). You will notice that there is a margin marker for each column. The white part of the bar represents the column width. The shaded part of the bar represents the gutter.

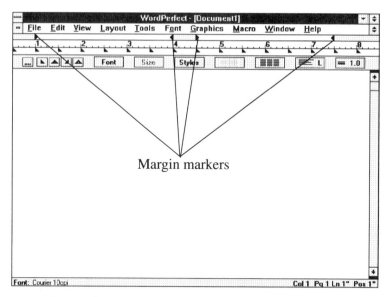

Figure 10.4—The Columns margin markers on the ruler.

4. To adjust the column widths, drag the margin markers to adjust the widths of the columns. The columns will adjust as you change the margins in the ruler. If you are working in newspaper columns, your insertion point can be in the columns anywhere on the first page before you adjust the ruler. If you are working with parallel columns, your insertion point must be in the first column group if you want to change the margins of all of the columns groups that follow. If your insertion point is not in the first column group, a new column definition will be inserted at the insertion point, and only the column groups that follow the insertion point will change.

Review Exercises for Chapter 10

◆ Open a new window and insert a column definition for newspaper columns. You should have two columns, with .5" gutters.

◆ Enter a page of text in the newspaper columns.

◆ Edit the text, inserting and deleting words and sentences.

◆ Turn columns off and return to normal text.

◆ Close the document.

◆ In a new window, create a column definition for three parallel columns with block protect.

◆ Using the ruler, make the second column wider.

◆ Type at least four column groups.

◆ Move the second column group to the end.

◆ Turn columns off using the ruler.

◆ Type in regular text and then turn columns back on.

◆ Enter two more column groups. Close the document.

Before You Go On...

Before you continue on to the next chapter, you should understand the differences between newspaper and parallel columns, and know how to create each. You should know how to adjust column widths using the dialog box and the ruler. You should be able to edit text in the columns and move, cut, and copy column groups.

Chapter 11

Working with Tabular Columns and Tables, Importing Spreadsheets

What You Will Learn in this Chapter

- ◆ How to set up and format tabular columns
- ◆ How to use leader dots
- ◆ How to create tables
- ◆ How to format data in cells
- ◆ How to name and identify cells
- ◆ How to add and delete rows
- ◆ Adding, deleting, and changing column widths
- ◆ How to use math formulas
- ◆ How to join and split cells
- ◆ How to lock and unlock cells
- ◆ How to format tables
- ◆ How to use a keyboard merge with tables
- ◆ Converting text to tables and vice versa
- ◆ Creating a table within a graphics box
- ◆ How to import and link a spreadsheet
- ◆ How to use the DDE spreadsheet link

This chapter is concerned with numbers and math. You can set up a spreadsheet-like table using the Decimal Tab Align feature and create columns of numbers separated by tabs, you can set up the same chart by using tables, or, if the table exists in a spreadsheet program, you can import it directly into WordPerfect.

Setting Up Numeric Columns (Shift+F9)

Numeric columns are simply lines of text separated by decimal align tabs. When you type in several lines, the text appears to be in columns. These are known as tabular columns. To set a decimal align tab:

1. Click on Layout.
2. Click on Line.
3. Click on Tab Set to display the Tab Set dialog box, as shown in Figure 11.1.

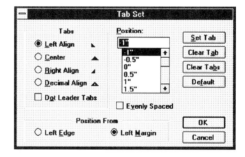

Figure 11.1—The Tab Set dialog box.

4. Clear all tabs.
5. Set decimal align tabs at 2.5", 3.5", 4.5", and 5.5" (or use your ruler to set the tabs). Setting tabs using either the Tab Set dialog box or the ruler is discussed in detail in Chapter 4.
6. Choose OK.

Now type in the following:

```
Jan. 1991    457.23      23.00 342.87   456.92
Feb. 1991     34.50     541.00  67.89 2345.67
March 1991 6788.99   23456.00   5.67    23.45
April 1991  890.00     673.00  45.89    22.00
```

Note that when you are typing numbers or text on a decimal align tab, all numbers or text preceding the decimal point move to the left, and all that follows the decimal point moves to the right.

Copying or Moving Text within Tabular Columns

After you have typed your tabular columns you may have a need to either move or copy a column. Type in the following tabular columns. Be sure to clear all tabs before you create your decimal align tab settings.

```
 25.00   45.00   65.00    85.00
105.00  115.00  135.00   155.00
175.00  195.00  215.00   235.00
```

To copy one of the above columns to another location, or to move one of the columns to another spot in your table:

1. Place your insertion point on the first number in the column you want to move or copy.
2. Select to the last number in the column you want to move or copy.
3. Click on Edit.
4. Click on Select.
5. Select Tabular Column.
6. Select either Cut or Copy.
7. Place your insertion point where you want the column to appear.
8. Click on Edit.
9. Click on Paste.

Changing the Value of the Decimal Align Character

You do not have to align your numbers on a decimal point. WordPerfect allows you to chose a different alignment character if you desire. To change the alignment character:

1. Click on Layout.
2. Click on Line.
3. Click on Special Codes to display the Insert Special Codes dialog box, as shown in Figure 11.2.

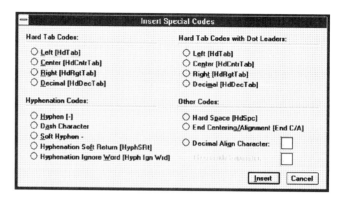

Figure 11.2—The Insert Special Codes dialog box.

4. Select Decimal Align Character. In the Decimal Align Character text box, type a slash mark [/].
5. Choose Insert. **Shortcut:** Use the Quick key Alt+Shift+F8 to access the Insert Special Codes dialog box.

6. Click on Layout.
7. Click on Line.
8. Click on Tab Set.
9. Clear all tabs.
10. Set your decimal align tabs.
11. Choose OK.

You must change your decimal align character *before* you set your tabs if you want to use anything other than the default decimal align character.

Type in the same table as above, using a slash mark instead of a decimal point. The following appears. Notice that now all of the numbers are aligned on the slash mark.

```
Jan. 1991    457/23        23/00   342/87    456/92
Feb. 1991     34/00       541/00    67/89   2345/67
March 1991  6788/99   123456/00     5/67     23/45
April 1991   890/00       673/00    45/89     22/00
```

Adding Headings to Your Table

You will probably also want to put headings above the columns in your table. Put your insertion point on the decimal align character code. Set center tabs at 2.5", 3.5", 4.5", and 5.5". Now tab over and type in the first four days of the week and two hard returns. Your table now looks like this:

```
             Mon.       Tues.     Wed.     Thurs.
Jan. 1991    457/23        23/00   342/87    456/92
Feb. 1991     34/00       541/00    67/89   2345/67
March 1991  6788/99   123456/00     5/67     23/45
April 1991   890/00       673/00    45/89     22/00
```

It is strongly suggested that you work in Reveal Codes whenever you are working with tabs and columns.

Using Dot Leaders

Dot leader tabs are used to connect text across the page with a series of dots. For example, in a book's Table of Contents, the headings are followed by dots leading to the page number. In WordPerfect this type of formatting is accomplished most efficiently by the use of dot leaders. To set up dot leader tabs:

1. Click on Layout.
2. Click on Line.
3. Click on Tab Set to open the Tab Set dialog box.
4. Clear all tabs.

5 Set a dot leader tab at 6". Set a decimal align tab at 6.5". Your ruler looks like the one shown in Figure 11.3. (Detailed information on how to set tabs using the Tab Set dialog box or the ruler is contained in Chapter 4.)

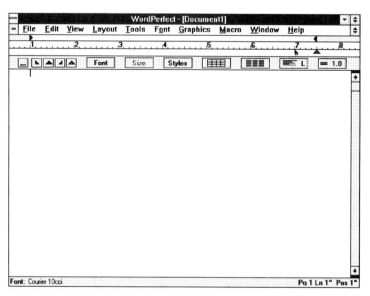

Figure 11.3—The WordPerfect ruler showing leader dot tab set.

Now, type the following text (tab after you type Chapter 1, tab after the leader dots end):

```
Chapter 1 ................  5
Chapter 2 ................  23
Chapter 3 ................ 100
```

Notice that the first tab (the dot leader tab) produces a series of dots starting at the 6" dot leader tab and moving to the left on the page until a character or number is encountered (in this case 1, 2, and 3 following the word Chapter). The second tab (the decimal align tab) moves all of the page numbers to the left. Remember that a decimal align tab anchors all characters preceding the decimal point to the left of the tab point (6.5") and all characters following the decimal tab to the right of it.

Creating Tables (Ctrl+F9)

Word Perfect's Table feature allows you to create multiple columns without using tabs. The Table feature also allows you to add, subtract, multiply, and divide across rows or down columns. Once you have created a table, you have the option of deleting the table structure, leaving only the text. There are two ways to create a table. The first is to:

1. Position your insertion point where you want to place the table.
2. Click on Layout.
3. Click on Tables.
4. Click on Create to display the Create Table dialog box, as shown in Figure 11.4.

Figure 11.4—The Create Table dialog box.

5. Type the number of columns you want in the Columns text box.
6. Type the number of rows you want in the Rows text box.
7. Choose OK.

The second way to create a table is to:

1. Position your insertion point where you want to place the table.
2. Click on the Table icon in your ruler.
3. Drag your mouse to select the number of columns and rows you want.
4. Release the mouse button.

You cannot create a table within either newspaper or parallel columns; you must create the table in a graphics box, which can then be included in either your newspaper or parallel columns. This will be discussed in greater detail later in this chapter.

Use one of the above methods to create a table with four columns and three rows. Your table should look like this:

Each column and row is separated by a line. The boxes created by these lines are known as **cells**. Cells can contain text, numbers, or calculation formulas. Each cell can be formatted individually, or you can select a group of cells and format them simultaneously. To move to the next cell press Tab; to move to the previous cell, press Shift+Tab. If you press Enter, you insert a hard return and move the insertion point to the next line in the same cell. Move your insertion point to the first cell and type the following information into your table:

January 1991	5000.00	450.00	325.00
February 1991	250.00	3400.00	1111.22
March 1991	12245.67	23.89	789.12

Once you have entered data into a cell in your table, it can be edited in exactly the same way as any other data. You can select data in cells and use cut, copy, and paste to move or copy data.

Formatting the Data in Cells

Notice that any formatting codes that were inserted into the document before you created this table are used in the table. You can format a table using either the standard document formatting codes or the table formatting codes.

Document format codes override table format codes.

You decide that you want to change the formatting in column 2 to include a decimal align tab. To do this:

1. Position your insertion point in any cell in the column..
2. Click on Layout.
3. Click on Tables.
4. Click on Column to open the Format Column dialog box, as shown in Figure 11.5.

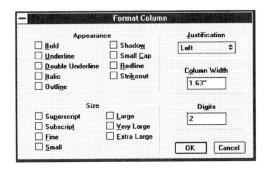

Figure 11.5—The Format Column dialog box.

5. Select Decimal Align in the Justification list box.
6. Choose OK.

The numbers in column 2 of your table are now decimal aligned.

January 1991	5000.00	450.00	325.00
February 1991	250.00	3400.00	1111.22
March 1991	12245.67	23.89	789.12

To change the tab alignment in columns 3 and 4 to decimal align:

1. Select the text from a cell in each column.
2. Click on Layout.
3. Click on Tables.
4. Click on Column to open the Format Column dialog box.
5. Select Decimal Align in the Justification list box.
6. Choose OK.

The numbers in columns 3 and 4 of your table are now decimal aligned.

January 1991	5000.00	450.00	325.00
February 1991	250.00	3400.00	1111.22
March 1991	12245.67	23.89	789.12

You can also change the appearance or justification of a column (or several columns) by selecting all of the cells you wish to affect, clicking on Layout, clicking on Tables, and clicking on Cell. You will access the Format Cell dialog box shown in Figure 11.6. Any selections you make in the Format Cell dialog box will be reflected in every cell that was selected.

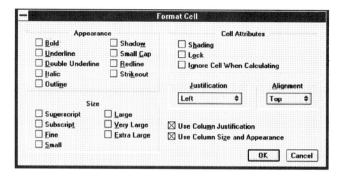

Figure 11.6—The Format Cell dialog box.

Changing One Cell in a Column

Positioning your insertion point in a cell and making changes in the Column dialog box will affect every cell in the column. To override the column formatting and change just one cell:

1. Position your insertion point in the cell you want to format.
2. Click on Layout.
3. Click on Tables.
4. Click on Cell to open the Format Cell dialog box.
5. Select the formatting change you want.
6. Choose OK.

In the following table, January 1991 was changed to italics using this method.

January 1991	5000.00	450.00	325.00
February 1991	250.00	3400.00	1111.22
March 1991	12245.67	23.89	789.12

Setting Lines Per Row and Row Height

The WordPerfect Tables feature allows you to choose the option of permitting one line or several lines of data in every cell in a row. The default is for several lines. When the default is selected, a hard return in a cell will wrap the text in that cell to the next line in the cell. In the sample table, a second line of text has been added after January 1991.

January 1991 to the present	5000.00	450.00	325.00
February 1991	250.00	3400.00	1111.22
March 1991	12245.67	23.89	789.12

Notice that all of the cells in the top row of the table have been expanded to accommodate the addition of the second line in the first cell. Notice also that additional data added to the cell continues in the same format. To change the lines per row designation:

1. Position your insertion point anywhere in the row you wish to affect.
2. Click on Layout.
3. Click on Tables.
4. Click on Row to display the Format Row dialog box, as shown in Figure 11.7.

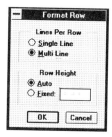

Figure 11.7—The Format Row dialog box.

5. Select Single.
6. Click on OK.

If you have more than one line of text in a cell and you change the Lines Per Row designation to Single, the text in any subsequent lines in the cell will not appear in your document, nor in the Print Preview window. It will not show in Reveal Codes and it will not print. The text is retained in a buffer. If you want to include the text, reset the Lines Per Row designation back to Multi and the text will reappear.

Row height defaults to Auto. This allows WordPerfect to calculate the row height according to the height of the text in a cell. When you change the size of the text, the height of the row will change to accommodate the new size. February 1991 has been enlarged in the sample table. The row height has been automatically changed to accommodate the new data size.

January 1991 to the present	5000.00	450.00	325.00
February 1991	250.00	3400.00	1111.22
March 1991	12245.67	23.89	789.12

If you want to set a fixed row height:

1. Position your insertion point in the row you wish to change.
2. Click on Layout.
3. Click on Tables.
4. Click on Row to open the Format Row dialog box.
5. Select Fixed and type in the row height measurement.
6. Choose OK.

Any data that does not fit within the fixed row height will not appear in your document window or in Reveal Codes, and will not print.

Naming and Identifying a Cell by Its Position in a Table

Cells are identified and correspondingly named according to their position in the table. The columns going across are given letters of the alphabet. The rows going down are numbered. The following table shows cell identification:

	A	B	C
1	*January 1991*	5000.00	450.00
2	February 1991	250.00	3400.00
3	March 1991	12245.67	23.89

Figure 11.8—Cell identification.

Using this formula, the cell address for January 1991 would be A1. February 1991 would be located in cell A2, and 5000.00 would be located in cell B1.

Adding and Deleting Rows

Once you have created your table, you might need to add or delete rows. WordPerfect has two ways in which you can accomplish this. The first way adds or deletes one or more rows to or from the last row on the bottom:

1. Position your insertion point anywhere within the table.
2. Click on Layout.
3. Click on Tables.
4. Click on Options to display the Table Options dialog box, as shown in Figure 11.9.

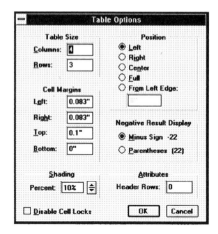

Figure 11.9—The Table Options dialog box.

5. In the Rows text box, type in the new number of rows you want. Either increase the number by the number of rows you want to add to the bottom of the table or decrease the number by the number of rows you want to delete from the bottom of the table. The sample table below now has one row added to the bottom.

January 1991 to the present	5000.00	450.00	325.00
February 1991	250.00	3400.00	1111.22
March 1991	12245.67	23.89	789.12

To add or delete a row anywhere else in the table:

1. Position your insertion point anywhere in the row directly below where you want to add a new row. New rows are added directly above the row in which you have placed your insertion point.
2. Click on Layout.
3. Click on Tables.
4. Click on Insert to open the Insert Columns/Rows dialog box, as shown in Figure 11.10.

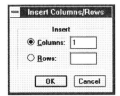

Figure 11.10—The Insert Columns/Rows dialog box.

5. Select Rows. In the Rows text box, type the number of rows you wish to add.
6. Choose OK.

The sample table below has a new row added directly above what was row 3.

January 1991 to the present	5000.00	450.00	325.00
February 1991	250.00	3400.00	1111.22
March 1991	12245.67	23.89	789.12

To delete a row from your table:

1. Position your insertion point anywhere in the row you wish to delete.
2. Click on Layout.
3. Click on Tables.
4. Click on Delete to display the Delete Columns/Rows dialog box.
5. Select Rows. In the Rows text box, type the number of rows you want to delete. If you type in more than 1, you will delete the row on which you have placed your insertion point and the specified number of rows that follow it.
6. Choose OK.

The sample table below has had the extra row deleted.

January 1991 to the present	5000.00	450.00	325.00
February 1991	250.00	3400.00	1111.22
March 1991	12245.67	23.89	789.12

Adding and Deleting Columns

There are also two ways to add and delete columns from a table. To add or delete a column at the extreme right of the table:

1. Position your insertion point anywhere in the table.
2. Click on Layout.
3. Click on Tables.
4. Click on Options to open the Table Options dialog box, as shown in Figure 11.9.
5. Select Columns. In the Columns text box, type in the number of columns you wish to add or delete.
6. Choose OK.

The sample table below has two columns added to it.

January 1991 to the present	5000.00	450.00	325.00		
February 1991	250.00	3400.00	1111.22		
March 1991	12245.67	23.89	789.12		

To add or delete columns at any other location within the table:

1. To add a column, place your insertion point in the column to the right of where you want the new column or columns to be. To delete a column, place your insertion point anywhere within the column you want to delete. If you specify more than one column to be deleted, the column that contains the insertion point and however many columns to its right will be deleted.

2. Click on Layout.
3. Click on Tables.
4. Click on Insert or Delete to open either the Insert Columns/Rows dialog box or the Delete Columns/Rows dialog box.
5. Select Columns. In the Columns text box, type the number of columns you want to add or delete.
6. Choose OK.

The sample table below has had a column deleted.

January 1991 *to the present*	450.00	325.00
February 1991	3400.00	1111.22
March 1991	23.89	789.12

Changing the Width of Columns

When you create a table, WordPerfect automatically assigns each column the same width and allows as much space for the table as your page size, font selections, and margins will permit. When you add additional columns, WordPerfect takes the needed space from the last column to the right and assigns it to the added columns. This does not always look the way you want it to. The sample table at the bottom of page 246 originally had four columns. Two more were added to it. Now columns B and C have too much space, and columns D, E, and F do not have enough. To change the width of your columns:

1. Position your insertion point anywhere in the column you wish to change.
2. Click on Layout.
3. Click on Tables.
4. Click on Column to open the Format Column dialog box, as shown in Figure 11.5.
5. In the Column Width text box, type in the width you wish your column to be.
6. Choose OK.

Continue these steps until all of the columns you wish to change are done. In the sample table below, columns B, C, D, E, and F have been changed to the same size.

January 1991 to the present	5000.00	450.00	325.00		
February 1991	250.00	3400.00	1111.22		
March 1991	12245.67	23.89	789.12		

Entering Math Formulas in a Table

The WordPerfect Table feature allows you not only to do math calculations, but to copy existing calculations between cells. To create a math formula:

1. Position your insertion point in the cell in which you wish to calculate.
2. Click on Layout.
3. Click on Tables.
4. Click on Formula to open the Tables Formula dialog box, as shown in Figure 11.11.

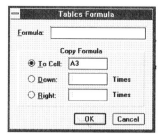

Figure 11.11—The Tables Format dialog box.

5. In the Formula text box, type the formula. **Formulas** include cell addresses—A1, B2, and so forth—and **operators**—addition (+), subtraction (–), multiplication (*), and division (/). To add all of the numbers in the B column, you would type B1+B2+B3 in the Formula text

box. In the To Cell text box you see the cell address in which your insertion point is located.

6. Choose OK.

The sample table now looks like this:

January 1991 to the present	5000.00	450.00	325.00		
February 1991	250.00	3400.00	1111.22		
March 1991	12245.67	23.89	789.12		
	17,495.67				

WordPerfect uses what are known as **relative cell references**. This means that if you have a formula in cell B4 to total all of the figures in cells B1 through B3, and you copy the formula to cell D4, WordPerfect will adjust the copied formula to total all of the figures in cells D1 through D3.

To copy the formula from cell B4 to cells C4 and D4:

1. Place your insertion point in the cell that contains the formula you wish to copy.
2. Click on Tables, then click on Tables again.
3. Click on Formula to open the Formula text box.
4. Select the Right text box and enter 2 to copy the formula to the two cells to the right of B4.
5. Choose OK.

The sample table now looks like this:

January 1991 to the present	5000.00	450.00	325.00		
February 1991	250.00	3400.00	1111.22		
March 1991	12245.67	23.89	789.12		
	17,495.67	3,873.89	2,225.34		

Notice that WordPerfect adjusted the cell addresses when it copied the formulas. The formula for cell C4 has been changed to C1+C2+C3. The formula for D4 is changed to D1+D2+D3. If you are not sure whether or not a cell contains a formula or what formula a cell contains, position your insertion point on the cell in question. If the cell contains a formula, it appears on the left of your status line.

Recalculating Totals When You Have Changed a Number

To recalculate totals when you have changed a number:

1. Position your insertion point on the cell you want to recalculate (or select the cells if there is more than one).
2. Click on Layout.
3. Click on Tables.
4. Click on Calculate.

Using the Subtotal, Total, and Grand Total Functions

You can use functions to calculate subtotals, totals, and grand totals. To instruct WordPerfect to subtotal a column of numbers:

1. Place your insertion point in the cell where you want the subtotal to appear.
2. Click on Layout.
3. Click on Tables.
4. Click on Formula to open the Tables formula dialog box.
5. Type a plus sign [+] in the Formula text box.
6. Choose OK.
7. To calculate the subtotal, click on Layout.
8. Click on Tables.
9. Choose Calculate.

The Total function adds all of the subtotals in the column directly above the Total function. To insert a Total function in a cell follow the same steps for subtotal above, but change step 5 as follows:

5. Type an equal sign [=] in the Formula text box.

The Grand Total function adds all of the totals in the column that precede the cell in which the Grand Total function is inserted. To insert a Grand Total function in a cell, follow the steps for subtotal above, but change step 5 as follows:

5. Type an asterisk [*] in the Formula text box.

You cannot calculate a total if you have no subtotals in your column. You cannot calculate a grand total if your column does not have any totals. The Subtotal function totals the individual cells, the Total function only totals the subtotal, and the Grand Total function totals only the totals.

Joining Cells

The Join Cells feature in WordPerfect Tables allows you to combine selected data in one or more columns or rows and combine it into one cell. To access this feature:

1. Select the columns or rows you want to combine.
2. Click on Layout.
3. Click on Tables.
4. Click on Join. The Join feature has no dialog box and no choices other than selecting the data you want joined.

All of the cells in Column A in the sample table have been joined. The table now looks like this:

January 1991 to the present February 1991 March 1991	5000.00	450.00	325.00		
	250.00	3400.00	1111.22		
	12245.67	23.89	789.12		
	17,495.67	3,873.89	2,225.34		

Notice that all the text has picked up the formatting of cell A1.

Splitting Cells into Rows or Columns

WordPerfect makes it possible for you to take a single cell and split it into multiple columns or rows. To access this feature:

1. Position your insertion point in the cell or select the cells you wish to split.
2. Click on Layout.
3. Click on Tables.

4. Click on Split to open the Split Column/Row dialog box, as shown in Figure 11.12.

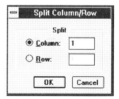

Figure 11.12—The Split Column/Row dialog box.

5. Select either the Column or Row text box. Type in the number of columns or rows you wish to create from the cell. If you select several cells, the number you type reflects the number of columns or rows you want to create from each cell.

6. Choose OK.

The insertion point was placed in cell B1 in the sample table. The number 2 was typed in the Row text box in the Split Row/Column dialog box. The sample table now looks like this:

January 1991 to the present February 1991 March 1991	5000.00	450.00	325.00		
	250.00	3400.00	1111.22		
	12245.67	23.89	789.12		
	17,495.67	3,873.89	2,225.34		

Save your tables before you join or split cells. It is not always possible to return your table to its original setup.

Locking and Unlocking Cells

When a cell is locked, you can not place your insertion point in it. You cannot edit the existing data in the cell, type any data in the cell, insert formulas into the cell, paste selections into the cell, or import any spreadsheet data into the cell. The only editing function you can perform in a locked cell is to select it. When you select a locked cell, the cell address appears in the left of the status bar in brackets.

Locking a Cell

1. Position your insertion point in the cell you want to lock.
2. Click on Layout.
3. Click on Tables.
4. Click on Cell to open the Format Cell dialog box.
5. Turn on the Lock attribute.
6. Choose OK.

Unlocking a Cell

1. Position your insertion point in the cell you have locked. Use the I-beam cursor to select the cell. (If you position your insertion point almost directly on the graphic line separating the cell, you will access the I-beam cursor.)
2. Click on Layout.
3. Click on Tables.
4. Click on Cell to open the Format Cell dialog box.
5. Turn off the Lock attribute.
6. Choose OK.

Disabling Cell Locks

When you disable cell locks, you are not removing the lock. If you turn off the Disable Cell Locks attribute, the cell is locked once more. This feature is generally used to gain temporary access to a locked cell. To access this feature:

1. Position your insertion point in the cell you have locked. Use the I-beam cursor to select the cell. (If you position your insertion point almost directly on the graphic line separating the cell you will access the I-beam cursor.)
2. Click on Layout.
3. Click on Tables.
4. Click on Options to open the Table Option dialog box.
5. Turn on the Disable Cell Locks attribute.
6. Choose OK.

To relock the cell, turn off the Disable Cell Locks attribute in the Table Option dialog box.

Using Headers in Tables

Headers can be put in the top rows of your table. They are especially handy when your table is longer than a page and you want the header information to repeat at the top of the next page. To create a header:

1. If your table already exists and you want to add a header row or rows with information that is different from the information in the existing top rows of the table, you must insert new rows at the top.
2. Click on Layout.
3. Click on Tables.
4. Click on Options to open the Table Options dialog box.
5. Type the number of header rows you want in the Header Rows text box.
6. Choose OK.

In the sample table, a row has been added to the top of the table (Click on Layout, click on Tables, click on Insert, and type the number of rows you want to insert in the Row text box. Choose OK). Text for the header has been typed in, and the first row has been selected as a header row. When your insertion point is placed in a header row, an asterisk as well as the cell address appear to the right in the status bar. The first page of the sample table now looks like this:

CELL A	CELL B	CELL C	CELL D	CELL E	CELL F
January 1991	5000.00	450.00	325.00		
February 1991	250.00	3400.00	1111.22		
March 1991	12245.67	23.89	789.12		

In order for your header to take effect, it must be on the same page as at least one row of the table.

Controlling Page Breaks in Tables

Sometimes a table can be split by a page break. To prevent this, you can use Block Protect, which is covered in Chapter 5.

To force a page break inside a table, position your insertion point where you want the table to break and press Ctrl+Enter. WordPerfect will break a table only at a new row. Text within rows cannot be broken.

Designing Table Formats

You can change the appearance of your table by changing the type of lines that surround the table and each individual cell. To do this:

1. Place your insertion point within the cell you want to change or select a group of cells.
2. Click on Layout.
3. Click on Tables.
4. Click on Lines to open the Table Lines dialog box.
5. The Top, Bottom, Left, and Right selections change the top, bottom, left, and right borders of the cell or group of cells you have selected. If you have selected a group of cells, selecting Outside changes the borders on the outside of the selection, and selecting Inside changes the borders on the inside of the selection.
6. Choose OK.

The sample table has been given some line changes. This is how it now appears:

CELL A	CELL B	CELL C	CELL D	CELL E	CELL F
January 1991	5000.00	450.00	325.00		
February 1991	250.00	3400.00	1111.22		
March 1991	12245.67	23.89	789.12		

Setting Up a Keyboard Merge in a Table

The Keyboard Merge (or Form Fill) feature can be used to create a table with some data that are permanent and some that are filled in or changed during the merge. For example, perhaps you want to compute the difference between your income and expenses every month. Your income remains the same, but your expenses are variable. The month, of course, changes in every report. You want to have to type in only the variable data and have the table recalculate your figures for each month. To accomplish this using the Table feature:

1. Position your insertion point where you want your table to start.
2. Click on Layout.
3. Click on Tables.
4. Click on Create to open the Tables Create dialog box.
5. Type in 4 in the Columns text box.
6. Type in 5 in the Rows text box.
7. Choose OK.

Or you can use your ruler to create the table. Make the first row of your table a header (click on Layout, click on Tables, click on Options, type 1 in the Header Rows text box). Join cells B1, B2, and B3 (select your cells, click on Layout, click on Tables, click on Join). In the joined cell type "INCOME AND EXPENSES" and position the words in the center of the cell (press Shift+F7). In cell A2, type "INCOME." In cell A3, type "EXPENSE." In cell A5, type "AMT. LEFT." In cell C2 type in 550.00. In cell C3 type in 2500.00. In cell C4 type in 465.00. Format columns B, C, and D for decimal align (select columns from B2 to D5, click on Layout, click on Tables, click on Columns, select decimal justification, choose OK). With your insertion point in cell B5, type in the formula to calculate the difference between your income and expenses (click on Layout, click on Tables, click on Formula, in the Tables Formula dialog box type B2–B3). Copy this formula to cells C5 and D5 (click on Layout, click on Tables, click on Formula, select Rows in the Tables Formula dialog box). Type 2 in the Rows text box. Your table now looks like this:

	INCOME AND EXPENSES		
INCOME	550.00	2500.00	465.00
EXPENSE			
AMT. LEFT	550.00	2,500.00	465.00

Now, add the merge codes that will turn this table into a form fill.

1. Position your insertion point in cell A1.
2. Click on Tools.
3. Click on Merge.
4. Click on Input to open the Insert Merge Code dialog box.
5. Type the message you want as a form fill prompt when you merge. In this table, type "MONTH:"
6. Choose OK.

Repeat these steps, typing "EXP. 1" in cell B2, "EXP. 2" in cell B3, and "EXP. 3" in cell B4. Your table now looks like this:

MONTH:	INCOME AND EXPENSES		
INCOME	550.00	2500.00	465.00
EXPENSE	EXP. 1⁻	EXP. 2⁻	EXP. 3⁻
AMT. LEFT	550.00	2,500.00	465.00

Before you can merge your table you must save it. Call it POVERTY. Close your document. At a blank window:

1. Click on Tools.
2. Click on Merge.
3. Click on Merge to open the Merge dialog box, as shown in Figure 11.13.
4. In the Primary File text box, type POVERTY.
5. The Secondary File text box is left blank. This is because there is no secondary file to merge. You are merging from the keyboard.
6. Choose OK.
7. A prompt appears on the bottom of your window asking the month. Type in "NOVEMBER" and press Alt+Enter. Continue until the merge is complete.

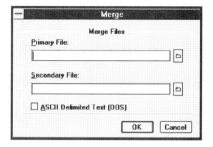

Figure 11.13—The Merge dialog box.

8. To recalculate the AMT. LEFT, select cells B5, C5, and D5.
9. Click on Layout.
10. Click on Tables.
11. Click on Calculate.

The month and expenses have been filled in and your totals have been recalculated. Your table now looks like this:

NOVEMBER	INCOME AND EXPENSE		
INCOME	550.00	2500.00	465.00
EXPENSE	555.00	2985.00	459.95
AMT. LEFT	-5.00	-485.00	5.05

Converting Existing Tabular or Parallel Columns into Tables

Converting existing tabular or parallel columns into tables is easy. When you convert a tabular column to a table, WordPerfect uses the tab settings to define table columns, and hard returns to define rows. In a table created with the Table feature, WordPerfect uses parallel column definitions to define table columns, and hard page codes to define rows. Type the following tabular columns. Remember to clear all tabs except those used in the columns themselves.

```
Row 1        456.00      3456.00      4578.98
Row 2        444.00      45.78        453.21
Row 3        222.33      444.55       1234.67
```

Now, to convert the tabular columns into a table:

1. Select the tabular columns you have typed (you could also select a portion of the text).
2. Click on Layout.
3. Click on Tables.
4. Select Create to open the Convert Table dialog box.
5. Select Tabular.
6. Choose OK.

The table you have created looks like this:

Ro w 1	456.00	3456.00	4578.98
Ro w 2	444.00	45.78	453.21
Ro w 3	222.33	444.55	1234.67

Next you can change the column widths and formatting if you so choose. Change the widths on columns A and B to 1" each. Set the Format Column Justification in Columns B, C, and D to decimal tab. Your converted table now looks like this:

Row 1	456.00	3456.00	4578.98
Row 2	444.00	45.78	453.21
Row 3	222.33	444.55	1234.67

Parallel columns are converted in exactly the same way.

Converting Tables into Text

To convert tables into text:

1. Highlight the table definition code in Reveal Codes.
2. Press Delete to display the Table Delete dialog box.
3. Select Table Structure.
4. Choose OK.

WordPerfect has converted all row and cell codes into hard tabs and hard returns. When you delete a Table Structure, you cannot use Undo to restore it.

Creating a Table Within a Graphics Box

You cannot create a table within newspaper or parallel columns. To insert a table in either of them you must first create a graphics box and put the table in it. You can then put the graphics box in either the newspaper or parallel columns. To create a graphics box:

1. Click on Graphics.
2. Click on Table Box.
3. Select Create.
4. In the Select Editor dialog box, select Text Editor.
5. Choose OK to open the Text Editor text box.
6. Click on Layout.
7. Click on Tables.
8. Click on Create to display the Create Table dialog box.
9. Type the number of columns in the Columns text box.
10. Type the number of rows you want in the Rows text box.
11. Choose OK.
12. You can now type the text into your table.
13. Click on Box Position to open the Box Position and Size dialog box.
14. In Size, click on Select Both.
15. In the Width text box, enter the width of table to accommodate your text box.
16. In the Height text box, enter the height of the table to accommodate your text box.
17. In the Vertical Position text box, type the vertical position at which you want the text box to appear on the page.
18. In the Horizontal Position text box, type the horizontal position at which you want the text box to appear on the page.
19. If you want to be able to wrap text around the box, enable Wrap Text Around Box.

20. Put your highlight on the Table Box code in Reveal Codes.

21. Click on Graphics.

22. Click on Options to open the Table Box Options.

23. In Border Styles, choose the border you want to surround your text box.

24. In Gray Shading, choose the amount of shading you want to appear in the background of your text box. You can choose between 0 (white) and 100% (black).

25. In Caption Numbering, choose the type of numbering and style of caption you want for your text box. If you do not want a numbered caption, set both the first and second levels to Off.

26. In Border Spacing, choose the amount of space you want between your text (the table) and the border of your text box. If you don't want any space at all, change the border spacing to 0.

27. In Caption Position, choose where you want your caption to be placed. If you don't have a caption, ignore this selection.

28. To see exactly how your graphics box will look when it is printed, use Print Preview. Chapter 17 has more detailed information on the Graphics feature.

Figure 11.8 shows a table created inside a graphics box.

Importing and Linking Spreadsheets

Importing a Spreadsheet

WordPerfect for Windows imports spreadsheets from PlanPerfect, Quattro, Quattro Pro, Lotus 1-2-3, and Microsoft Excel. When you import a spreadsheet, you are inserting a table into your document. It is not linked to the original spreadsheet, so any changes made in the source spreadsheet are not automatically reflected in the imported table. If you have imported a spreadsheet into WordPerfect and later decide to link it to the source spreadsheet, you can create such a link.

To import a spreadsheet:

1. Place your insertion point where you want the spreadsheet to be located.
2. Click on Tools.
3. Click on Spreadsheet.
4. Click on Import to display the Import Spreadsheet dialog box, as shown in Figure 11.14.

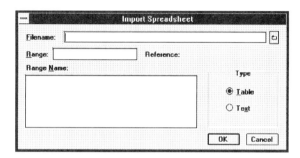

Figure 11.14—The Import Spreadsheet dialog box.

5. Type in the full path and name of the spreadsheet you want to import in the Filename text box. (In the example, we imported F:\EXCEL\ANNUAL.XLS.)
6. Unless you want to import your entire spreadsheet, type the range or select the range name you want to import in the Range text box or the Range Name text box. (A **range** includes all data from the first cell address you choose to the last cell address you choose.) In our example, the spreadsheet was imported using a range of A1.D14. This means that all the data between the cells A1 and D14 were imported into WordPerfect. The proper syntax to identify a range is any one of the following: A1.D14, A1..D14, A1:D14. If you have already defined ranges in your spreadsheet program and named them, you can type in the name of the range you want in the Range Name text box.
7. Select either Table or Text Type. If you select Table, you have three options:
   a. If you want your table to have the same formatting defaults as the spreadsheet you are importing, skip to step 9.

b. If you want to specify the size of your table and control cell formatting inside WordPerfect, you should create and format a table, position your insertion point anywhere in the table, and import or link the spreadsheet.

c. If you do not want to specify the size of your table, but do want to control cell formatting from within WordPerfect, you can import the data and then create a link to the same data in the first cell of your table.

Imported spreadsheets have the same size limitations as tables. WordPerfect will import only as much data as the left and right margins allow. To import the largest amount of data there are several steps you can take. You can reduce the column widths in the spreadsheet, you can reduce your left and right margins in WordPerfect, you can change to a smaller font size in your document before you import the spreadsheet, or you can choose a landscape paper size (your printer must be capable of printing in landscape format).

8. If you select Text, WordPerfect imports your spreadsheet as tabular columns with each column separated by a tab and each line separated by a hard return. If the text is too long for the page width, WordPerfect will wrap the line.

9. Choose OK.

Once you have imported your spreadsheet, you can use any of the table formatting options available in WordPerfect to alter its appearance.

The following table was imported using the Table option in the Import Spreadsheet dialog box.

Annual Summary, 1984-1986			
	Fiscal Year 1984	Fiscal Year 1985	Fiscal Year 1986
Net sales			
Total expenses	$303,070	$242,816	$270,468
Operating income	($303,070)	($242,816)	($270,468)
Income tax rate	0.414	0.473	0.439
Taxes on income	($125,471)	($114,852)	($118,735)
Net income	($177,599)	($127,964)	($151,733)
Earnings	($3.22)	($2.24)	($2.58)
Shares outstanding	55,211	57,034	58,764

Linking an Imported Spreadsheet

If you decide to link your spreadsheet after importing it:

1. Position your highlight in Reveal Codes on the Table Definition Code.
2. Click on Tools.
3. Click on Spreadsheet to open the Create Spreadsheet Link dialog box.
4. All of the information reflected in the text boxes should be correct. If not, change the information to match the information you used to import the spreadsheet.
5. Choose OK.

Two codes have been inserted into the document. These codes indicate where a link begins and ends. The begin link code indicates the filename and the range of cells you are linking to in the source spreadsheet. The end link code simply indicates the end of the link.

 When you link a spreadsheet into a table or columns, the begin and end link codes do not show in your document and they are not printed.

Importing and Linking Simultaneously

1. Place your insertion point where you want the spreadsheet to be located.
2. Click on Tools.
3. Click on Spreadsheet.
4. Click on Create Link to open the Create Link dialog box, as shown in Figure 11.15.

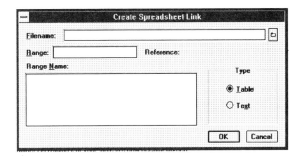

Figure 11.15—The Create Spreadsheet Link dialog box.

5. Type in the full path and name of the spreadsheet you want to import in the Filename text box.
6. Unless you want to import and link your entire spreadsheet, type the range in the Range text box or select the range name you want to import in the Range Name text box.
7. Select either Table or Text Type.
8. Choose OK.

Editing a Link

At some time you may want to edit your link to the original spreadsheet. For example, you may have changed spreadsheet programs and copied all of your spreadsheets into a new directory. In order for the link to work, WordPerfect must be able to locate the source spreadsheet. You must change the path of the source spreadsheet in your WordPerfect link. To do this:

1. Place your insertion point between the begin and end link codes.
2. Click on Tools.
3. Click on Spreadsheet.
4. Click on Edit Link to display the Edit Spreadsheet Link dialog box, as shown in Figure 11.16.

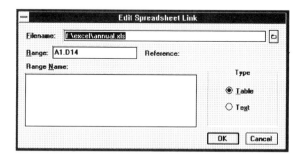

Figure 11.16—The Edit Spreadsheet Link dialog box.

5. Make the necessary changes to the Filename text box, Range text box, or Range Name text box.
6. Choose OK.

Deleting a Link

To delete a link, place your insertion point in either the begin link code or the end link code in Reveal Codes, and press Delete.

Manually Updating Multiple Links

To manually update all links in your document to reflect changes made in the source spreadsheets:

1. Open your document.
2. Click on Tools.
3. Click on Spreadsheet.
4. Click on Update All Links to open the Update All Spreadsheet Links dialog box.
5. Choose Yes to update all links in your document.

Manually Updating a Single Link

To update just one linked table:

1. Position your insertion point between the begin and end link codes of the table you wish to update.
2. Click on Tools.
3. Click on Spreadsheet.
4. Click on Edit to open the Edit Spreadsheet Link dialog box.
5. Choose OK.

Your table is now updated.

Linking Options

The Spreadsheet Link Options feature allows you to choose whether or not you want to reveal the begin and end link codes in your document, and whether or not you want WordPerfect to automatically update all links in your document when you retrieve it. To access this feature:

1. Click on Tools.
2. Click on Spreadsheet.
3. Click on Link Options to display the Link Options dialog box, as shown in Figure 11.17.

Figure 11.17—The Link Options dialog box.

4. Select either or both of the options (Update on Retrieve and Show Link Codes).
5. Choose OK.

Linking Three-Dimensional Spreadsheets

If your spreadsheet program allows you to produce three-dimensional spreadsheet files, you can import them into WordPerfect and maintain the links. Each worksheet is imported as a separate table and has its own link codes. The tables or text are separated by hard returns. To import and link three-dimensional spreadsheets:

1. Place your insertion point where you want the spreadsheet to be located.
2. Click on Tools.
3. Click on Spreadsheet.
4. Click on Create Link to open the Create Link Spreadsheet dialog box, as shown in Figure 11.15.
5. Type in the full path and name of the spreadsheet you want to import and link in the Filename text box. (The example spreadsheet was imported from Excel; its path is F:\EXCEL\ANNUAL.XLS.)
6. Specify a range that includes all worksheets in the spreadsheet. A range includes all data from the first cell address you choose to the last cell address you choose. The proper syntax to identify a range is any one of the following: A1.D14, A1..D14, A1:D14.
7. Select either Table or Text Type.

 Imported spreadsheets have the same size limitations as tables. WordPerfect will import only as much data as the left and right margins allow. To import the largest amount of data, there are several steps you can take. You can reduce the column widths in the spreadsheets, you can reduce your left and right margins in WordPerfect, you can change to a smaller font size in your document before you import the spreadsheets, or you can choose a landscape paper size (your printer must be capable of printing in landscape format).

8. If you select Text, WordPerfect imports your spreadsheets as tabular columns with each column separated by a tab and each line separated by a hard return. If the text is too long for the page width, WordPerfect will wrap the line.
9. Choose OK.

The DDE Link

The DDE (Dynamic Data Exchange) Link works only with Microsoft Windows applications. There are two basic differences between the WordPerfect link and the DDE Link.

1. The DDE Link will automatically update the tables in your document at the time you make a change in the source spreadsheet. In order for this to work, both files must be open and the source spreadsheet file must be opened first.
2. The DDE Link allows you to paste data from a source spreadsheet into a WordPerfect document and create a link. To accomplish this:
    a. Open both files.
    b. Switch your window to the source file and copy the data to the Clipboard.
    c. Switch your window to the WordPerfect document and place your insertion point where you want to put your table.
    d. Click on Edit.
    e. Click on Link.
    f. Select Paste.

You have imported the data from the source spreadsheet and linked it to the table in WordPerfect.

Creating a DDE Link

If you do not want to open the file in which your source spreadsheet is contained, or switch windows, you can create a DDE link by doing the following:

1. Place your insertion point where you want the imported, linked data to appear in your WordPerfect document.
2. Click on Edit.
3. Click on Link.
4. Click on Create to open the Create DDE Link dialog box.

5. Type the application, file, and item names (separate each with a vertical line) in the Source File and Item text boxes.

6. Choose OK.

7. Type a name for the link in the Link Name text box.

8. Select Automatic or Manual option for link updates.

9. If you want to import your source data as Text or Graphics, make the selection.

10. Choose OK.

Review Exercises for Chapter 11

◆ Create a tabular column.
◆ Use character align tabs and center tabs to format your column.
◆ Create a document using leader dot tabs.
◆ Create a table.
◆ Use the table formatting features to change the appearance of your table.
◆ Insert math calculation formulas in your table.
◆ Add and delete rows in your table.
◆ Add and delete columns in your table.
◆ Change the column widths in your table.
◆ Change some of the numbers in your table and recalculate.
◆ Create a table in a graphics box.
◆ Import and link a spreadsheet.
◆ Delete the spreadsheet link.

Before You Go On...

Before you continue on to the next chapter, you should feel comfortable setting up tabular columns, you should be able to create tables and employ math calculation formulas, and you should be able to import and link spreadsheets.

Chapter 12

Mass Producing with Merge and Document Assembly

What You Will Learn in this Chapter

- How to plan and create a secondary file
- How to create a primary merge file
- How to merge a primary file with a secondary file
- How to merge directly to the printer
- How to stop a merge
- How to prevent blank lines and spaces
- How to do a keyboard merge
- How to create a boilerplate document
- How to build a new document using a boilerplate

WordPerfect allows you to combine information from two or more sources to produce a new document. This is known as **merging**. It is often used to produce multiple copies of the same letter with different names and addresses. Two documents are required in a merge—a primary file and a secondary file.

Planning and Creating a Secondary File

Your secondary document contains all of the information you want to be able to merge into a master document. Assume that you want to mail the same letter to several people. You need to produce a secondary file containing the names and addresses of all the people to whom you will be sending this letter. You can then use this secondary file to merge with either label or envelope forms, as well as with the letter form.

The first step in creating a secondary merge file is planning. Your original goal may be to send a letter to everyone on a list, but in the future you might want to extract a portion of the list for limited mailings. You might want the sort the list alphabetically by last name, by zip code, by phone number, and so on. (The WordPerfect Sort and Select feature is covered in Chapter 13.) All of these considerations should be taken into account in planning your secondary merge file. Every secondary merge file consists of records. Each **record** is comprised of fields. Each **field** contains information that will be merged into a primary merge file. Records are identified in WordPerfect by an {END RECORD} code followed by a hard page break. Fields are identified by an {END FIELD} code followed by a hard return. To access these codes:

1. Click on Tools in the menu bar.
2. Click on Merge to open the Merge cascading menu, as shown in Figure 12.1.
3. Click on End Field or End Record.

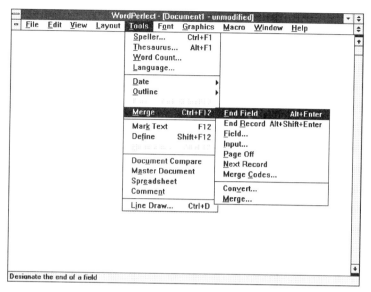

Figure 12.1—The Merge cascading menu.

Shortcut: To produce an {END FIELD} code from the keyboard, type Alt+Enter. To produce an {END RECORD} code from the keyboard type Alt+Shift+Enter.

To create a secondary merge file, type:

```
Mr.{END FIELD}
John{END FIELD}
Jones{END FIELD}
1 Main Street{END FIELD}
New York{END FIELD}
NY{END FIELD}
10000{END FIELD}
212-444-6666{END FIELD}
{END RECORD}
==========================================
Ms.{END FIELD}
Priscilla{END FIELD}
Smith{END FIELD}
23 Elm Street{END FIELD}
Greenwich{END FIELD}
CT{END FIELD}
{END FIELD}
```

continued...

... from previous page

```
719-888-4567{END FIELD}
{END RECORD}
=========================================
Professor{END FIELD}
Robert{END FIELD}
Johnson{END FIELD}
1 University Place{END FIELD}
Chicago{END FIELD}
IL{END FIELD}
{END FIELD}
444-555-6666{END FIELD}
{END RECORD}
=========================================
Mr.{END FIELD}
George{END FIELD}
Doe{END FIELD}
700 East 22nd Street[END FIELD}
New York{END FIELD}
NY{END FIELD}
{END FIELD}
212-444-1234{END FIELD}
{END RECORD}
=========================================
```

Save your secondary merge file and name it PRODUCT.DB.
You will notice that there are eight fields, and that each of these
fields comprises one record. Each field in the record is numbered
from top to bottom, Field 1, Field 2, and so on. You have created
separate fields for beginning addresses (Mr., Ms., and so on), first
names, last names, street addresses, cities, states, zip codes, and
phone numbers. Notice that in the last record, Field 7 is blank. You
must have the same number of fields in each record. If there is no
information for that field, it should be left empty except for an
{END FIELD} code. Do not insert hard returns between fields or
records, and do not put any spaces between the last word in a field
and the {END FIELD} code. By setting up your secondary merge
file with eight fields, you can, at a later date, retrieve the file and
alphabetize by Field 3 (last name), sort by Field 5 (state, zip code,
or even extract a portion of the file—such as all records for the state
of New York). All of these features are covered in Chapter 13. Re-

member, all of the information contained in a field will be merged; you cannot merge a portion of a field. Before you type in a secondary merge file, try to envision all of the possibilities for which it will be used.

Creating a Primary Merge File

Now that you have a secondary merge file, you need to create the primary merge file. This is the document into which the names and addresses in the secondary merge file will be placed. Type the following text for the body of your letter:

```
You have been chosen to test our new product,
Super Duper Nifty House and Clothing Cleaner.
A sample product is enclosed for you to try.
We would appreciate any comments you may have
concerning this product.


Please address any comments or suggestions to:

    The Super Duper Nifty Cleaning Corp.
    1 Main Street
    Anywhere, USA

Thank you for your help.



Very truly yours,



Mary Jones
Production Manager
```

Save this document and name it PRODUCT.PRI. You want to merge this letter with the names and addresses in your secondary merge file. Before you can do this, you must indicate in your letter (the primary merge file) what fields from the secondary merge file you want to include. If your letter is not on the screen, retrieve it now. You want Field 1, Field 2, Field 3, Field 4, Field 5, Field 6, and Field 7 to appear before the text. To do this:

1. Place your insertion point where you want the person's name to appear in the letter.
2. Use the Quick key (Ctrl+F12) to access the Merge cascading menu, as shown in Figure 12.1.
3. Click on Field to display the Insert Merge Codes dialog box, as shown in Figure 12.2.

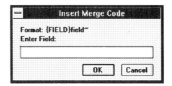

Figure 12.2—The Insert Merge Codes dialog box.

4. Type the number 1 in the Enter Field text box.
5. Click on OK or press Enter.
6. {FIELD}1~ now appears on your screen. Type a space after the ~.
7. Use the Quick key (Ctrl+F12) to access the Merge cascading menu (see Figure 12.1).
8. Click on Field to display the Insert Merge Codes dialog box (see Figure 12.2).
9. Type the number 2 in the Enter Field text box.
10. Click on OK or press Enter.
11. {FIELD}2~ now appears on your screen. Type a space after the ~.
12. Use the Quick key (Ctrl+F12) to access the Merge cascading menu (see Figure 12.1).
13. Click on Field to display the Insert Merge Codes dialog box (see Figure 12.2).
14. Type the number 3 in the Enter Field text box.
15. Click on OK or press Enter.
16. {FIELD}3~ now appears on your screen. Type a hard return after the ~.

The text on your screen should now look like this:

```
{FIELD}1~ {FIELD}2~ {FIELD}3~
```

You have been chosen to test our new product, Super Duper Nifty House and Clothing Cleaner. A sample product is enclosed for you to try. We would appreciate any comments you may have concerning this product.

Please address any comments or suggestions to:

    The Super Duper Nifty Cleaning Corp.
    1 Main Street
    Anywhere, USA

Thank you for your help.

Very truly yours,

Mary Jones
Production Manager

Now you will add the street address, city, state, zip code, and salutation to the letter, which is the primary merge file.

1. Place your insertion point on the line immediately following Fields 1, 2, and 3.
2. Use the Quick key (Ctrl+F12) to access the Merge cascading menu (see Figure 12.1).
3. Click on Field to display the Insert Merge Codes dialog box (see Figure 12.2).
4. Type the number 4 in the Enter Field text box.
5. Click on OK or press Enter.
6. {FIELD}4~ now appears on your screen. Type a hard return after the ~.
7. Place your insertion point on the line immediately following Field 4.
8. Use the Quick key (Ctrl+F12) to access the Merge cascading menu (see Figure 12.1).

9. Click on Field to open the Insert Merge Codes dialog box (see Figure 12.2).

10. Type the number 5 in the Enter Field text box.

11. Click on OK or press Enter.

12. {FIELD}5~ now appears on your screen. Type a comma and a space after the ~.

13. Use the Quick key (Ctrl+F12) to access the Merge cascading menu (see Figure 12.1).

14. Click on Field to display the Insert Merge Codes dialog box (see Figure 12.2).

15. Type the number 6 in the Enter Field text box.

16. Click on OK or press Enter.

17. {FIELD}6~ now appears on your screen. Type a space after the ~.

18. Use the Quick key (Ctrl+F12) to access the Merge cascading menu (see Figure 12.1).

19. Click on Field to display the Insert Merge Codes dialog box (see Figure 12.2).

20. Type the number 7 in the Enter Field text box.

21. Click on OK or press Enter.

22. {FIELD}7~ now appears on your screen. Type a hard return after the ~.

23. Type two more hard returns and then type "Dear." Type a space after "Dear."

24. Use the Quick key (Ctrl+F12) to access the Merge cascading menu (see Figure 12.1).

25. Click on Field to display the Insert Merge Codes dialog box (see Figure 12.2).

26. Type the number 1 in the Enter Field text box.

27. Click on OK or press Enter.

28. {FIELD}1~ now appears on your screen. Type a space after the ~.

29. Use the Quick key (Ctrl+F12) to access the Merge cascading menu (see Figure 12.1).

30. Click on Field to display the Insert Merge Codes dialog box (see Figure 12.2).

31. Type the number 3 in the Enter Field text box.

32. Click on OK or press Enter.

33. {FIELD}3~ now appears on your screen. Type a colon after the ~.

The text on your screen will look like this:

```
{FIELD}1~ {FIELD}2~ {FIELD}3~
{FIELD}4~
{FIELD}5~, {FIELD}6~ {FIELD}7


Dear {FIELD}1~ {FIELD}3~:

You have been chosen to test our new product,
Super Duper Nifty House and Clothing Cleaner.
A sample product is enclosed for you to try.
We would appreciate any comments you may have
concerning this product.

Please address any comments or suggestions to:

    The Super Duper Nifty Cleaning Corp.
    1 Main Street
    Anywhere, USA

Thank you for your help.


Very truly yours,



Mary Jones
Production Manager
```

The first line of your letter now contains Fields 1, 2, and 3 (beginning address, first name, and last name) with a space between each word. The second line contains Field 4 (street address). The third line contains Fields 5, 6, and 7 (city, state, and zip code) with a comma and a space after city, and a space between state and zip code. Fields 1 and 3 (beginning address and last name) follow "Dear." Field 3 is followed by a colon. Resave the letter.

Merging a Primary File with a Secondary File

Now that you have a primary file and a secondary file, you are ready to merge them into one document. At a blank document window:

1. Use the keyboard Quick key (Ctrl+F12) to access the Merge cascading menu.
2. Click on Merge to open the Merge dialog box.
3. Type the name of your primary file (PRODUCT.PRI) in the Primary File text box.
4. Type the name of your secondary file (PRODUCT.DB) in the Secondary File text box. The Merge dialog box now looks like Figure 12.3.
5. Click on OK or type Enter.

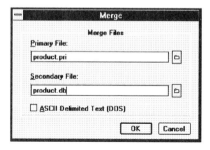

Figure 12.3—The Merge dialog box.

You now have four identical letters; each one contains the names and addresses in one record of the secondary file. Each letter in the merged document is separated by a hard page break. The text of your letters now look like this:

```
Mr. John Jones
1 Main Street
New York, NY 10000

Dear Mr. Jones:

You have been chosen to test our new product,
```

Super Duper Nifty House and Clothing Cleaner.
A sample product is enclosed for you to try.
We would appreciate any comments you may have
concerning this product.

Please address any comments or suggestions to:

    The Super Duper Nifty Cleaning Corp.
    1 Main Street
    Anywhere, USA

Thank you for your help.

Very truly yours,

Mary Jones
Production Manager
==
Ms. Priscilla Smith
23 Elm Street
Greenwich, CT

Dear Ms. Smith:

You have been chosen to test our new product,
Super Duper Nifty House and Clothing Cleaner. A
sample product is enclosed for you to try. We
would appreciate any comments you may have
concerning this product.

Please address any comments or suggestions to:

        The Super Duper Nifty Cleaning Corp.
        1 Main Street
        Anywhere, USA

Thank you for your help.

continued...

... from previous page

Thank you for your help.

Very truly yours,

Mary Jones
Production Manager
===
Professor Robert Johnson
1 University Place
Chicago, IL

Dear Professor Johnson:

You have been chosen to test our new product,
Super Duper Nifty House and Clothing Cleaner. A
sample product is enclosed for you to try. We
would appreciate any comments you may have
concerning this product.

Please address any comments or suggestions to:

   The Super Duper Nifty Cleaning Corp.
   1 Main Street
   Anywhere, USA

Thank you for your help.

Very truly yours,

Mary Jones
Production Manager
===

continued...

... from previous page

```
Mr. George Doe
700 East 22nd Street
New York, NY


Dear Mr. Doe:

You have been chosen to test our new product,
Super Duper Nifty House and Clothing Cleaner.
A sample product is enclosed for you to try.
We would appreciate any comments you may have
concerning this product.

Please address any  comments  or  suggestions
to:

   The Super Duper Nifty Cleaning Corp.
   1 Main Street
   Anywhere, USA

Thank you for your help.


Very truly yours,



Mary Jones
Production Manager
=========================================
```

You can have as many words and/or lines in a field as you wish.
The following example has five fields:

```
Mr.{END FIELD}
Jones{END FIELD}
1 Main Street
Apt. 4C{END FIELD}
New York{END FIELD}
NY{END FIELD}
{END RECORD}
=========================================
```

Field 3 has two lines but is still only one field. WordPerfect recognizes the end of a field when it sees the {END FIELD} code. Any data typed before the {END FIELD} code is considered part of the field. If you merged this record with your primary merge file, the name and address would look like this:

```
Mr. Jones
1 Main Street
Apt. 4C
New York, NY
```

Merging Directly to the Printer

There may be times when you will want to send your merged document directly to the printer. In order to do this you must add the {PAGE OFF} and {PRINT} merge code to your primary merge document:

1. Retrieve your primary merge document.
2. Move your insertion point to the end of the document.
3. Use the keyboard Quick key (Ctrl+F12) to access the Merge cascading menu.
4. Click on Merge Codes to display the Insert Merge Codes dialog box.
5. Click twice on {PAGE OFF}.
6. Click twice on {PRINT}.

Your primary merge document is now set up this way:

```
{FIELD}1~ {FIELD}2~ {FIELD}3~
{FIELD}4~
{FIELD}5~, {FIELD}6~ {FIELD}7


Dear {FIELD}1~ {FIELD}3~:

You have been chosen to test our new product,
Super Duper Nifty House and Clothing Cleaner.
A sample product is enclosed for you to try.
We would appreciate any comments you may have
concerning this product.
```

```
Please  address  any  comments  or  suggestions
to:

    The Super Duper Nifty Cleaning Corp.
    1 Main Street
    Anywhere, USA

Thank you for your help.


Very truly yours,



Mary Jones
Production Manager
{PAGE OFF}{PRINT}
```

Now, merge your primary and secondary merge documents directly to the printer:

1. Use the keyboard Quick key (Ctrl+F12) to access the Merge cascading menu.
2. Click on Merge to display the Merge dialog box.
3. Type the name of your primary file (PRODUCT.PRI) in the Primary File text box.
4. Type the name of your secondary file (PRODUCT.DB) in the Secondary File text box. The Merge dialog box now looks like Figure 12.3.
5. Click on OK or press Enter.

Your merged document will now print out. Each letter will be printed on a separate page.

When you send a merged document directly to the printer, it does not create a file. Your primary and secondary merge files still exist, but there is no actual final merged file.

Stopping a Merge

To stop a merge, simply press Cancel (Esc). If Cancel does not take effect, press Ctrl+Break to stop the merge.

Preventing Extra Lines when Merging Blank Fields

You want to merge your primary and secondary merge files to create a list or letters but, because at least one field is blank, the merged document will have unwanted blank lines. Retrieve your secondary merge file (PRODUCT.DB). Your screen now looks like this:

```
Mr.{END FIELD}
John{END FIELD}
Jones{END FIELD}
1 Main Street{END FIELD}
New York{END FIELD}
NY{END FIELD}
10000{END FIELD}
212-444-6666{END FIELD}
{END RECORD}
==========================================
Ms.{END FIELD}
Priscilla{END FIELD}
Smith{END FIELD}
23 Elm Street{END FIELD}
Greenwich{END FIELD}
CT{END FIELD}
{END FIELD}
719-888-4567{END FIELD}
{END RECORD}
==========================================
Professor{END FIELD}
Robert{END FIELD}
Johnson{END FIELD}
1 University Place{END FIELD}
Chicago{END FIELD}
IL{END FIELD}
{END FIELD}
444-555-6666{END FIELD}
{END RECORD}
==========================================
Mr.{END FIELD}
George{END FIELD}
Doe{END FIELD}
```

continued...

...from previous page

```
700 East 22nd Street[END FIELD}
New York{END FIELD}
NY{END FIELD}
{END FIELD}
212-444-1234{END FIELD}
{END RECORD}
=========================================
```

Notice that in three out of the four records in the secondary merge file, Field 7 is blank. Say your primary merge file is set up as follows:

```
{FIELD}1~ {FIELD}2~ {FIELD}3~
{FIELD}4~
{FIELD}5~, {FIELD}6~
{FIELD}7~
{FIELD}8~
```

If you merge the secondary merge file with a primary merge file such as this, the text in your final merged document will look like this:

```
Mr. John Jones
1 Main Street
New York, NY
10000
212-444-6666
=========================================
Ms. Priscilla Smith
23 Elm Street
Greenwich, CT

719-888-4567
=========================================
Professor Robert Johnson
1 University Place
Chicago, IL

444-555-6666
=========================================
Mr. George Doe
700 East 22nd Street
New York, NY

212-444-1234
=========================================
```

Notice that in three of the four merged records, there is a blank line between the city and state and the phone number. This is because the zip code field was left blank in those records. To avoid blank lines in your merged documents, do the following when setting up a primary merge document:

1. Place your insertion point where you want the person's name to appear in the letter.

2. Use the Quick key (Ctrl+F12) to access the Merge cascading menu (see Figure 12.1).

3. Click on Field to display the Insert Merge Codes dialog box (see Figure 12.2).

4. Type the number 1 in the Enter Field text box.

5. Click on OK or press Enter.

6. {FIELD}1~ appears on your screen. Type a space after the ~.

7. Use the Quick key (Ctrl+F12) to access the Merge cascading menu (see Figure 12.1).

8. Click on Field to display the Insert Merge Codes dialog box (see Figure 12.2).

9. Type the number 2 in the Enter Field text box.

10. Click on OK or press Enter.

11. {FIELD}2~ now appears on your screen. Type a space after the ~.

12. Use the Quick key (Ctrl+F12) to access the Merge cascading menu (see Figure 12.1).

13. Click on Field to display the Insert Merge Codes dialog box (see Figure 12.2).

14. Type the number 3 in the Enter Field text box.

15. Click on OK or press Enter.

16. {FIELD}3~ now appears on your screen. Type a hard return after the ~.

17. Place your insertion point on the line immediately following Fields 1, 2, and 3.

18. Use the Quick key (Ctrl+F12) to access the Merge cascading menu (see Figure 12.1).

19. Click on Field to display the Insert Merge Codes dialog box (see Figure 12.2).

20. Type the number 4 in the Enter Field text box.

21. Click on OK or press Enter.

22. {FIELD}4~ appears on your screen. Type a hard return after the ~.

23. Place your insertion point on the line immediately following Field 4.

24. Use the Quick key (Ctrl+F12) to access the Merge cascading menu (see Figure 12.1).

25. Click on Field to display the Insert Merge Codes dialog box (see Figure 12.2).

26. Type the number 5 in the Enter Field text box.

27. Click on OK or press Enter.

28. {FIELD}5~ now appears on your screen. Type a comma and a space after the ~.

29. Use the Quick key (Ctrl+F12) to access the Merge cascading menu (see Figure 12.1).

30. Click on Field to display the Insert Merge Codes dialog box (see Figure 12.2).

31. Type the number 6 in the Enter Field text box.

32. Click on OK or press Enter.

33. {FIELD}6~ now appears on your screen. Type a hard return after the ~.

34. Use the Quick key (Ctrl+F12) to access the Merge cascading menu (see Figure 12.1).

35. Click on Field to display the Insert Merge Codes dialog box (see Figure 12.2).

36. Type 7? in the Enter Field text box, as shown in Figure 12.4.

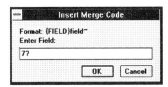

Figure 12.4—The Enter Field text box.

37. Click on OK or press Enter.

38. {FIELD}7?~ now appears on your screen. Type a hard return after the ~.
39. Use the Quick key (Ctrl+F12) to access the Merge cascading menu (see Figure 12.1).
40. Click on Field to display the Insert Merge Codes dialog box (see Figure 12.2).
41. Type the number 8 in the Enter Field text box.
42. Click on OK or press Enter.
43. {FIELD}8~ now appears on your screen. Type a hard return after the ~.

The text on your screen will look like this:

```
{FIELD}1~ {FIELD}2~ {FIELD}3~
{FIELD}4~
{FIELD}5~, {FIELD}6~
{FIELD}7?~
{FIELD}8~
```

If you merge your primary merge document with your secondary merge document, the final merged document will not contain any blank lines. The question mark instructs WordPerfect not to put a blank field in the final document. Instead, WordPerfect will go to the next field and put the text where a blank would have been. This command will work only when there is one field in a line.

 If you have an existing primary merge document and you have forgotten to allow for possible blank fields, you do not have to redo your merge codes. Simply move your insertion point to the field in which you want to insert a question mark and type it in between the field number and the ~.

Preventing Extra Spaces when Merging Blank Fields

There will be times when your primary merge document will contain more than one field on a line. These fields are usually separated by a space, and sometimes are separated by a comma and a blank space. (Retrieve your primary merge document, PRODUCT.PRI, as an example). If one of the fields on the line is blank, WordPerfect will skip the blank field and go on to the next field, but it will not remove extra spaces or commas. In order to do this, you must use the codes included in the Insert Merge Codes dialog box. For example, say you have a secondary merge file that contains the following fields:

```
Mr.{END FIELD}
John{END FIELD}
Jones{END FIELD}
{END FIELD}
=========================================
{END FIELD}
George{END FIELD}
Johnson{END FIELD}
Esq.{END FIELD}
=========================================
```

You have set up your primary merge document to look like this:

```
{FIELD}1~ {FIELD}2~ {FIELD}3~, {FIELD}4~
```

When you merge your primary merge document with your secondary merge document, the result will look like this:

```
Mr. John Jones,
    George Johnson, Esq.
```

To avoid this, when setting up a primary merge document:

1. Use your keyboard Quick key (Ctrl+F12) to access the Merge cascading menu.
2. Click on Merge to display the Insert Merge Codes dialog box.
3. Click twice on {IF BLANK} to display the Insert Merge Code text box.
4. Type 1 (to indicate Field 1).
5. Click on OK or Enter. You are in the Insert Merge Codes dialog box.
6. Click twice on {FIELD}.
7. Type 2 in the Insert Merge Code text box.
8. Click on OK or Enter.
9. Click twice on {FIELD} in the Insert Merge Codes dialog box.
10. Type 3 in the Insert Merge Code text box.
11. Click on OK or Enter.

12. Click twice on {FIELD} in the Insert Merge Codes dialog box.

13. Type 4 in the Insert Merge Code text box.

14. Click on OK or Enter.

15. Click twice on {ELSE} in the Insert Merge Codes dialog box.

16. Click twice on {FIELD} in the Insert Merge Codes dialog box.

17. Type 1 in the Insert Merge Code text box.

18. Click on OK or Enter

19. Click twice on {FIELD} in the Insert Merge Codes dialog box.

20. Type 2 in the Insert Merge Code text box.

21. Click on OK or Enter.

22. Click twice on {FIELD} in the Insert Merge Codes dialog box.

23. Type 3 in the Insert Merge Code text box.

24. Click on OK or Enter.

25. Click twice on {END IF} in the Insert Merge Codes dialog box.

26. Click on Cancel.

Your window should look like the one shown in Figure 12.5

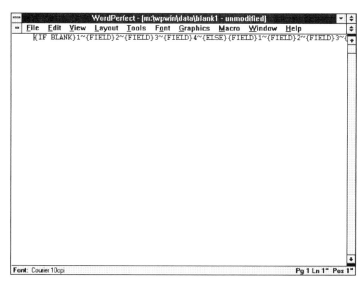

Figure 12.5—IF BLANK...ELSE...END IF statement before formatting.

There is one more step to do before you can use this primary merge document. Position your insertion point between Fields 2 and 3 and insert a space. Insert a comma and then a space between Fields 3 and 4. Position your insertion point after the {ELSE} and insert a space between Fields 1 and 2 and between Fields 2 and 3. (Your screen will scroll as you move your insertion point.) Your window now looks like the one shown in Figure 12.6

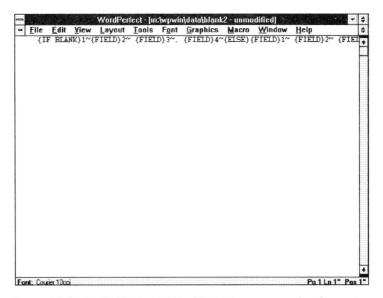

Figure 12.6—IF BLANK...ELSE...END IF statement after formatting.

{IF BLANK}1~{FIELD}2~ {FIELD}3~, {FIELD}4~ means that if Field 1 is blank, use Field 2(space)Field 3(,space)Field 4.

{ELSE}{FIELD}1~ {FIELD}2~ {FIELD}3~ means that if Field 1 is not blank, use Field 1(space)Field 2(space)Field 3.

{END IF} denotes the end of the If statement.

Merging to a List

Once you have created a secondary merge file, you will want to be able to print out the entire file. If you print the secondary merge file as it was originally typed in, each record will be a separate page. To avoid this, the secondary merge file should be merged with a primary merge file. Type in the following secondary merge file.

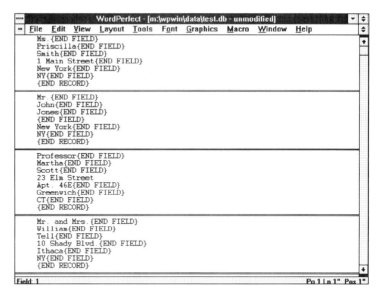

Figure 12.7—The sample secondary merge file.

 Shortcut: Alt+Enter will produce the {END FIELD} code and Alt+Shift+Enter will produce the {END RECORD} code.

Next, type in the primary merge file shown in Figure 12.8. For each field you want to incorporate into your final merged document:

1. Use the Quick key (Ctrl+F12) to access the Merge cascading menu (see Figure 12.1).
2. Click on Field to display the Insert Merge Codes dialog box (see Figure 12.2).
3. Type the number of the field you want in the Enter Field text box.
4. Click on OK or press Enter.

Place Fields 1, 2, and 3 on the first line of your primary merge document, Field 4 on the second line, and Fields 5 and 6 on the third line. (If you have forgotten how to create a primary merge document, refer to "How to Create a Primary Merge Document" at the beginning of this chapter.) Once you have entered all of the required fields in your primary merge document, insert a couple of hard returns. Then insert a {PAGE OFF} code. To do this:

1. Use the Quick key (Ctrl+F12) to access the Merge cascading menu (see Figure 12.1).
2. Click on Page Off.

The {PAGE OFF} code instructs WordPerfect to ignore the hard page break at the end of each record. Your primary merge document should look like the one shown in Figure 12.8.

Figure 12.8—The sample primary merge document.

Finally, you want to merge your primary merge document with your secondary merge document to produce a final merged list. To do this:

1. Use the Quick key (Ctrl+F12) to access the Merge cascading menu.
2. Click on Merge to display the Merge dialog box.
3. Type the name of your primary file in the Primary File text box.
4. Type the name of your secondary file in the Secondary File text box.
5. Click on OK or type Enter.

The final merged list in your window looks like the one shown in Figure 12.9.

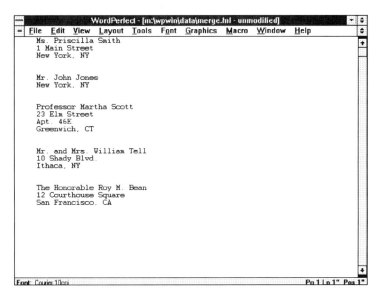

Figure 12.9—The sample final merged list.

Doing a Keyboard Merge

Now that you know how to create a primary merge document and a secondary merge document by merging two existing documents, you should learn how to create a document that lets you input different information into your primary merge document each time you merge. This is known as a **keyboard merge**, or, sometimes, as a **form-fill document**. To create a keyboard merge document, type:

M E M O R A N D U M

> **TO:**   **DATE:**
> **FROM:**   **PHONE:**
> **RE:**

----

1. Place your insertion point one tab after "TO."
2. Use your Quick key (Ctrl+F12) to access the Merge cascading menu.
3. Click on Merge Codes.
4. Click twice on {KEYBOARD}.

5. Place your insertion point one tab after "DATE."
6. Use your Quick key (Ctrl+F12) to access the Merge cascading menu.
7. Click on Merge Codes.
8. Click twice on {DATE}.
9. Place your insertion point one tab after "FROM."
10. Use your Quick key (Ctrl+F12) to access the Merge cascading menu.
11. Click on Merge Codes.
12. Click twice on {KEYBOARD}.
13. Place your insertion point one tab after "PHONE."
14. Click on Merge Codes.
15. Click twice on {KEYBOARD}.
16. Place your insertion point one tab after "RE."
17. Click on Merge Codes.
18. Click twice on {KEYBOARD}.

The document on your window should look like the one shown in Figure 12.10. Save your primary document.

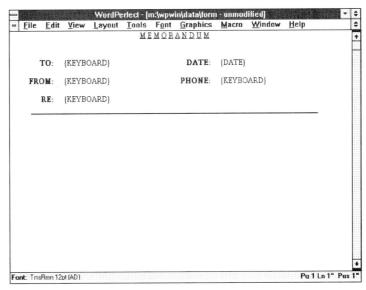

Figure 12.10—The keyboard merge form.

Merging a Primary File with the Keyboard

1. Use the Quick key (Ctrl+F12) to access the Merge cascading menu.
2. Click on Merge to display the Merge dialog box.
3. Type the name of your primary file in the Primary File text box.
4. Leave the name of your secondary file blank in the Secondary File text box.
5. Click on OK or type Enter.

The merge will stop at each point where you inserted a {KEYBOARD} code and wait for you to type in information. Once you have typed in the information for that field, use Alt+Enter to go on to the next field. Continue until you have finished. Your document now looks like the one shown in Figure 12.11.

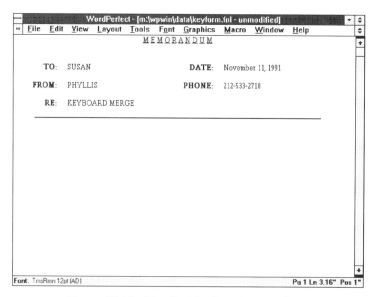

Figure 12.11—The final keyboard merge form.

Creating a Boilerplate Document

A boilerplate document can be created in one of two ways. If you have a document that already exists, you can select and save parts of it to create several different documents, then combine them in any order you wish. If no document exists, you must type in each separate document. Type in the following text to use as a sample:

```
AMENDMENT 1

    Congress shall make no law respecting an es-
tablishment of religion, or prohibiting the
free exercise thereof; or abridging the freedom
of speech, or of the press; or the right of the
people peaceably to assemble, and to petition
the Government for a redress of grievances.

AMENDMENT 2

    A well regulated Militia, being necessary to
the security of a free State, the right of the
people to keep and bear Arms shall not be in-
fringed.

AMENDMENT 3

    No Soldier shall, in time of peace, be
quartered in any house, without the consent
of the Owner, nor in time of war, but in a
manner to be prescribed by law.

AMENDMENT 4

    The right of the people to be secure in
their persons, houses, papers, and effects,
against unreasonable searches and seizures,
shall not be violated, and no Warrants shall
```

continued...

...from previous page

```
issue, but upon probable cause, supported by
Oath or affirmation, and particularly de-
scribing the place to be searched, and the
persons or thing to be seized.
```

Save this document and name it RIGHTS. You might wish to create a new directory for this boilerplate document. To create a directory see Chapter 8.

To take this document and create a boilerplate out of it, first retrieve the document.

1. Select AMENDMENT 1 and save that portion of text. Call this document something easy to identify like AMEND1.
2. Select AMENDMENT 2 and save that portion of text.
3. Select AMENDMENT 3 and save that portion of text.
4. Select AMENDMENT 4 and save that portion of text.

You now have four separate documents that you have created from one larger document. If the original document did not exist, you would have to type in each document separately.

Building a New Document Using Boilerplate Text

You now have the basis upon which to build a new document from the existing boilerplate. In this new document, you want to change the order of the amendments. To do this:

1. Retrieve AMEND1.
2. Go to the end of the document [Ctrl+End].
3. Retrieve AMEND2.
4. Go to the end of the document [Ctrl+End].
5. Retrieve AMEND4.
6. Go to the end of the document [Ctrl+End].
7. Retrieve AMEND3.
8. Save the document.

Your window should now look like the one shown in Figure 12.12.

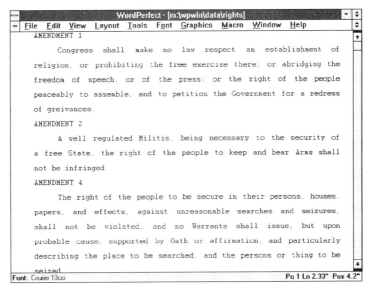

Figure 12.12—The sample boilerplate document.

Review Exercises for Chapter 12

- ◆ Create a secondary merge file.
- ◆ Create a primary merge letter file.
- ◆ Merge primary and secondary files.
- ◆ Edit your primary merge file to eliminate blank lines and spaces caused by blank fields.
- ◆ Create a primary merge list file.
- ◆ Merge to a list.
- ◆ Create a keyboard merge document.
- ◆ Do a keyboard merge.
- ◆ Create a boilerplate document.
- ◆ Create a new document using boilerplate text.

Before You Go On...

Before you continue on to the next chapter, you should be familiar with the most commonly used merge codes. You should be able to create primary and secondary merge files and merge them into a final document. You should be able to create and execute a keyboard merge. You should be familiar with boilerplating.

Chapter 13

Sort and Select

What You Will Learn in this Chapter

- ◆ How to do a line sort
- ◆ How to do a paragraph sort
- ◆ How to do a merge sort
- ◆ How to do a table sort
- ◆ How to select types of sorts
- ◆ How to select sort order
- ◆ How to use key definitions
- ◆ How to use select operators
- ◆ How to enter selection criteria
- ◆ How to globally select

The WordPerfect Sort feature allows you to take an entire document or portions of a document and reorder sections of text. You can sort by line, paragraph, secondary merge records, or rows of a table.

Any codes included on a line of text that is sorted will be sorted with that line. If you are going to sort a document that contains codes, be sure that the codes were defined in Document Initial Codes (see Chapter 5).

To sort part of a document, select the portion you want to sort before you begin the sort.

Doing a Line Sort (Ctrl+Shft+F12)

WordPerfect identifies text as a line when the last character is either a hard or soft return. Each line is identified by the WordPerfect Sort feature as a **record**. The words within each record are identified as **Words**. Type the following list at the left margin:

```
Kansas City
Alabama
San Francisco
New York
Boston
Chicago
Athens
Buffalo
```

Save your document before sorting. A sort cannot be undone. After you save the document, perform the sort. If you make a mistake while sorting, close the document without saving it again. The original file will not be overwritten and you can open it and sort again.

To sort this list alphabetically:

1. Click on Tools in the menu bar.
2. Click on Sort to open the Sort dialog box, as shown in Figure 13.1.
3. Select Line as your Record Type. Remember, we want the lines to be in alphabetical order.
4. Select Ascending as your Sort Order. Ascending starts at the lowest number or letter (a) and sorts in order to the highest number or letter (z). Descending sorts numbers or letters in reverse order.

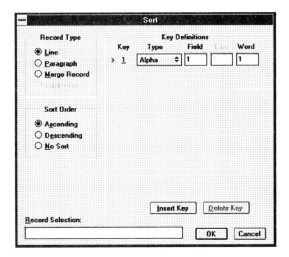

Figure 13.1—The Sort dialog box.

5. Look at Key Definitions. Key 1 has as its Type Alpha, for alphabetical. Since we are sorting by letter, we do not need to change this. Field is 1 and Word is 1. This indicates to the Sort feature that we want the records to be sorted by the first word (such as "San" in San Francisco) in the first field. Since this list contains only one field, this information is correct.

6. Click on OK. The Sort Status dialog box will show you the status of the sort in progress.

Your list should now look like this:

```
Alabama
Athens
Boston
Buffalo
Chicago
Kansas City
New York
San Francisco
```

This is the simplest type of sort. Now let's do a line sort with more than one field. In line and paragraph sorts, **fields** are the sections of text that are separated by tabs or indents within each line. Type the following, separating names and states by a single tab:

```
John Smith      New York
John Adams      Massachusetts
John Doe        New York
Mary Johnson    Massachusetts
George Doe      New York
```

You want to sort this list by state, then by last name, and, finally, by first name. To accomplish this:

1. Click on Tools in the menu bar.
2. Click on Sort to open the Sort dialog box, as shown in Figure 13.1.
3. Click on Line in Record Type.
4. Click on Ascending in Sort Order.
5. Look at Key Definitions. Key Definitions determine the order in which your list will be sorted. You may use up to nine Key Definitions. In this example, we will use three. Click on Insert Key twice. Three Key Definitions are now in the Key Definition dialog box. We have a list with five lines. Each line has two fields (remember, each field is separated by a tab; therefore, John Smith is Field 1 and New York is Field 2). Each field contains one or two words. We start with Key 1. The Type is Alpha. This is correct. The Field is 1. We want to sort on state first. In our list, this is Field 2. Click on Field and change the 1 to 2. Word is 1. We want to sort on the first word in Field 2, so we leave Word alone. We want to sort next by last name. To do this, go to Key 2 in the Key Definition dialog box. Once again, the Type is Alpha. The name column is the first field we typed, and is Field 1. We want to sort on last name, which is the second Word in Field 1. Go to Word in Key 2 and change 1 to 2. We have now instructed WordPerfect to sort our list alphabetically, first by state (Field 2) and then by last name (the second word of Field 1). We also want to sort by first name. Go to Key 3 in the Key Definition dialog box. The Type remains Alpha. The first name is included in the first field, so Field is 1. The first name is the first word in the first field, so Word is also 1. Your Sort dialog box should now look like the one shown in Figure 13.2.

6. Click on OK. The Sort Status dialog box appears and shows you the progress of the sort.

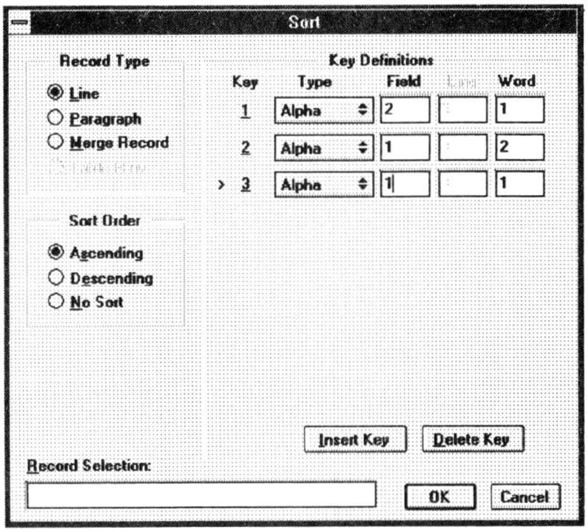

Figure 13.2—The Sort dialog box with multiple key definitions.

Your list should now look like this:

```
John Adams      Massachusetts
Mary Johnson    Massachusetts
George Doe      New York
John Doe        New York
John Smith      New York
```

Notice that the state of Massachusetts is before the state of New York. Next WordPerfect sorted the list by last name. Finally, it sorted by first name, putting John Doe and George Doe in alphabetical order.

Doing a Paragraph Sort (Ctrl+Shft+F12)

The WordPerfect Sort feature identifies text that is followed by two or more hard returns as a paragraph. Each paragraph can have as many words and lines as you wish, as long as the paragraphs are separated by two or more hard returns. As with Line Sort, fields within a paragraph are identified by a tab or an indent. Type the following, using either the Tab key or the Indent key to separate columns in the paragraphs, and remembering to press Return twice at the end of each paragraph.

```
10/12/91        Mary Martin
                New York, New York
                10000

10/25/91        John Smith
                Brooklyn, New York
                10010

11/01/91        Bob Smith
                Brooklyn, New York
                10012
```

There are three lines in each paragraph. Each line has two fields. Remember, a tab or indent identifies fields. It is not necessary to have text in a field. In the second line of the first paragraph, Field 1 is blank, Field 2 is New York, New York. You must be consistent in your use of lines and fields. If city and state are located in Line 2, Field 2 in the first paragraph, city and state should be located in Line 2, Field 2 throughout the list. We want to sort this document by zip code and then by state:

1. Click on Tools in the menu bar.
2. Click on Sort to display the Sort dialog box, as shown in Figure 13.1.
3. Click on Paragraph in Record Type.
4. Click on Insert Key to create a second Key Definition. In Key 1 we want to sort by zip code.
5. The zip code is comprised of numbers, so click on the Type list box in Key Definition 1 and select Numeric.
6. Click on Field in Key Definition 1, and type 2. Even though no text appears in Field 1, the tab or indent separates the blank Field 1 from the zip code (Field 2).
7. Click on Line in Key Definition 1, and type 3, since the zip code is the third line in the paragraph.
8. Word in Key Definition remains at 1. The zip code is the first word in the second field in the third line.
9. The Type in Key Definition 2 remains Alpha, since we are sorting by state.
10. Click on Field in Key Definition 2, and type 2.
11. Click on Line in Key Definition 2, and type 2.

12. Word in Key Definition 2 presents a problem. In paragraph 1 of our list the state is the third word in the field (New York, New York). In paragraphs 2 and 3, the state is the second word in the field (Brooklyn, New York). In order for the Sort feature to identify the location of the Key Word in Key Definition 2, we will have to count from right to left. The first word on the right is York—this would be Word-1, the second word is New—this would be Word-2, and so on. We want to sort on the second word from the right. Click on Word in Key Definition 2, and type -2. The Sort dialog box looks like the one shown in Figure 13.3.

13. Click on OK.

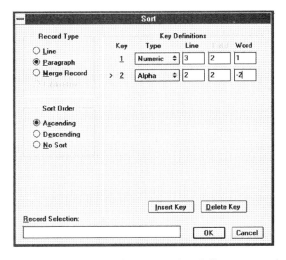

Figure 13.3—The Sort dialog box with a different record type.

Your list now looks like this:

```
10/12/91        Mary Martin
                New York, New York
                10000
10/25/91        John Smith
                Brooklyn, New York
                10010
11/01/91        Bob Smith
                Brooklyn, New York
                10012
```

Remember, use only one tab or indent between fields. Two tabs or indents (such as `10/21/91[Tab][Tab]Mary Martin`) indicates to WordPerfect that this line contains three fields. Field 1 is 10/21/91, Field 2 is identified by the first tab and WordPerfect interprets it as a blank field, and Field 3 is Mary Martin.

Doing a Merge Sort (Ctrl+Shft+F12)

Merge records are identified in the Sort feature by their merge codes. Each record ends with an {END RECORD} code. Each field ends with an {END FIELD} code. Each field can have more than one line, separated by a hard or soft return. Each line can contain several words. Merge codes are covered in Chapter 12.

Type the following merge document.

```
Mary Martin{END FIELD}
1 Main Street{END FIELD}
New York{END FIELD}
New York{END FIELD}
10000{END FIELD}
{END RECORD}
==========================================
John Smith{END FIELD}
{END FIELD}
Brooklyn{END FIELD}
New York{END FIELD}
10010{END FIELD}
{END RECORD}
==========================================
George Johnson{END FIELD}
34 Elm Street{END FIELD}
Chicago{END FIELD}
Illinois{END FIELD}
14086{END FIELD}
{END RECORD}
==========================================
```

Each record contains five fields: name, street address, city, state, and zip code. In Record 2 we do not know the street address. Since the fields must be consistent, this field is identified by an {END

FIELD} code only. This way, in every record, Field 3 is city, Field 4 is state, and Field 5 is zip code. To sort this merge document by state:

1. Click on Tools in the menu bar.
2. Click on Sort to display the Sort dialog box.
3. Click on Merge Record in the Record Type dialog box.
4. Sort Order remains at Ascending.
5. Select Type Alpha in Key 1.
6. Select Field and type 4 in Key 1.
7. Select Line and type 1 in Key 1.
8. Select Word and type 1 in Key 1.
9. Click on OK.

Your merge document will now look like this:

```
George Johnson{END FIELD}
34 Elm Street{END FIELD}
Chicago{END FIELD}
Illinois{END FIELD}
14086{END FIELD}
{END RECORD}
==========================================
John Smith{END FIELD}
{END FIELD}
Brooklyn{END FIELD}
New York{END FIELD}
10010{END FIELD}
{END RECORD}
==========================================
Mary Martin{END FIELD}
1 Main Street{END FIELD}
New York{END FIELD}
New York{END FIELD}
10000{END FIELD}
{END RECORD}
==========================================
```

Doing a Table Sort (Ctrl+Shft+F12)

Tables are discussed in detail in Chapter 11. Briefly, a table consists of rows and columns. Each row is divided into cells. Each cell can contain several lines, and each line can contain several words. For a sort, cells are counted from left to right. The first cell in the row is numbered 1, the second cell is numbered 2, and so forth. We want to sort the following table by ascending numerical order in cell 2.

Row 1		10000	20000	10/21/90	10/21/91	.750
Row 2		20000	30000	09/01/89	09/01/90	.500
Row 3		5000	10000			.625
Row 4			7500	05/30/90	05/30/91	.250
Row 5		2500	15000	07/05/88	07/05/90	.450
Row 6		22000	32000			.800

To accomplish this:

1. Click on Tools in the menu bar.
2. Select Sort to display the Sort dialog box.
3. Select Table Row in Record Type.
4. Select Ascending in Sort Order.
5. Select Type numeric in Key Definition 1.
6. Select Cell and type 2 in Key Definition 1.
7. Select Line and type 1 in Key Definition 1.
8. Select Word and type 1 in Key Definition 1.
9. Click on OK.

Your table should now look like this:

Row 4			7500	05/30/90	05/30/91	.250
Row 5		2500	15000	07/05/88	07/05/90	.450
Row 3		5000	10000			.625
Row 1		10000	20000	10/21/90	10/21/91	.750
Row 2		20000	30000	09/01/89	09/01/90	.500
Row 6		22000	32000			.800

Sorting by Date (Ctrl+Shft+F12)

The WordPerfect Sort feature recognizes either a forward slash or hyphen as a word separator in a date. If you have typed your date as 10-21-91, the Sort feature will identify 10 as Word 1, 21 as Word 2, and 91 as Word 3. In order for the hyphen to be identified, you must type Ctrl+-. If you use the Hyphen key alone, the Sort feature will not identify it as a dash character and will treat the date as a single number.

Selecting (Ctrl+Shft+F12)

Using the WordPerfect Select feature, you can extract from a merge document records that match specific criteria. You have the ability to either select these records in the order in which they are currently listed, or to sort and select them simultaneously. If you wish to both sort and select, first you have to choose your sort criteria. If you want to select records only, and do not wish to sort them, select No Sort in the Sort Order dialog box.

Save your document before you select. After the select is complete, the document will contain only the records that match your selection criteria. In order not to lose the original merge document containing all of the records, you must save the new document to a different name using Save As.

To select a group of records that match a specified criteria, you must create a Selection Statement in the Record Selection text box using the conditions in the following table:

Symbol	Criteria
+	or
*	and
=	is equal to
< >	is not equal to
>	is greater than
<	is less than
> =	is greater than or equal to
< =	is less than or equal to

Let's assume that Key 1 is a name field and that Key 3 is a state field. To select those records that have someone named Smith living in the State of New York, you would type "key1=Smith * key2=New York."

To select records for the State of New York only, you would type "key3=New York."

To select all records *except* those in the State of New York, you would type "key3<>New York."

To select all records of people whose names appear after Smith in the alphabet, you would type "key1>Smith."

To select all the records for people named Smith or people living in Ohio, you would type "key1=Smith + key3=Ohio."

Using Global Select (Ctrl+Shft+F12)

You can use a global key to select records where the key matches a certain word anywhere in the record. In the Record Selection text box in the Sort dialog box, a global key is identified as "keyg." For example: if you type "keyg=New" in the Record Selection text box, all records that contain the word "New" in any field will be selected.

Review Exercises for Chapter 13

◆ Type a short list.

◆ Sort the list alphabetically. Remember to save the list before you sort.

◆ Type a list with two or more fields separated by Tab or Indent, with at least one of the fields containing more than one word.

◆ Sort the list on more than one field.

◆ Resort the list on more than one field and on the second word in one of the fields.

◆ Type a merge list using {END FIELD} and {END RECORD}.

◆ Sort and select on several fields (remember to save the document first).

◆ Do a global select using the global key "keyg."

Before You Go On...

Before you go on to the next chapter, you should be familiar with line, paragraph, merge, block, and table sort. You should be able to identify fields and sort on several fields. You should know how to select records to match your specified selection criteria.

Chapter 14

Working with Reference Aids

What You Will Learn in this Chapter

How to work with the following reference aids:

- Index and concordance files
- Lists
- Table of contents
- Table of authorities
- Cross-referencing
- Document compare
- Master document

What Are Reference Aids?

When working with particularly long documents, such as books or dissertations, it is helpful to include reference aids that enable the reader to locate information in the document. Indexes, tables of contents, tables of authorities, and so on are examples of reference aids. WordPerfect has several powerful features that can automate referencing. Most of them involve three basic steps:

1. Mark the text to be referenced.
2. Define the style of the reference aid.
3. Generate the reference aid.

Once a reference aid is defined, WordPerfect will automatically update it if changes are made to the document.

Creating an Index

An **index** is a list at the end of the document of pertinent items and where in the document they can be located. You can use both headings and subheadings, and you can choose one of five numbering styles.

There are basically two ways to create an index: one is to create a concordance file to generate the index and the other is to manually mark entries throughout the document. When you create a concordance file, you list each index entry in a file. WordPerfect then searches the entire document for each occurrence of the entry and inserts the page numbers in the index. This is usually more efficient because it saves you the trouble of having to manually mark each item you want to appear in the index. If you decide not to use a concordance file, you must search the document for each index entry and mark it manually. This is much more time consuming.

You can combine these methods, marking some entries manually and using a concordance file for others.

Creating a Concordance File and Marking Text for an Index

To create a concordance file:

1. Open a new window.
2. Type a list of the entries as you want them to appear in the index. Each entry should be no longer than one line, so that it does not wrap (if the line wraps, sorting it will be more difficult). At the end of each entry press Enter.
3. Sort the list alphabetically. (See Chapter 13 for information on how to do a line sort.)
4. Save the file.

WordPerfect automatically marks each entry in the concordance file as a heading. If you want an entry in the file to be a subheading, you must mark it as such. If you want the text to be a heading and a subheading, you must mark it twice, once as a heading and once as a subheading. To mark the text, make sure the concordance file is in the window. Then:

1. Select the text you want to be a subheading.
2. Click on Tools in the menu bar.
3. Click on Mark Text (F12).
4. Click on Index to open the Mark Index dialog box, as shown in Figure 14.1. The text you selected in step 1 will appear in the Heading text box.
5. To mark this text as a heading only, choose OK.
6. To mark this text as a subheading as well, type a heading in the Heading text box, then select Subheading. The selected text appears in the Subheading text box.
7. Choose OK.
8. Continue until you have marked all of the entries that you want to be subheadings or headings and subheadings.
9. Save the file.

If you decide not to create a concordance file, you must mark each index entry manually in the document. To do this:

1. Open the document you want to index.
2. Select an entry you want to index.
3. Click on Tools in the menu bar.
4. Click on Mark Text (F12).
5. Click on Index to open the Mark Index dialog box, as shown in Figure 14.1. The text you selected in step 2 will appear in the Heading text box.

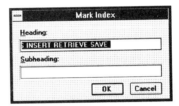

Figure 14.1—The Mark Index dialog box.

6. To mark this text as a heading only, choose OK.
7. To mark this text as a subheading, type a heading in the Heading text box, then select Subheading. The selected text appears in the Subheading text box.
8. Choose OK.
9. Continue until you have marked all of the entries that you want to be in the index.
10. Save the file.

Shortcut: You can use the WordPerfect Search feature to locate each entry. Mark the entry and then search for its next occurrence. Continue marking and searching until all the entries have been found.

You are now ready to define a style for your index.

Defining the Index

The second step in producing a reference aid is defining the style. WordPerfect provides the following five numbering styles to choose from:

Style	Result	Example
No Numbering	No page numbers.	
Text #	Entries followed by page numbers (separated by one space).	Index Entry 25
Text (#)	Entries followed by page numbers in parentheses (separated by one space).	Index Entry (25)
Text #	Entries followed by flush right page numbers.	Index Entry 25
Text......#	Entries followed by flush right page numbers with leader dots.	Index Entry.....25

The numbering format affects only the placement of numbers. You can also change the number type from arabic to roman by changing the Style option in the Page Number dialog box (see Chapter 5).

To define your index style:

1. Insert a hard page break Ctrl+Enter at the end of your document. You insertion point should be at the top of the new page.
2. If you are going to add a title or heading for the index, press Enter a few times.
3. Click on Tools in the menu bar to open the Tools menu.
4. Click on Define (Shift+F12).
5. Click on Index to open the Define Index dialog box.
6. If you are using a concordance file, type the complete filename (including the path if it is in another directory) in the Optional Concordance File text box. (You can use the List button at the right of the text box to open the Select File dialog box to view files.)
7. Select a format from the Number Format drop-down list.
8. Choose OK.

You are now ready to generate your index.

Generating the Index

To generate your index:

1. Click on Tools in the menu bar to open the Tools menu.
2. Click on Generate (Alt+F12).
3. Choose Yes. Your index will begin generating.

Index entries are listed in alphabetical order.

When you generate a reference aid, all other references aids in the document will also regenerate.

Creating Lists

You can use the Lists reference aid to list graphics, illustrations, tables, captions, and so on in your document. If you want to create several lists, you should assign a number to each list before marking the text. You will mark text, define, and generate each list separately.

Marking Text for Lists

WordPerfect will generate a maximum of ten lists in each document. Marked text should be assigned to list numbers 1-5. List numbers 6 to 10 are reserved for Graphics captions. Number six is reserved for figure captions, seven for table box captions, eight for text box captions, nine for user box captions, and ten for equation box captions.

If you created captions using WordPerfect's Graphics feature, the captions are automatically included in a list using the preassigned list numbers (six to ten). These captions do not have to be marked. However, if you created a caption outside of the Graphics feature, it must be marked to be included in the list, then assigned to the correct number.

Defining Lists

To define lists:

1. Place the insertion point anywhere that you want the list to appear.

2. If you want a heading for the list, type it in and press Enter a few times.
3. Click on Tools in the menu bar to open the Tools menu.
4. Click on Define (Shift+F12).
5. Click on List to display the Define List dialog box, as shown in Figure 14.2.

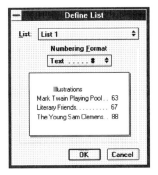

Figure 14.2—The Define List dialog box.

6. Select the List Number using the List drop-down list.

7. Select a numbering format from the Numbering Format drop-down list.

8. Choose OK.

9. Repeat the above steps for each list you want to define.

Generating Lists

To generate a list:

1. Click on Tools in the menu bar to open the Tools menu.
2. Click on Generate (Alt+F12).
3. Choose Yes. Your list will begin generating.

List entries are listed in the order in which they appear in the document.

When you generate a reference aid, all other references aids in the document will regenerate.

Creating a Table of Contents

You can have up to five levels of headings in a table of contents. Each level can have its own numbering format.

Marking Text for a Table of Contents

To mark text for a table of contents:

1. Select the text you want to appear in the table of contents.
2. Click on Tools in the menu bar to open the Tools menu.
3. Click on Mark Text (F12).
4. Click on Table of Contents to open the Mark Table of Contents dialog box, as shown in Figure 14.3.

Figure 14.3—The Mark Table of Contents dialog box.

5. Specify the table level number for this entry. Each line will be indented according to its level.
6. Choose OK.
7. Repeat the above steps for each table of contents entry.

Defining the Table of Contents

To define a table of contents:

1. Place the insertion point where you want the table of contents to be generated. Use a hard page break (Ctrl+Enter) if you want the table of contents on a separate page.
2. Type in the heading for the table. Press Enter a few times.
3. Click on Tools in the menu bar to open the Tools menu.
4. Click on Define (Shift+F12).
5. Click on Table of Contents to open the Define Table of Contents dialog box, as shown in Figure 14.4.

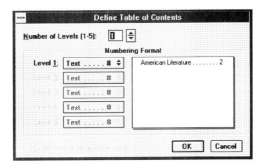

Figure 14.4—The Define Table of Contents dialog box.

6. In the Number of Levels text box, specify the number of levels you want in the table of contents.

7. Select a numbering format for each of the levels you have selected. If you have more than one level, you might want all of the entries in each last level to wrap at the end of the line. If so, select Last Level in Wrapped Format. If you select this option, the page number in the last level cannot be flush against the right margin, and it cannot have a dot leader. Therefore, only the first three numbering formats are available.

8. Choose OK.

9. Insert a hard page break (Ctrl+Enter) so that your document starts on a new page.

10. Change your page numbering after the hard page break, so that the document begins numbering with page 1 (see Chapter 5).

Generating the Table of Contents

To generate a table of contents:

1. Click on Tools in the menu bar to open the Tools menu.

2. Click on Generate (Alt+F12).

3. Choose Yes. Your table of contents will begin generating.

Table of contents entries are listed in the order in which they appear in the document.

Creating a Table of Authorities

A table of authorities is usually used with legal briefs. It lists the location of citations that appear in the document, and can be divided into sections for the different types of citations (cases, statutes, and so forth). Each section is sorted alphanumerically, and each can have its own format.

Marking Text for a Table of Authorities

Before you mark the entries for your table of authorities, you should decide how many sections you want and the order in which they will appear. For example, you might have sections for cases, statutes, U.S. Constitution, miscellaneous, and so on. Each section will be assigned a number from one to six.

When you mark text for a table of authorities, be sure to include citations in footnotes, headers, footers, graphics, and so forth.

Usually, when you cite an authority in a document, it is fully typed out only the first time; thereafter, a shorter form of the citation is used. When you mark an authority the first time, you will be asked to supply the **full form**. This is the way the authority will appear in the table of authorities. You are also asked to assign a **short form**. You will mark all subsequent occurrences of the authority with the short form. If you are careful to cite the authority exactly the same way throughout the document, you can use the WordPerfect Search feature to find each occurrence of the citation.

To mark an authority:

1. Find the first occurrence of the authority and select the text.
2. Click on Tools in the menu bar to open the Tools menu.
3. Click on Mark Text.
4. Click on ToA Full Form. The Mark ToA Full Form dialog box is displayed.
5. Specify the section number in which you want the authority included.
6. A suggested short form name is in the Short Form text box. If you want a different short form, change it. This is the form you will use to identify additional occurrences of this authority. You cannot have two authorities with the same short form.

7. Choose OK. The dialog box closes and the Full Form editing window appears.

8. Edit the full form exactly as you want it to appear in the table of authorities. You may use up to thirty lines. You may also use formatting features (such as hanging indents) and most font attributes (bold, italics, underline, and so forth).

9. Choose Close to return to the document window.

Once you have completed steps one to nine, you must proceed to mark each subsequent occurrence of the same authority, using the short form.

1. Select the next occurrence of the authority.
2. Click on Tools in the menu bar to open the Tools menu.
3. Click on Mark Text.
4. Click ToA Short Form. The Mark ToA Short Form dialog box appears.
5. Type the short form in the text box (or accept the existing name if it is correct). If you enter a short form name that does not match any existing full forms, the short form name will appear with an asterisk beside it at the beginning of the table of authorities.

The preceding five steps must be performed for each occurrence of the authority. If you used the same text each time you typed the authority, you can use the WordPerfect Search feature (see Chapter 6) to find each occurrence of the authority.

Repeat the above procedure for every authority in the document. When you are finished, proceed to Defining a Table of Authorities.

Editing the Full Form

The full form determines exactly how the authority will appear in the table of authorities. It is sometimes necessary to make changes in the authority after the table of authorities has been generated. To do this, you must edit the full form. (You can edit the actual table of authorities after it has been generated, but if you do this rather than editing the full form, each time you generate the table you will have to edit it, since it will appear as it does in the full form.)

1. Find the first occurrence of the authority in the document.
2. In Reveal Codes, find the [ToA:] code. Place the insertion point at the immediate right of the code.
3. Click on Tools in the menu bar to open the Tools menu.
4. Click on Mark Text.
5. Click on ToA Edit Full Form.
6. Edit the full form text.
7. If you need to change the short form or the section number, choose Edit Short Form and make your changes.
8. Choose Close to save the changes.
9. Generate the Table of Authorities again.

Defining a Table of Authorities

When you define a table of authorities, you decide the location and format of the sections, and give each section its own heading. To define a table of authorities:

1. Place your insertion point where you want the table to appear when it is generated. If you want the table to start on a new page, insert a hard page break (Ctrl+Enter).
2. Type a heading for the section (such as Cases or Statutes), and if necessary a subheading. Format the headings as you want them to appear in the table of authorities (center, left margin, and so forth). After you type the headings, press Enter a few times.
3. Click on Tools in the menu bar to open the Tools menu.
4. Click on Define.
5. Click on Table of Authorities to open the Define Table of Authorities dialog box, as shown in Figure 14.5.
6. Specify the number of the section you want to define.
7. Specify the Numbering Format Options you want:
   a. Use the Blank Line Between Authorities option if you want double-spacing between authorities. If you do not select it, the table will be single-spaced.

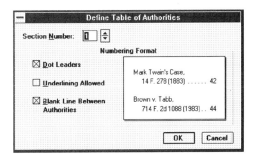

Figure 14.5—The Define Table of Authorities dialog box.

  b. If you select the Dot Leaders option, the table will have right-aligned numbers with leader dots. If you do not select it, the table will have right aligned numbers without leader dots.

  c. Most authorities include underlining in the text. If you want the underlining to remain in the table, select this option. If you do not select the Underlining Allowed option, the underlining in authorities will be removed in the table.

 8. Choose OK.

 9. Change your page numbering after the hard page break, so that the next section in the document begins with page 1 (see Chapter 5).

Follow steps one to eight for each section in the table. Each section can have its own formatting.

You can also change the page numbering from arabic to roman in your table of authorities by changing the Style option in the Page Number dialog box (see Chapter 5).

Generating a Table of Authorities

To generate a table of authorities:

 1. Click on Tools in the menu bar to open the Tools menu.

 2. Click on Generate (Alt+F12).

 3. Choose Yes. Your table of authorities will begin generating.

Tables of authorities entries are listed alphabetically within sections.

Editing Reference Aids

You can edit reference aids once they have been generated. However, any errors you edit in the generated aids still exist in the marked entries. If you generate the reference aid again, you will have the same errors all over again. It is much better to edit the marked reference in the document and then regenerate the reference aid. This way, if you generate it again in the future, it will always be correct. When editing marked text, be very careful not to delete or corrupt the reference codes around the text.

Cross-Referencing

Documents often contain cross-references. For example, on page 25 of a document, you might have a cross-reference (the **reference**) to text on page 15 (the **target**). If you edit the document, the target text on page 15 might fall on another page. With cross-referencing, you can direct WordPerfect to automatically update reference text to the correct page number.

Cross-referencing involves two processes: marking the reference and target text; and generating the cross-references.

Marking Text For Cross-Referencing

You can mark the reference and target separately or you can mark them together. You can cross-reference the following reference types: footnotes and endnotes, pages, paragraphs, outlines, figures, and graphics boxes (figures are also considered graphics boxes).

Marking Reference Only

To mark the reference only:

1. Place the insertion point where you want to create the reference.
2. Type in any introductory text you want, such as "See page," plus a space.
3. Click on Tools in the menu bar to open the Tools menu.
4. Click on Mark Text.

5. Click on Cross-Reference to open the Mark Cross-Reference dialog box, as shown in Figure 14.6.

Figure 14.6—The Mark Cross-Reference dialog box.

6. Select the Reference option in the Mark box.
7. Select a reference type from the Tie Reference To drop-down list.
8. Type a name in the Target Name text box. This must be the same for the reference and corresponding target.
9. Choose OK.

Repeat steps one to nine for each additional reference.

Marking Target Only

You can mark the target text separately after you have created a reference. To mark a target only:

1. Place the insertion point immediately after the target.
2. Click on Tools in the menu bar to open the Tools menu.
3. Click on Mark Text.
4. Click on Cross-Reference to open the Mark Cross-Reference dialog box, as shown in Figure 14.6.
5. Select the Target option in the Mark box.
6. Type a name in the Target Name text box. This must be the same for the reference and corresponding target.
7. Choose OK.

Repeat steps one to seven for each additional target.

Marking Both Reference and Text

You can mark both the reference and target in one operation:

1. Place the insertion point where you want to create the reference.
2. Type in any introductory text you want, such as "See page," plus a space.
3. Click on Tools in the menu bar to open the Tools menu.
4. Click on Mark Text.
5. Click on Cross-Reference to display the Mark Cross-Reference dialog box, as shown in Figure 14.6.
6. Select the Reference and Target option in the Mark box.
7. Select a reference type from the Tie Reference To drop-down list.
8. Type a name in the Target Name text box.
9. Choose OK.
10. A Mark Cross Reference Both message box appears, telling you to move the insertion point to the target.
11. Choose OK.
12. Move the insertion point the position immediately *after* the target and press Enter. Both reference and target are marked.

Repeat steps one to twelve for each additional reference and target you want to mark.

Multiple Targets

You may want to cross-reference several targets with one reference. For example, at a reference you might type "See pages," to be followed by several target page numbers. To do this, you have to mark the reference only once. Then, mark each target, using the same target name as the reference. When you generate the cross-reference, each target will be separated by a comma and a space.

Generating Cross-References

After you have marked your references and targets, to generate a cross-reference:

1. Click on Tools in the menu bar to open the Tools menu.
2. Click on Generate (Alt+F12).
3. Choose Yes. Your cross-reference will begin generating.

Document Compare

Document Compare uses redline and strikeout to show changes to a document. It does this by comparing the document in the window with the version stored on the disk, and then marking the document when differences are found. You can then print out the marked document and compare that version with the original document for changes. For example, you might print out a document and give it to somebody else to mark for revision. After you make revisions to the document, you can use Document Compare to mark the changes. Then you can proof the marked copy against the original to make sure that the changes were made.

Document Compare marks differences phrase-by-phrase, not word-by-word. If you want word-by-word comparisons, use the redline and strikeout font attributes (see Chapter 16). A phrase is marked by punctuation marks, hard returns, hard page breaks, footnotes, endnotes, and the end of the document.

Text that has been added to the document is Redlined (usually shaded in the printout). Deleted text is marked with Strikeout (usually shown with a line through it in the printout). "The Following Text Was Moved" is inserted before and "The Preceding Text Was Moved" is inserted after any text that was moved. You can change the printed appearance of marked text by selecting options in the Document Redline dialog box:

1. Click on Layout in the menu bar to open the Layout menu.
2. Click on Document.
3. Click on Redline Method to open the Document Redline dialog box.
4. Select the options you want and choose OK.

The Redline Method you choose depends upon your printer's capability to support it.

To compare the current document with the document on disk:

1. Make your revisions to the document in the window. Save the document to another name using the Save As command.
2. Click on Tools in the menu bar to open the Tools menu.
3. Click on Document Compare.
4. Click on Add Markings to open the Add Markings dialog box.
5. In the File to Compare text box, type in the name of the original file on the disk (not the name you just saved the file to).
6. Choose Compare. When the comparison is finished, the current document is marked with the changes.
7. Print out the marked document if you wish to check the original against the revised document.

Removing Markings

It is a good idea to save the document to another name before running Document Compare. However, if you did not, you may want to remove the markings. To do this make sure the marked document is in the window. Then:

1. Click on Tools in the menu bar to open the Tools menu.
2. Click on Document Compare.
3. Click on Remove Markings to open the Remove Markings dialog box.
4. If you want a version of the document that marks only added text, select Leave Redline Marks.
5. Choose OK.

Using Master Document

If you are working on a very large document, you can break the project into manageable segments called subdocuments, then use Master Document to put the whole project together. For example, if you are writing a book, each chapter can be a subdocument or separate file, then when you are finished, you can combine all of the subdocuments. Each subdocument can have its own page numbering, footnotes, endnotes, graphics, and so on, which will be combined into the master as if they were one document.

Once you combine all of the subdocuments into a master document, you can create a table of contents, an index, lists, and other referencing aids for all of the documents as if they were one.

When you create a master document, you insert **subdocument links** at specific locations. Then, when you generate the master document, the subdocuments are inserted at the location of their subdocument links. Subdocument links look like document comments in the document window.

Creating a Master Document

To create a master document:

1. Open a new window.
2. At the beginning of the document insert any introductory text you want (headings, cover page, introductory remarks), as well as any formatting codes.
3. Place the insertion point where you want the first subdocument to be inserted.
4. Click on Tools in the menu bar to open the Tools menu.
5. Click on Master Document.
6. Click on Subdocument to open the Include Subdocument dialog box, as shown in Figure 14.7.
7. Type in the name of the subdocument you want to insert at that location, including the path.
8. Choose Insert.

Continue creating subdocument links in the master document until all of the links have been inserted.

After you have expanded the master document, the codes in the subdocuments will work the same way they do in any document. Any formatting code will be effective until the program encounters another formatting code to replace.

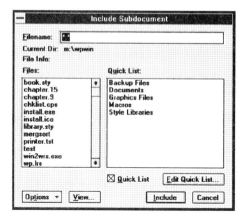

Figure 14.7—The Include Subdocument dialog box.

Codes that generate numbers (page numbering, footnotes, graphics, and so forth) continue numbering throughout the document as though the document had never been broken into segments.

Expanding a Master Document

For the subdocument codes to take effect in the master document, the master document must be expanded. When you expand a master document, the subdocuments are retrieved into the master document at the subdocument links. You should expand a master document before you generate any reference aids or print it.

To expand a master document, make sure it is in the window. Then:

1. Click on Tools in the menu bar to open the Tools menu.
2. Click on Master Document.
3. Click on Expand Master. The master document will be expanded to include all of the subdocuments.
4. You can edit any part of the master document, including subdocuments, as though it were one document. If you save the master document, or condense it (see below), WordPerfect will give you the opportunity to save the changes to the subdocuments.

Condensing a Master Document

After you have expanded a master document, you can condense it again, should you find it unwieldy in its expanded version. For instance, if you want to make a change in any of the subdocuments, it is easier to condense the master document, make the change, and then expand it again. Condensing a master document removes the subdocuments.

To condense a master document:

1. Click on Tools in the menu bar to open the Tools menu.
2. Click on Master Document.
3. Click on Condense Master to open the Condense Master dialog box, as shown in Figure 14.8, which lets you decide if you want to save changes to the subdocuments before you condense the master document. If you choose Yes, you will be prompted to confirm the replacement for each subdocument.

Figure 14.8—The Condense Master Document dialog box.

Saving a Master Document

You can save a master document in its expanded form or condensed form, just as you would save any other document. However, if you save it in its expanded form, WordPerfect will display a prompt asking you if you want to condense the document before saving. If you choose No, WordPerfect will save the document in its expanded form, and will not display this prompt on subsequent saves. If you say Yes, WordPerfect will display a dialog box allowing you to save the changes made to the subdocuments while they were in the master document.

Review Exercises for Chapter 14

◆ Type a short document with appropriate headings for a table of contents.

◆ Using the document, type a short concordance file, and alphabetize the list using the Sort feature.

◆ Mark entries as headings and subheadings.

◆ Define and generate an index.

◆ Mark text for a table of contents.

◆ Define and generate a table of contents.

◆ Cross-reference two items in the document.

◆ Generate the cross-references.

◆ Save the document.

◆ Make changes in the document, then use Document Compare to mark the changes.

◆ Print out the marked document.

◆ Remove the marking and save the document.

Before You Go On...

Before you continue on to the next chapter, you should know how to create an index, a table of contents, lists, and a table of authorities. You should know how to cross-reference text and compare documents. You should be able to build a master document from subdocuments.

Chapter 15

Working with Styles

What You Will Learn in this Chapter

- Styles versus macros
- Types of styles
- How to create a paired style
- How to create an open style
- How to turn a style on
- How to turn a style off
- How to edit a style
- How to change a style type
- How to delete a style
- How to create a style library
- How to retrieve a different style library

The WordPerfect Styles feature lets you control the formatting of all or parts of the text in your document without have to retype the formatting codes each time. As a example of how styles are used, consider this book. The original typed copy has a footer that reads "Chapter ?? — Page #" (with the appropriate chapter number typed in, of course). The third page of each chapter is numbered 2. Rather than creating a footer and changing the page numbering for each chapter, a style is being used. The style is turned on in the appropriate location and the footers in every chapter of the book are consistent. Styles can be used to set formatting defaults for an entire document if you wish. You might have a style that instructs WordPerfect to use a different font, double space, and create 1.5 inch left and right margins for every draft you type. Rather than reformatting for every draft, you simply turn on your style and type.

Styles Versus Macros

Why bother to create styles when a keystroke macro could accomplish the same thing? While it is true that a macro will insert your coding for you, if you decide to change your coding throughout the document and you have used macros you will have to go through the entire document and change every relevant code. If you have used styles, you need only change the original style in your style library, and all of the relevant styles in your document will automatically change. Obviously, for consistency and ease of formatting, styles have a lot to offer.

Types of Styles

There are two types of styles: open and paired. Open styles have only a Style On code, and cannot be turned off in the document. The style you select remains in effect until the end of the document. The only way to change the formatting defaults in a document when you are using an open style is to manually insert a new code. Paired styles have both a Style On and a Style Off code. Everything done in a document within these two codes will reflect the active style. Once you turn the style off, your document will return to whatever defaults were active before you turned your style on. When you create a paired style, you can also include codes to take effect after the style is turned off. There are two exceptions to this: left and right margins and tab settings will not take effect. When you use paired codes, such as [Und On][Und Off], you do not have to include the end code. When you turn the style off, you also turn off the code.

Some codes remain in effect throughout the document even if they are part of a paired style that has been turned off. These codes are: center page, force odd/even page, page numbering, footers, headers, suppress page format, top and bottom margins and paper/size type.

Creating a Paired Style (Alt+F8)

Before you can use a style, you must create one. To create a style that will automatically insert the coding for a centered boldface heading:

1. Click on Layout.
2. Click on Styles to open the Styles dialog box, as shown in Figure 15.1. You will see a list of styles already in the dialog box. These are sample styles included in WordPerfect's style library. The name of the style library you are currently accessing is LIBRARY.STY. Later in this chapter we will create another style library.

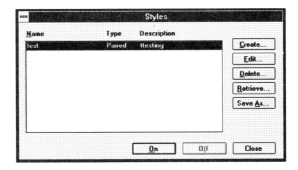

Figure 15.1—The Styles dialog box.

3. Select Create. You have accessed the Style Properties dialog box (see Figure 15.2).

Figure 15.2—The Style Properties dialog box.

4. Type "Heading 3" in the Name text box.

5. Type "Centered and Bolded" in the Description text box.

6. Leave the Type option set at Paired.

7. The Enter Key Inserts option allows you three choices to determine what the Enter key will do when you are using a paired style.

   a. When you choose Hard Return, the Enter key works exactly as it always does.

   b. When you choose Style Off, Enter turns the style off. This is useful for styles that are meant to be one line or one paragraph, such as headings.

   c. When you choose Style Off/On, pressing the Enter key turns a style off and then turns it on again. To return the Enter key to its standard use, use your arrow key to move the insertion point past the Style Off code. Style Off/On is useful if you have text in which the formatting of the first line is different in each paragraph and the style needs to be repeated to reflect that difference, such as a paragraph in which the first line is indented.

   Since we are creating a heading style that requires only one line, choose Style Off to automatically turn the style off when you press Enter.

8. Choose OK. You are in the Style Editor window. In the Style Editor window a comment code already exists. All of the codes placed above the comment code will take effect when the style is on. All of the codes below the comment code will take effect when the style is turned off.

9. Insert the center and bold codes using either the menu or the keystroke commands.

10. Choose Close.

Your new style now appears in the Styles dialog box.

Styles are saved with your document when your document is saved. You must save your style permanently in order for it to be available in any document you wish. To do this:

1. Click on Layout and then Styles to access the Styles dialog box.

2. Place your insertion point on Heading 3.

3. Choose Save As to open the Save Style dialog box.

4. Type LIBRARY.STY in the Save As text box.

5. Choose Save.

Creating an Open Style

1. Click on Layout.

2. Click on Styles to open the Styles dialog box, as shown in Figure 15.1.

3. Select Create to access the Style Properties dialog box, as shown in Figure 15.2.

4. Fill in the Name text box.

5. Fill in the Description text box.

6. Change the Type option to Open.

7. The Enter Key Inserts option is dimmed. An open style is turned on throughout the entire document, and the Enter key functions exactly as it would in a document that is not formatted with a style.

8. Choose OK to open the Style Editor window.

9. Insert the center and bold codes using either the menu or the keystroke commands.

10. Choose Close.

Turning a Style On

1. Place your insertion point where you want to style to begin.
2. Click on Layout.
3. Click on Styles.
4. In the Styles dialog box, select the style you want to use.
5. Choose On.

Turning a Paired Style Off

To turn off a paired style (other than a style with the Style Off option selected):

1. Click on Layout.
2. Click on Styles.
3. Choose Off.

Editing a Style

To change the coding or text in a style:

1. Click on Layout.
2. Click on Styles to open the Styles dialog box.
3. Select Edit. Using all of the WordPerfect standard editing features, make the changes to your style.
4. Choose Close to return to the Styles dialog box.
5. Select Save As and resave your style.
6. Choose Close.

Changing a Style Type

To change a style from open to paired or vice versa, or to change an Enter Key Inserts option in a paired style:

1. Click on Layout.
2. Click on Styles.
3. Select Edit in the Styles dialog box.
4. In the Style Editor window, select Properties to display the Style Properties dialog box.
5. Change the Type or Enter Key Inserts options.
6. Choose OK.
7. Choose Close in the Style Editor window.
8. Choose Close in the Styles dialog box.

Deleting a Style

You can delete a style from a section of text in your document by selecting the style code in Reveal Codes and pressing Delete. To delete a style that has been used several times in the document:

1. Click on Layout.
2. Click on Styles. Select the style you wish to delete.
3. Select Delete to open the Delete Style dialog box, as shown in Figure 15.3. You have three options.

   a. If you select Leave Format Codes, WordPerfect will delete the style from the Styles dialog box and will delete all of the selected style codes from your document. The style codes will be replaced by the coding contained in the style.

   b. If you select Delete Format Codes, WordPerfect will delete the style from the Styles dialog box, and all of the selected style codes from your document. When the style codes are deleted, all of the formatting codes contained in the style will also be deleted.

   c. If you select Delete Definition Only, WordPerfect will delete the style from the Styles dialog box. The style codes in your document will remain and will still be in effect. If you scroll through your document and pass any text that contains the deleted style, it will reappear in the Styles dialog box.

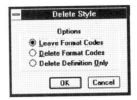

Figure 15.3—The Delete Style dialog box.

4. Select one of the options in the Delete Style dialog box.
5. Choose OK.

When you delete a style using the Delete Style dialog box, you can no longer use the deleted style, in your current document or any other document, unless you have saved the style using the Save As option in the Styles dialog box.

Creating a Style Library

You can create more than one style library. When you create a style in a document that style is active only in that document unless you save it using the Save As option in the Styles dialog box. If you wanted to save styles to use with all documents of a certain kind in their own Style library, you would:

1. Click on Layout.
2. Click on Styles to open the Styles dialog box.
3. Select Save As.
4. In the Save As text box, type in the name of the style library to which you want to save the style (for instance, for public relations styles you might type PR.STY). If the style library does not already exist, WordPerfect will create it and store the style to it.
5. Choose Save.

Retrieving a Different Style Library

If you have created more than one style library, you might want to use the styles from two or more of them in one document. If you are using the default Location of Files (located in Preferences, Files) you will always default to the LIBRARY.STY, which is included in the WordPerfect program. To change to another style library:

1. Click on Layout.
2. Click on Styles.
3. Select Retrieve to display the Retrieve Styles dialog box.
4. Select the style library you want to retrieve.
5. Choose Retrieve.
6. WordPerfect should then check your default list of styles for duplicate style names. If a match is found, WordPerfect will then display the message "Style(s) Already Exist. Replace?" If you choose No, WordPerfect should retrieve only the non-matching styles, if you choose Yes, WordPerfect should retrieve all of the styles, including those with matching names. At the time of this writing, this function is not perfected. After you have used one style library, WordPerfect will always display the message "Style(s) Already Exist. Replace?" Whether you choose No or Yes, WordPerfect will retrieve all of the styles in both the default style library and in the style library you have chosen. WordPerfect is aware of this problem.
7. Choose Retrieve. You will see a list of all of the styles in your default style library and all of the styles in the style library you have just retrieved.

Review Exercises for Chapter 15

◆ Create a paired style.
◆ Insert the style in a document.
◆ Edit the style. Note the changes in the document.
◆ Change the paired style to an open style.
◆ Save your style to a new style library.
◆ Close your document.
◆ Open a new document. Retrieve your new style library.

Before You Go On...

Before you continue on to the next chapter, you should be able to create a style to make your formatting easier. You should be able to edit the style, change the style type, and delete the style from your document. You should be able to create a new style library and retrieve it.

Chapter 16

Using Printing Enhancements

What You Will Learn in this Chapter

- ◆ How WordPerfect processes a print job
- ◆ How to monitor a print job
- ◆ How to print with different paper sizes
- ◆ How to use multi-bin printers
- ◆ How to use line numbering
- ◆ How to use Print Preview
- ◆ How to advance to different locations on a page
- ◆ How to use WordPerfect character sets
- ◆ How to use fonts and font attributes
- ◆ How to redline
- ◆ How to use the typesetting feature
- ◆ How to deal with common printing problems

WordPerfect has many features that can enhance the appearance of your document. If your printer has the capability, you can use character sets to insert such characters as $\frac{1}{2}$, +, and ♫. You can use soft fonts or font cartridges to access different typefaces, and you change the size and appearance of the text in your document. This chapter will discuss the ways you can use WordPerfect's printer enhancements to improve the appearance of your documents, how print jobs are handled by WordPerfect, and some of the things that can go wrong.

Using the Control Printer Dialog Box

The Control Printer dialog box appears in the window after you have sent a job to print. It tells you the status of your print job. How it works depends upon how WordPerfect has been configured to handle printing. When you send a document to a printer in WordPerfect for Windows, it is can be handled in one of three ways:

1. It can be sent directly from WordPerfect using a WordPerfect driver to the printer. In this situation, Print Manager in Windows is disabled (refer to your Windows manual for information on the Print Manager), and you have configured WordPerfect to use a WordPerfect driver (see Appendix A). If your program is configured to work this way, the Control Printer dialog box relays the status of your job as it is being sent to the printer.

2. It can be sent from WordPerfect, using a WordPerfect driver, to the Windows Print Manager. In this situation, Print Manager in Windows is enabled, and you have configured WordPerfect to use a WordPerfect driver. If your program is configured this way, the Control Printer dialog box relays the status of your job as it is being sent to the Windows Print Manager.

3. It can be sent from WordPerfect, using a Windows driver, to the Windows Print Manager. In this situation, Print Manager in Windows is enabled, and you *must* have configured WordPerfect to use a Windows driver. If your program is configured this way, the Control Printer dialog box relays the status of your job as it is being sent to the Windows Print Manager.

How you configure WordPerfect to print depends upon many factors, some of which are discussed in Appendix A.

The Control Printer dialog box reports the following information:

Status:	This field informs you that the print job has started processing. Depending upon how you configured WordPerfect, it is being sent either to the printer or to the Windows Print Manager.
Page Number:	This field tells you what page number is currently being processed (out of the total number of pages to be printed).
Current Copy:	This field tells you which copy is being processed. This is useful if you are printing multiple copies of a job.
Message:	This field relays messages that can help you solve certain problems. For example, if your printer is not turned on, you might get a message telling you that the printer is not accepting characters.
Action:	If there is a problem, this field might suggest an action you can take that may solve it.

If you are sending the job directly to the printer and there is a problem, a Cannot Print dialog box usually appears. Cancel the job, correct the problem, and send the job again. (See "Common Print Problems" later in this chapter for help with troubleshooting).

If you are sending the job to the Windows Print Manager and there is a problem, a Print Manager dialog box will appear stating the nature of the problem. You should switch programs to the Windows Print Manager and delete the job from the Print Manager, then correct the problem and send the job again. To cancel the job in the Print Manager:

1. Press Ctrl+Esc to access the task list (see Chapter 19 for information about switching programs).
2. Double-click on Print Manager to access the Windows Print Manager.
3. Select the job and choose Delete (refer to your Windows manual for information about the Windows Print Manager).

4. The job is deleted from the Print Manager.

5. To return to WordPerfect for Windows, bring up the task list again and double-click on WordPerfect.

You can also cancel a print job from the Current Print Job dialog box by choosing Cancel. This will cancel whatever portion of the job has not yet been sent to the printer or the Windows Print Manager. However, once the Current Print dialog box disappears from the window, the job has already been sent to the printer or the Windows Print Manager, and can no longer be cancelled from WordPerfect. If the job has been sent to the Windows Print Manager, you might still be able to cancel the print job through that facility.

1. Press Ctrl+Esc to access the task list (see Chapter 19 for information about switching programs).

2. If the Print Manager is still on the list, it means that at least part of the job is still being held in that facility. Double-click on Print Manager to access the Windows Print Manager.

3. Select the job and choose Delete (refer to your Windows manual for information about the Windows Print Manager).

4. The job is deleted from the Print Manager. However, some of the job may already be in the printer's memory buffer and will continue to print. Either let it finish printing, or turn the printer off and then back on. This will delete anything that is being held in the printer's memory buffer.

5. To return to WordPerfect for Windows, bring up the task list again and double-click on WordPerfect.

If the job has been sent directly to the printer, any part of the job that was not cancelled in the Current Print Job dialog box is already being held in the printer's memory buffer. You must turn off the printer to stop the job from printing out.

Selecting a Paper Size Definition

WordPerfect defaults to a paper size of 8.5" x 11", with portrait **orientation** (this is the U.S. default; it varies for non-U.S. versions of the program). However, you are not limited to only one paper size. WordPerfect comes with the most common paper size definitions already set up and available for use. You can select any of these by using the Paper Size command.

Orientation refers to whether the text is printed straight up and down on a page with the text parallel to the short edge of the paper (portrait), or sideways on a page with the text parallel to the long edge of the paper (landscape). These are shown in Figure 16.1.

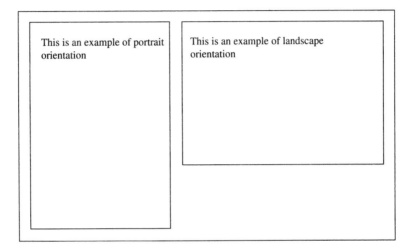

This is an example of portrait orientation

This is an example of landscape orientation

Figure 16.1—Portrait and landscape orientation.

You cannot have two orientations on a page. If you are printing a page that requires text in both orientations (for example, a red herring on a legal document), you must print the page twice. Set up the text on two separate pages in your document, with portrait orientation on one page and landscape orientation on another. Then print one of the pages. Insert the printed page back into the printer, and print the other page.

Paper size codes should be placed at the top of a page. If Auto Code Placement is turned on, paper size codes are automatically moved to the top of the page, no matter where the insertion point is when you turn on the code. You can select as many paper size definitions as you want in a document, but you may select only one per page. Changing your paper size will affect only the current document. To change the default paper size definition, you have to reconfigure initial codes (see Appendix A).

You cannot insert a paper size definition into a column or table.

To select a paper size definition:

1. Click on Layout in the menu bar to open the Layout menu.
2. Click on Page to display the Page cascading menu.
3. Click on Paper Size to display the Paper Size dialog box, as shown in Figure 16.2.
4. Highlight a paper size definition from the list.
5. Choose Select.

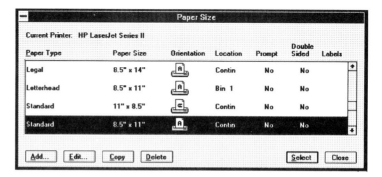

Figure 16.2—Paper Size dialog box.

 If you are using a Windows print driver (see above), you can only select one paper size for your entire document. In addition, orientation and other paper size features are limited. Consult your Windows manual.

Adding a Paper Size Definition

Though WordPerfect comes with a number of paper sizes already defined, you may want to add another to the list. To do this, you will have to define a new paper size. To add a paper size definition:

1. Click on Layout in the menu bar to open the Layout menu.
2. Click on Page to open the Page cascading menu.
3. Click on Paper Size to display the Paper Size dialog box (see Figure 16.2).
4. Choose Add. The Add Paper Size dialog box appears.

   Fill in the information requested in the dialog box.
5. Select a paper type from the Paper Type drop-down list. If you want to make up your own, select Other and type the name in the Other text box.

6. Select a paper size from the Paper Size drop-down list. If the size you want is not in the list, choose Other and type the size in the text boxes.

7. Select an orientation in the Paper Orientation box. Printers handle landscape orientation differently. Most laser printers **rotate** fonts to get them to print sideways on the paper. If your printer can rotate fonts, and you want landscape orientation, choose Rotated Font. If you are using a printer that cannot rotate fonts (such as most dot matrix printers), and you want landscape orientation, select Wide Form. If you are not sure, check your printer manual.

8. The Print Location box allows you to determine whether the paper will be loaded continuously (for example, from a paper tray), or manually (by hand). If your printer has multiple bins, you should select a bin for the paper size you chose. Unless you change it, paper printed with this paper size definition will always come from the designated bin. If you select Prompt to Load Paper, the computer will beep you during printing and display the Current Print Job dialog box. Insert the required paper and choose Go to continue printing.

9. The Text Adjustments box allows you to adjust where the text starts printing on the page. For example, if your top margin is set for 1 inch and text is printing 1.5 inches from the top edge of the page, you can set the Top to adjust up .5 inch to compensate for the problem.

10. If your printer is capable of double-sided printing, choose that option in the Print Options box. When printing double-sided, the printer rotates the paper around the specified binding edge. For example, if you specify a top binding edge, the printer will print to the bottom of the page, turn the paper over bottom to top (like a standard writing pad), and print top to bottom again.

11. You can set up Label paper size definitions in WordPerfect to print with almost any size label. If you choose Label, an Edit Labels dialog box appears. Fill in the information to correspond to your label size. Once you have the Label

paper size definition set up, you can use it as a form to merge with a secondary file (see Chapter 12 for information on how to merge a form with a secondary file). Select the appropriate Label paper size definition, and set up the document as a form with the required merge codes. Then merge the form with the secondary file.

 The types of paper and paper sizes you can use may be limited by your printer. Refer to your printer manual.

Editing a Paper Size Definition

You might decide you want to make a change in an existing paper size definition. To edit a definition:

1. Open the Paper Size dialog box.
2. Highlight the paper size definition you want to edit.
3. Select Edit to open the Edit Paper Size dialog box, as shown in Figure 16.3.
4. Fill in the information using the guidelines set forth above in the section entitled "Adding a Paper Size Definition."
5. Choose OK.

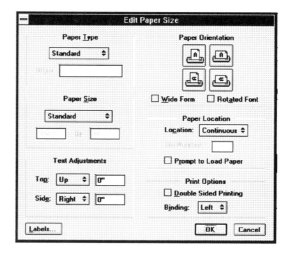

Figure 16.3—Edit Paper Size dialog box.

Deleting a Paper Size Definition

To delete a paper size definition:

1. Open the Paper Size dialog box.
2. Highlight the paper size definition you want to delete.
3. Select Delete. You will be asked to confirm the deletion. Choose Yes. The paper size definition is now deleted.

Copying a Paper Size Definition

To copy a paper size definition:

1. Open the Paper Size dialog box.
2. Highlight the paper size definition you want to copy.
3. Select Copy. An exact copy of the paper size definition is inserted into the Paper Size dialog box.
4. Edit the new paper size definition. You *must* change either the Paper Type name or the Paper Size. Any other changes are optional.

Working with Multi-Bin Printers

If your printer has more than one bin, you can specify which bin you want by identifying a specific bin in your paper size selection. For instance, assume that your printer has two bins and you want to be able to print all first pages of letters from one bin, and all succeeding pages from the other bin. Let's add a paper size definition for the first page:

1. Click on Layout in the menu bar to open the Layout menu.
2. Click on Page to open the Page cascading menu.
3. Click on Paper Size to display the Paper Size dialog box.
4. Choose Add.
5. From the Paper Type drop-down list, select Letterhead.
6. From the Paper Location drop-down list, select Bin.
7. Enter the Bin number in the Bin text box (enter a bin number that has not been selected for use by standard 8.5" x 11" paper).

8. Fill in the rest of the information requested by the dialog box.

9. Choose OK.

10. You have returned to the Paper Size dialog box. You now have a Letterhead definition listed.

11. Choose Close.

When you type the first page of the letter, select letterhead as your paper size:

1. Open the Paper Size dialog box.
2. Highlight Letterhead.
3. Choose Select.

If your letter extends to more than one page, put your insertion point anywhere on page 2. Then:

1. Open the Paper Size dialog box.
2. Highlight Standard (8.5" x 11").
3. Choose Select.

As long as this paper size instruction remains somewhere on page two, the printer will automatically switch to the bin assigned to this particular paper size.

Using Line Numbering (Shift+F9)

You may at one time or another want to number each line of text in a document, either starting at page one and continuing throughout the document, restarting the numbering at each new page, or numbering only a selected group of lines in your text. This is done through the Line Numbering command. To use Line Numbering:

1. Place your insertion point where you want line numbering to begin. If Auto Code Placement is turned on, WordPerfect automatically places the Line Numbering code at the beginning of the paragraph.

2. Click on Layout in the menu bar to open the Layout menu.

3. Click on Line to open the Line cascading menu.

4. Click on Numbering to display the Line Numbering dialog box, as shown in Figure 16.4.

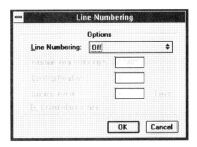

Figure 16.4—Line Numbering dialog box.

5. In the Line Numbering drop-down list, select either Restart Each Page or Continuous.

   a. If you selected Restart Each Page, your numbering will begin all over again at the top of each page.

   b. If you selected Continuous, line numbering will start at the insertion point and continue throughout the document until it is turned off.

6. In the Position from Left Edge text box, indicate the position from the left edge of the paper at which you want line numbering to print.

7. In the Starting Number text box, type in the number with which you wish to begin numbering.

8. In the Number Every [ ] Lines text box, tell WordPerfect which lines you want numbered. You can chose to have every line numbered, every other line numbered, every fourth line numbered, or any other variation. This numbering applies only to lines that contain text.

9. If you want line numbering to include blank lines as well, enable the Count Blank Lines option.

10. Choose OK.

Line numbering will continue until you turn it off. To turn off line numbering:

1. Place your insertion point where you want line numbering to stop.

2. Click on Layout in the menu bar to open the Layout menu.

3. Click on Line to open the Line cascading menu.

4. Click on Numbering to display the Line Numbering dialog box.

5. In the Line Numbering drop-down list, select Off.

6. Choose OK.

Line numbering will not appear on your window. To actually see the numbers, you must either print the document or use Print Preview.

Using Print Preview (Shift+F5)

The document window in WordPerfect will allow you to see font and size changes, but it will not show headers, footers, footnotes, or line numbering. If you want to see exactly how a page is going to look before it is printed, you must use Print Preview. To access Print Preview:

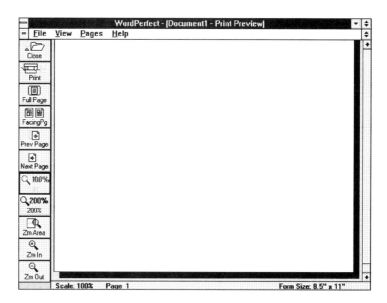

Figure 16.5—Print Preview window.

1. Click on File in the menu bar to open the File menu.

2. Click on Print Preview to open the Print Preview window, as shown in Figure 16.5. To move around in the Print Preview window, use your arrow keys or the scroll bar to move to different sections of a page. PgUp and PgDn will move up or down the page a screen at a time.

3. Click on File in the Print Preview menu bar to open the File menu.

   a. Click on Print if you want to print the job. The Print dialog box is displayed.

   b. Click on Exit to leave the Print Preview window and return to your document.

4. Click on View in the Print Preview menu bar to open the View menu.

   a. Click on 100% to see the current page of the document you are viewing at approximately the size at which the text and graphics will be printed.

   b. Click on 200% to see the page you are viewing at twice the size at which the text and graphics at will be printed.

   c. Click on Zoom Area to enlarge a section of text. Position your insertion point at the upper-left edge of the text area you wish to view. Drag the mouse to form a box around the area. Release the mouse button. The area you have enclosed in the box will be enlarged and will fill the entire Print Preview window.

   d. Click on Zoom to Full Width to view the entire width of the page.

   e. Click on Zoom In to enlarge the size of the displayed text and graphics on the Print Preview window by 25%. You can continue to click on Zoom In until you have reached 400% magnification.

   f. Click on Zoom Out to shrink the size of the displayed text and graphics on the Print Preview window by 25%. You can continue to click on Zoom Out to return to normal page size.

   g. Click on View Reset to return the Print Preview window

to the conditions you established the last time you closed out of Print Preview.

h. Click on Button Bar to display the Print Preview button bar. Click on Button Bar again to toggle the display off.

i. Click on Button Bar Setup to add or delete buttons in the Print Preview button bar. See Chapter 18 for information concerning button bars.

5. Click on Pages in the Print Preview menu bar to open the Page menu.

a. Click on Full Page to show the entire page on the Print Preview window.

b. Click on Facing Pages to see two consecutive pages of your document in the Print Preview window. You must have consecutively numbered odd and even pages to view facing pages (for example, pages 1 and 2).

c. Click on Go To Page to specify a page in your document to view. Type the number of the page you want to see in the Go To dialog box, and click on OK or press Enter.

d. Click on Previous Page to view the preceding page.

e. Click on Next Page to go to the next page in your document.

You can also execute the above commands by using the button bar at the left side of the window. Chapter 18 explains how button bars work.

Using Advance

Advance allows you to place your text at a specified position on a page. If, for instance, you are using a sheet of letterhead, you might want your text on the first page to start 2 inches down from the top of the page. If the letter is longer than one page, you want all subsequent pages to start at the normal 1 inch default. The Advance command allows you to do this without having to change and rechange your top margin. This feature is also great for filling in preprinted forms. To use Advance:

1. Click on Layout to open the Layout menu.
2. Click on Advance to display the Advance dialog box, as shown in Figure 16.6. There are six possible choices in Advance Text.

Figure 16.6—Advance dialog box.

3. Select an Advance option, and type the distance you want to advance in the Advance text box.

a. Selecting Up advances your text a specified distance up from the insertion point.

b. Selecting Down advances your text a specified distance down from the insertion point.

c. Selecting Left advances your text a specified distance left from the insertion point.

d. Selecting Right advances your text a specified distance right from the insertion point.

e. Selecting To Line advances your text a specified distance down from the top edge of the paper.

f. Selecting To Position advances your text a specified distance from the left edge of the paper.

If you advance up, down, left, or right, the distance the text is advanced is always relative to the insertion point. For example, if your insertion point is 2" from the top of the page and you insert a code to advance Down 2", the next text you type will advance to a location 4" from the top of the page (2" down from the insertion point). If you select To Line or To Position, the text is advanced to an absolute location on the page. It does not matter where the insertion point is when you enter the code; the distance will be measured from the top edge or left edge of the page. For example, if your insertion point is at the bottom of the page and you insert a code to advance To Line 1 inch, the next text you type will advance to a position 1 inch from the top edge of the page. When you select To Line or To Position, a number automatically appears in the Advance text box. This number indicates the current location of your insertion point on the page.

Here are some examples of how the Advance command might be used:

1. You are typing a letter and want to paste a newspaper clipping in between two paragraphs. You no longer have to insert multiple returns to create what you hope is the right amount of blank space to leave between the paragraphs. Instead, you can measure the length of the clipping, and use the Advance Down option to advance the amount of space needed to accommodate it.

2. You want to fill in the answers on a preprinted form. You want to insert the form into a laser printer, and have the answers print in the correct locations on the form, you can measure where the answers have to be printed on the form and then use the Advance To Line and Advance To Position commands to insert them exactly where they belong. For example, suppose one of the answers is a date. With a ruler, measure the distance from the top edge of the page to where the date should be filled in. Then measure the distance from the left edge of the page. Using the Advance To Line and the Advance To Position commands, move to that location on the page. Type in the date. When the form is printed, the date will print at that location. Use this procedure to position all of the answers in the form.

   It is a good idea to print the answers on a blank sheet of paper first. Hold the paper up against the form to be sure all of the answers are in the correct location. When you are satisfied that they are, insert the form in the printer and print the answers directly to the form.

You can use the Advance command only to move to a location on the current page. If you try to advance past a page break, a message is displayed and you are returned to the Advance dialog box.

Using WP Characters (Ctrl+W)

No longer do you have to flip through pages of Appendices looking for character sets to accommodate special figures needed in your documents. Now, the ½ sign, the ¢ sign, and even a ☎, are all available to you at the click of a mouse. WordPerfect for Windows comes with thirteen predefined character sets. Each set contains its own group of symbols or characters. To access the character sets:

1. Position your insertion point at the location where you want to insert a character.
2. Click on Font to open the Font menu.
3. Click on WP Characters to display the WordPerfect Characters dialog box as shown in Figure 16.7.

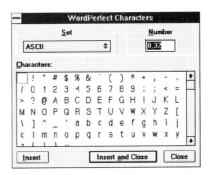

Figure 16.7—WordPerfect Characters dialog box.

4. Click on the Set drop-down list. Select the Character Set you want to use.
5. Click on the character you wish to select in the Characters dialog box.
6. Choose Insert to insert the character into your document.
7. Continue to select characters until you are finished. After you select the last character, choose Insert and Close.

The Numbers text box displays the Character Set number WordPerfect has assigned to the character. If you already know the number, you can type it in, and select Insert or Insert and Close.

The WP Character will print in the current font size. If your printer is not capable of recognizing the character you have selected as text, WordPerfect will convert it to a graphic character and it will print as a graphic.

Using Fonts to Enhance Your Text

The ability to recognize virtually every font available is one of the most powerful features of WordPerfect. Fonts allow you to enhance your text by changing the size and appearance of your type. For example, you might select a very large font, or an italic typeface. Using a variety of typefaces in your documents will add aesthetic appeal and sophistication to your work.

Your printer comes with its own internal set of fonts. Most laser printers also allow you to add additional fonts using either **soft fonts** or **print cartridges**. In order for you to be able to use soft fonts and cartridges, they must be properly installed, and your WordPerfect printer driver must be configured to recognize them (see Appendix A). Your default font is the one you selected when you installed and configured WordPerfect. When you select a font, it will remain in effect until you choose another one to replace it.

If you are using downloadable soft fonts, when you configured your WordPerfect printer driver, you decided how they would be downloaded to the printer. If you decided to download them with the print job, they will automatically download when the job is printed. If you decided that you wanted some fonts to be present when the job began, then you must **initialize** the printer before you print your documents. Initializing downloads selected fonts to the printer. These fonts are held in the printer's memory buffer until you turn the printer off. To initialize the printer:

1. Open the Print dialog box.
2. Choose Initialize Printer. (This box will be dimmed if you have not configured your printer driver to have fonts present when the job begins.)
3. The fonts will download to the printer.

The advantage of initializing your printer is that you can download the fonts you use most often. Once they are in the printer's memory buffer, they remain there until you turn the printer off. This way you do not have to wait for the fonts to download each time you send a job to print.

If you turn the printer off, you must initialize again when you turn it back on.

Selecting Fonts

To select a font:

1. Click on Font in the menu bar to open the Font menu.
2. Click on Font (F9) to display the Font dialog box, as shown in Figure 16.8.

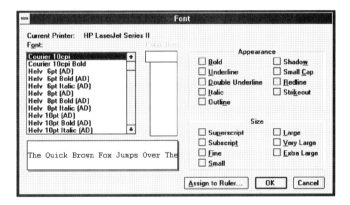

Figure 16.8—Font dialog box.

3. The Font list box contains a list of all of the fonts available to you. Select the font you wish to use. If you are using scalable fonts (fonts for which you can specify any point size), you will be prompted to fill in a point size.
4. Select OK. The font has now been selected.

You can also assign fonts to the ruler and then select those fonts from the ruler. To find out how this works, see below, "Selecting Fonts from the Ruler."

Using Font Attributes

You can also use font attributes to change the appearance or size of a font you have selected. For example, suppose you are printing in a particular font and you want the next few pages to be printed in italics. You can tell WordPerfect to start printing in italics by changing the appearance attribute in the Font dialog box. To change an attribute:

1. Open the Font dialog box.
2. Select an appearance or size attribute.
3. Choose OK.

You can also choose attributes from the Font menu. To apply an attribute to text you are about to type:

1. Open the Font menu.
2. Select an appearance attribute from the menu.
3. If you want to select a size attribute, click on Size (Ctrl+S) to open the Size cascading menu. Select a size.

To turn the attribute off, choose it again in the Font menu or in the Font dialog box.

When you turn an attribute on, the code that turns the attribute on and the code that turns the attribute off are both inserted into the document and are visible in Reveal Codes. As you type, the text is inserted between the two codes.

 Shortcut: When you are finished typing, you can use the right arrow key (→) to move the insertion point past the code that turns the attribute off. This is a quick way to turn the attribute off.

To turn off all attributes, choose Normal (Ctrl+N) from the Font menu.

To apply an attribute to existing text, select the text and then follow the steps listed above to apply attributes from the Font menu or the Font dialog box.

Your ability to use appearance attributes depends upon the fonts your printer has available to it. For example, if you select the Italic appearance attribute, and your printer does not have the ability to print italics, the attribute will not work. Likewise, if your printer has only one font size, you cannot change the size attribute. You can find out how your printer handles appearance attributes by retrieving and printing the PRINTER.TST file. This file is found in the same directory containing the WPWIN.EXE file.

The way font attributes appear on your screen depends on the monitor and video card you are using. The more sophisticated your hardware, the more accurate your attributes will appear.

Multiple Attributes

Use the Font dialog box to apply multiple attributes to text. The following restrictions apply:

1. You cannot apply both subscript and superscript at the same time.
2. You can only apply one size attribute at a time.

Using Redline and Strikeout

Redline and strikeout are appearance attributes that are used to mark text in order to compare documents. For example, a lawyer might send an agreement to a client. The client would then discuss certain changes with the lawyer, which the lawyer would incorporate into the agreement. By using redline and strikeout to mark the revised agreement, the client could tell at a glance where the changes in the document are located. Text that is redlined has been added to the document, and text marked with Strikeout has been deleted.

To Redline as you type:

1. Using either the Font menu or the Font dialog box, turn Redline on.
2. Type the text you are adding to the document.
3. After you have typed the text, use the right arrow key (→) to turn redline off.

To redline text that has already been typed:

1. Select the text to be redlined.
2. Choose Redline from the Font menu or the Font dialog box. The selected text has been redlined.

To indicate text that is to be deleted using strikeout:

1. Select the text that is to be deleted.
2. Using the Font menu or the Font dialog box, select Strikeout.

You can also use the Document Compare command in the Tools menu to mark text with redline and strikeout. Refer to Chapter 14 for information about this feature.

After you have printed out a marked copy of the document, you will want to remove redlining and strikeout and print the document out again without the marks. To remove redline and strikeout:

1. Click on Tools in the menu bar to open the Tools menu.
2. Click on Document Compare.
3. Click on Remove Markings to display the Remove Markings dialog box.
4. Be sure that the Leave Redline Marks option is *not* selected.
5. Choose OK.

Selecting Fonts from the Ruler

You can assign fonts to the ruler and then select those fonts using the ruler. To assign fonts to the ruler:

1. Double-click on the Font button on the ruler to open the Font dialog box.
2. Choose Assign to Ruler to display the Ruler Fonts Menu dialog box. Available fonts are listed in the Font list.
3. Select a font, then choose Add.
4. Repeat step number 3 until you have finished selecting fonts.
5. Choose OK. The fonts are now assigned to the ruler.

The number of fonts that can be displayed using the Ruler Font button depends on the window size. It is a good idea to limit the number of fonts you assign to the ruler to ensure that they will be able to be displayed in any size window.

To select a font from the ruler, click on the Font button. Select a font from the drop-down list.

Using the Typesetting Command

Typesetting can alter the way text appears in your document. You can change the amount of spacing between words, letters, or even lines of text. To use Typesetting:

1. Place your insertion point where you wish the changes to take effect.
2. Click on Layout in the menu bar to open the Layout menu.
3. Click on Typesetting to display the Typesetting dialog box, as shown in Figure 16.9.

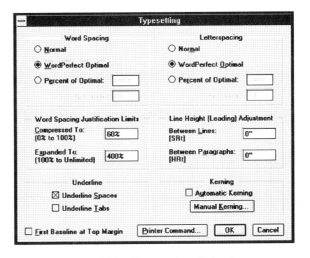

Figure 16.9—Typesetting dialog box.

4. To adjust Word Spacing, click on Percent of Optimal.
   a. If you want to increase the spacing between words, increase the Percent of Optimal to more than 100% (the default).
   b. If you want to decrease the spacing between words decrease the Percent of Optimal.
   c. If you are using a fixed font (a font in which each character takes up the same amount of space, like Courier), you can change the pitch in the Set Pitch text box.

5. To adjust Word Spacing in Justified Text, click on Word Spacing Justification Limits.

   a. If the words in your justified text are too close together, increase the minimum justification (the default is 60%).

   b. If the words are spaced too far apart, decrease the maximum justification (the default is 400%).

6. The Underline option in the Typesetting dialog box allows you to decide whether or not you wish to underline spaces and tabs in underlined text when you print your document. (See the section in Chapter 4 titled "Underlining Spaces and Tabs.")

7. Click on Letterspacing to adjust the spacing between letters in your document. To increase spacing between letters, increase the Percent of Optimal. To decrease spacing between letters, decrease the Percent of Optimal. If you are using a fixed font, use the Set Pitch text box to change the pitch.

8. Click on Line Height Adjustment to change the amount of vertical space assigned to soft returns and hard returns. The default is set to 0 inches. To increase the spacing after a soft return, increase the number in the Between Lines text box. To increase the spacing after a hard return, increase the number in the Between Paragraphs text box. This is a useful way to increase the spacing between paragraphs without increasing the spacing between lines.

9. Kerning adjusts the spacing between pairs of letters in your document to make them appear more evenly spaced. The pairs of letters that can be kerned automatically are predetermined by your printer. If you choose automatic kerning you can automatically adjust the spacing of pairs of letters throughout your entire document. If you choose manual kerning, you can adjust the spacing between pairs of letters in your document on a case-by-case basis. Manual kerning will also allow you the option of either increasing or decreasing the spacing between letter pairs.

10. When First Baseline at Top of Margin is not selected, WordPerfect makes the top of the first line of text even with

the top margin, and the bottom of the first line of text even with the baseline (the line the characters sit on). If you want to position text in precise locations on a page (for example, when using the Advance feature to fill in forms), the first baseline must remain constant. Normally this varies depending upon the font size you are using. If you turn this option on, the first baseline will always be in the same location (at the top margin), regardless of the font. First Baseline at Top of Margin must be inserted at the beginning of your document. You must also set a fixed line height (see "Line Height," below).

11. If you know how to use Escape Sequences, you can choose Printer Command to enter a printer instruction for them.

12. When you have finished making your typesetting changes, choose OK.

Changing Line Height

Changing the line height in WordPerfect is different from changing the line height adjustment (see above). Changing the line height adjustment allows you to adjust the vertical space after soft returns and hard returns, by adding or deleting from the default line height.

The **line height** is the distance from the baseline in one line to the baseline in the next line. Changing the line height allows you to override the default line height, which varies according to font size. This is called setting a **fixed line height**. The new line height remains constant, even if you change your font size (normally, the line height would adjust with different font sizes). You can use this feature if you have to fit a certain number of lines within a specified space.

To change the line height:

1. Place the insertion point at the beginning of the paragraph where you want the change to begin. If Auto Code Placement is turned on, the code will automatically move to the beginning of the paragraph.

2. Click on Layout in the menu bar to open the Layout menu.

3. Click on Line.
4. Click on Height to open the Line Height dialog box.
5. Select Fixed. The default line height for the current font is displayed in the Fixed text box.
6. Type a new line height in the text box.
7. Choose OK.

You can return to the default line height by selecting Auto. You can select a block of text and change its line height:

1. Select the text you want to change.
2. Follow steps 2 through 7 above.

Common Printing Problems

Listed below are some of the most common printing problems encountered and possible solutions. Your printer manual is also an excellent reference for troubleshooting.

Problem: You sent the job to the printer but it did not print.
Solution: Check the following items:
    1. Is the printer plugged in and turned on?
    2. Is the printer On Line?
    3. Are you using the correct cable, and is it securely plugged in at both ends?
    4. Is the correct printer selected? Is it set for the correct port?
    5. Is there paper in the printer?
    6. Check for a manual feed message in the Current Print Job dialog box.

Problem: Your paper keeps jamming in the printer.
Solution: Check the following:
    1. If you are using a printer with a tractor feed, do the tractor wheels line up? The pin feeds should be exactly even, or the paper will not line up properly. Is the paper securely locked in? Is it properly loaded? Check your printer manual.

2. If you are using a laser printer, check to make sure there is no paper trapped inside the printer. Take the paper out of the tray, fan the paper, and put it back. Reinsert the tray.

3. Check your printer manual to be sure you are using a paper size and weight that is acceptable to your printer.

4. If the problem persists, place a service call.

Problem: You receive a Not Enough Memory message code on your printer.

Solution: You are trying to send fonts or graphics that are too large to fit in your printer's memory buffer. Increase the memory in your printer, or send smaller fonts and graphics.

Problem: The print is uneven, too light, or there are vertical fade-outs on the page.

Solution: Make sure that your printer ribbon or cartridge is properly installed and does not need to be replaced. If the problem persists, place a service call.

Problem: You receive a Document Not Formatted for Current Printer message.

Solution: The document you are trying to print has been formatted for another printer. Open the document, select the correct printer, and save the job. Now it should be able to print.

Problem: You receive an Invalid Printer Definition String message.

Solution: If you have added commands to the .PRS file using the Printer Program, check to make sure they are correct. If you have not modified the .PRS file, and you get this message, the .PRS file is probably corrupt. Rename it and reselect the printer.

Review Exercise for Chapter 16

- ◆ Open a document. Change the paper size to 8.5" x 14".
- ◆ Turn on line numbering. Number the lines on the top half of the page.
- ◆ Turn off line numbering.
- ◆ Halfway through the page, advance down 1".
- ◆ Select a new font. Choose Large in the Font Size box.
- ◆ Type in a sentence or two. Insert a WP character.
- ◆ Return to the original font for the rest of the document.
- ◆ Change the letter spacing for a paragraph of text.
- ◆ Return to the beginning of the document. Increase the line height adjustment between paragraphs.
- ◆ Use Print Preview to view your document before you print it.

Before You Go On...

Before you continue on to the next chapter, you should understand how WordPerfect processes your print jobs and how to monitor them. You should be able to use the typesetting feature, as well as fonts and font attributes, to enhance the appearance of your documents. You should be able to insert WP Characters into a document, and know how to work with paper size definitions. You should be familiar with the Print Preview window.

Chapter 17

Creative Document Processing with Graphics

What You Will Learn in this Chapter

- ◆ How to create graphics boxes
- ◆ How to set the appearance options for boxes
- ◆ How to set the location and size of boxes
- ◆ How to use the mouse to move and size graphics
- ◆ What graphic images you can use with WordPerfect
- ◆ How to work with graphics lines
- ◆ How to use Line Draw

You can use graphics to add visual enhancement to your WordPerfect documents. It is not only desktop publishers who use graphics. Even the most conservative document can be made more attractive and professional by the use of lines and boxes.

You should plan graphics carefully before you insert them into your document. Consider where you want to place the graphic and how it should integrate with your text. How large should it be? Do you want your text to wrap around the graphic? Once you have made some basic decisions, you can begin to layout the page. You will want to use the Print Preview feature frequently to view the page. Most graphic artists rework their pages several times to get just the right effect.

The more you work with graphics, the more imaginative and expert you become. WordPerfect's graphics features are sophisticated and fun to work with. You will be amazed at the results you can get.

The graphics features in WordPerfect can accommodate sophisticated desktop publishing layouts. It is beyond the scope of this book to do more than just present the basics. For detailed applications of graphics, consult an advanced users manual.

Graphics boxes can be positioned anywhere in a document. WordPerfect allows you to create five types of graphics boxes: Figure, Text, Equation, Table, and User. Most of these boxes have identical capabilities, but slightly different default settings. Listed below are the defaults that can be set with graphics boxes. (Table boxes are covered in Chapter 11.)

Appearance Options

You can change the appearance of graphics boxes by editing the border style, the amount of shading in the box, the position, size, caption style, and text offset. When you set the options for a particular type of graphics box, the options remain effective throughout the document for all other graphics boxes of that type. For example, if you edit the options for a figure box, all succeeding figure boxes will have the same options, unless you change them again. Other types of graphics boxes (such as text boxes) will not be affected.

Borders, captions, shading, and text offset are edited in the Options dialog box. Each figure type has its own dialog box, although the options are the same.

To set an Appearance option:

1. Position the insertion point before the first graphics box of the type that you want to change (or set the options before you create the graphics box).
2. Click on Graphics in the menu bar to open the Graphics menu.
3. Click on the appropriate graphics box type.
4. Click on Options to display the Options dialog box, as shown in Figure 17.1.

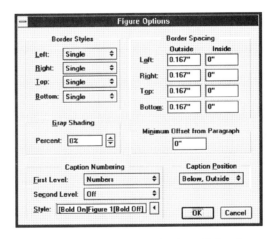

Figure 17.1—The Figure Options dialog box.

Border Style

Graphics boxes can have a number of border styles. Use the Border Styles options to select one of the following styles: None, Single, Double, Dashed, Dotted, Thick, or Extra Thick. You should specify a border style for the Left, Right, Top, and Bottom border of the box. You can also mix styles. For example, a text box might have a thick top and right border, and a single left and bottom border. You might decide to use None for the borders around graphic images.

Border Spacing

This option allows you to determine the amount of space between the border and information inside and outside the border. For example, you might want any text wrapping around a graphics box to be set off 1".

Gray Shading

This option lets you determine the amount of shading in a graphics box or line. You can choose from 0% to 100%, where 0% represents no shading and 100% represents black.

Minimum Offset from Paragraph

This feature is used with Paragraph anchors (see the "Position and Size" section below). When you set a paragraph anchor you usually set the minimum offset allowed between the box and the paragraph. If the paragraph and graphics box cannot fit on the same page, WordPerfect will reduce the offset. It the offset cannot be reduced enough to fit the box on the same page as the paragraph, WordPerfect will move it to the next page. Minimum Offset from Paragraph allows you to set the minimum offset allowed before the graphic is moved to the next page.

Caption Numbering

You can create captions to appear with your graphics boxes. WordPerfect assigns a number to each graphics box you create. Boxes are numbered consecutively by type throughout the document (for example, [Fig: Box1], [Fig: Box2], [Text Box:1], [Text Box:2], and so on). These numbers are assigned to captions. Caption Numbering allows you to change the numbering type and style of the captions for each type of graphics box. The numbering can be numbers, letters, or Roman numerals. The style can be any word you type (such as "Figure", "Table", etc.), in bold, italics, underline, or small caps. You can use a second numbering level to set a character after the first number (such as a decimal or a dash) followed by a second number. An example would be Figure 1-2. The number 2 would be set in the second level.

First Level

Set your numbering type to Numbers, Letters, or Roman Numerals from the First Level pop-up list. If you choose Off, caption numbers will not display or print. If you choose Letters or Roman Numerals in the first level, the number style will always be uppercase.

Second Level

Set your second level numbering type here. You can choose Numbers, Letters, or Roman Numerals from the Second Level pop-up list. If you do not want a second number level, choose Off. Type a character, such as a decimal or a dash, in the Style text box to separate the two numbering levels (for example: "Figure 1-2"). The second level numbering style is always lowercase. Second level numbering will only go as high as thirty-one. After that, the first level moves up one number and the second level starts over. For example, 1.31 is followed by 2.1.

Style

Use Style to change the caption number style for all boxes of a particular type. For example, typing "Figure 1-2" causes numbering codes in captions to display the word "Figure" followed by the first level number, then a dash, followed by the second level numbering. You can use the Style pop-up list to change the text to bold, italics, underline, or small caps. Delete the old attribute, position the insertion point before the text, and choose the new attribute.

Caption Position

Caption Position allows you to determine where the caption will print in relationship to the box. You can place it below or above the box, and inside or outside the border. In Equation boxes, you can place the caption inside the box, below, above, on the left, or on the right of the equation.

Appearance options set options only for the captions. You must still create the caption in the Caption Editor (see below). Captions will not display or print unless the Caption Editor has been opened and closed.

Position and Size Options

You can use the Box Position and Size dialog box to position and size a graphics box. To set the Box Position and Size dialog box options:

1. Click on Graphics in the menu bar to open the Graphics menu.
2. Click on the appropriate graphics box type.
3. Click on Position. A dialog box appears asking for the number of the box. Type in the appropriate number.
4. The Box Position and Size dialog box is displayed, as shown in Figure 17.2.

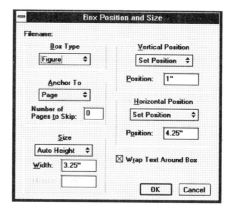

Figure 17.2—The Box Position and Size dialog box.

You can set the following options:

Box Type

Box Type lets you specify a different box type for purposes of appearance options and lists. It does not change the position, size, contents, or editor of the box. For example, if you are working on a text box and you change the box type to figure, the box will take on the appearance options of a figure box and will appear in lists (see Chapter 14) as a figure box.

Anchor To

You can anchor a graphics box to a paragraph, a page, or a character. If you anchor it to a paragraph, it moves with the paragraph; if you anchor it to a page, it remains fixed at a particular location on a page; and if you anchor it to a character, it is treated like any other character as part of text on a line. For example, if your paragraph instructs the reader to "See the figure to the right of this paragraph," you would anchor the graphics box to the paragraph. If the paragraph is moved, the box moves with it. If you have a graphics box that always belongs in a particular location on a page, irrespective of text, you would anchor it to the page. If you have a graphics box that you want to appear on a line as part of the text (for example, a check box ✔), you would anchor it to a character.

Number of Pages to Skip

This is used for graphics boxes that are anchored to a page. If the insertion point is on a different page than the one on which you want the box to appear, type in the number of pages to skip. For example, if your insertion point is on page 2 and you want the box to appear on page 4, type 2 in the Number of Pages to Skip text box.

Wrap Text Around Box

If you select this option, WordPerfect will wrap text around the graphics box. If you do not select this option, text will print from margin to margin, even if it means printing in the graphics box. If you do not select this option, you can use the Advance feature (see Chapter 16) to overlay text in a box.

Horizontal Position

The best way to set the horizontal position of a graphics box is to use the mouse (see below). If you want precise settings, you can use the Horizontal Position option in the Box Position and Size dialog box. The choices for setting this option depend upon the anchor type.

Page

If you have selected a page anchor type, you can set the horizontal position between margins, or you can select a position on the line between the left and right margin. Margin, Left and Margin, Right will position the box on the left or right margin. Margin, Center will position the box on the line between the left and right margins. If you select Margin, Full, the box fills the area between the left and right margins. Set Position will position the box a specified distance from the left edge of the page. Column, Left or Column, Right will align the box with the left or right edge of a column. Column, Full will align the box between specified column margins. Column, Center aligns the box between columns.

Paragraph

If you have selected a paragraph anchor type, you can set the horizontal position between margins. Margin, Left and Margin, Right will position the box on the left or right margin. Margin, Center will position the box on the line between the left and right margins. If you select Margin, Full, the box fills the area between the left and right margins.

Character

You cannot enter a horizontal position for a character graphic. It is automatically positioned to the right of its preceding character.

Vertical Position

The best way to set the vertical position of a graphics box is to use the mouse (see below). If you want precise settings, you can use the Vertical Position option in the Box Position and Size dialog box. The choices for setting this option depend upon the anchor type.

Page

With a page anchor, you can align the box with the top and bottom margin, or center it between the top and bottom margin. If you choose Offset Position, you can set the box a specified distance from the top edge of the page. If you choose Full Page, the box will fill the area between the top and bottom margins.

Paragraph

With a paragraph anchor, WordPerfect assumes that the graphics box will align with the first line of the paragraph. You can change this in the Vertical Position text box. The default is 0", which aligns the box with the first line of the paragraph. To adjust the offset, enter a new figure in the text box.

Character

With a character anchor type, you can align the box with the top, center, or bottom of the text around it. These align designations are based on the baseline of the text (Bottom aligns with the bottom edge of the text). For an Equation box, choose Baseline to align the baseline of the equation with the baseline of the text.

The position of a graphics box is measured from the border. Even if you choose not to have a visible border (by selecting None in the Appearance Options), a border still exists around a graphics box.

Size

The best way to size a graphic (make it larger or smaller) is to use the mouse (see below). If you want precise settings, you can use the dialog box to size a box. You can change the width, or height, or both. The default settings are determined for each graphics box by its type and contents.

The ability of your printer to handle large image graphics is limited by the amount of RAM in the printer's memory buffer. If you get a "not enough memory" error message on the printer's prompt panel, you may have to reduce the size of your graphic.

Setting Horizontal and Vertical Position and Resizing Graphics with a Mouse

The easiest way to set the horizontal and vertical position of the graphics box and to resize it is to drag it with the mouse. Select the graphics box by positioning the insertion point on the border and holding down the left mouse button. A dotted border appears around the box and the insertion point changes, as shown in Figure 17.3.

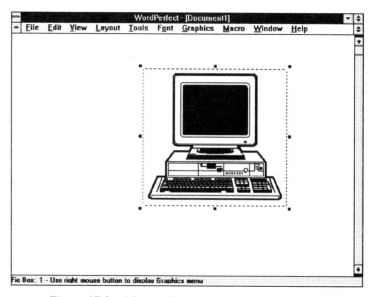

Figure 17.3—A box with dragging and sizing border.

To move the box, place the insertion point on the dotted border and use the mouse to drag the box to its new location. Be careful not to drag a size handle (these are the solid dots that appear at intervals outside of the dotted border).

To resize a graphics box, place the insertion point on a sizing handle (not the dragging border) and use the mouse to drag the box to its new size. Be careful not to position the mouse on the dragging border, or you will drag the box to a new location.

After you have positioned or resized the box, click outside of the border to deselect the box and return the border and insertion point to normal.

When moving a graphics box, be sure to move any options codes that relate to the box.

If you have not selected the Wrap Text Around Box option (see above), you cannot select the figure by using the left mouse button. You must press the right mouse button, then choose Select Box in the menu that appears. You will then be able to drag the box with the mouse.

Caption Editor

The Caption Editor is used to create or edit a caption for a graphics box. To open the Caption Editor:

1. Click on Graphics in the menu bar to open the Graphics menu.
2. Click on the appropriate box type.
3. Click on Caption and choose the number of the caption you want to create or edit. The Caption window is opened.
4. The current Box Number is in the window. You can accept it or edit it. To reinsert it, click on Box Number.
5. If you decide to edit it, you can use any font attributes that are normally available to you.
6. Choose Close to return to your document. The caption appears with the graphics box in the window.
7. To edit the caption, double-click on it in the window.

New Number

Graphics boxes are numbered consecutively by type. You can use this option to start renumbering at any box.

1. Position the insertion point immediately before the code for the box where you want to start renumbering.
2. Click on Graphics in the menu bar to open the Graphics menu.
3. Click on the appropriate box type.

4. Click on New Number, and type a new number in the dialog box that appears.

5. Choose OK.

You can choose a new number only for the first level of a caption number.

Creating a Figure Graphics Box

Now that you are familiar with the options you can use to change the appearance, size, and location of a graphics box, let's create a figure box and retrieve a WordPerfect image into it.

1. Click on Graphics in the menu bar to open the Graphics menu.

2. Click on Figure.

3. Click on Options to display the Options dialog box.

4. Change all four borders to None.

5. Choose OK to close the dialog box.

6. Click on Create to open the Figure Editor, as shown in Figure 17.4.

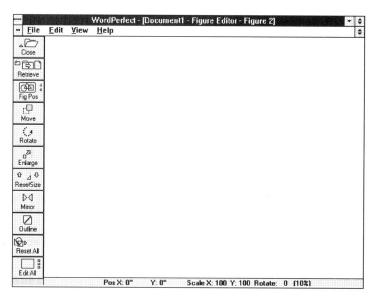

Figure 17.4—The Figure Editor.

7. Choose Retrieve from the button bar or from the File menu to open the Retrieve Figure dialog box.
8. Select COMPUTR.WPG from the list of graphics images in the list box.
9. Select Retrieve to retrieve the figure into the Figure Editor window, as shown in Figure 17.5.

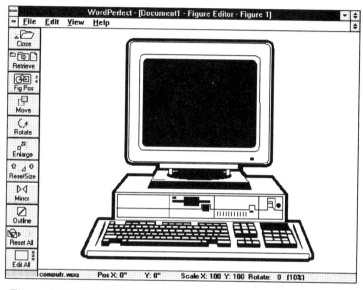

Figure 17.5—COMPUTER.WPG shown in Figure Editor window.

10. Choose Position from the button bar or the File menu to open the Position and Size dialog box.
11. Set the Horizontal and Vertical Position for Margins, Center.
12. Select OK to close the dialog box.
13. Choose Close in the button bar or File menu.
14. You can now use Print Preview to view the page with the graphic image. You can print it at this point or rework it some more by adding text or more graphics. If you insert another image, be sure it does not overlap with the one already created. Use Print Preview to view your changes before you print the page.

There are a number of options available in the Edit menu of the Figure Editor window that allow you to change the appearance of the figure.

You can use the Scale command to enlarge, reduce, or reset the size of the figure. You can use Enlarge Area to select any portion of the figure and enlarge it. Use the mouse to size the segment and enlarge that portion. Enlarge % and Reduce % enlarge and reduce the figure by a specific percentage.

Rotate allows you to rotate the figure. When you select Rotation, a rotation angle appears on the figure. You can drag the right end of the axis to rotate the figure any number of degrees. You can also rotate the figure without choosing Rotate, by pressing Ctrl and the left or right arrow. This will rotate the figure clockwise or counterclockwise a certain percentage each time you press the key.

You can use Move to move the figure horizontally and vertically in the border. Any segment of the figure moved out of the border will not print. To move the figure, drag it with the mouse or press the arrow keys in the direction you want to move the figure.

Mirror Image flips the figure on its vertical axis so that it appears from left to right. For example, an arrow that was pointing to the right will be pointing to the left when you use mirror image on it.

Black and White changes all colors in the figure to black and white.

Invert does not affect black and white graphics. Use Invert with color images to invert the colors like a photo negative.

Edit All allows you to edit all of the above features in one dialog box.

Graphic Images You Can Use with WordPerfect

Figure boxes are usually used for graphic images, such as pictures, diagrams, and so on. Word Perfect for Windows comes with thirty-five WordPerfect (.WPG) graphic images. When you choose Retrieve in the Figure Editor, the thirty-five images are listed in the File list box. In addition, WordPerfect can support the graphics formats listed in the following table. Any of these graphics formats will automatically convert into a .WPG (WordPerfect Graphic) when retrieved by the WordPerfect Graphics feature.

BMP	Windows (3.x) and OS/2 Presentation Manager Bitmap Format
CGM	Computer Graphics Metafile
DHP	Dr. Halo PIC Format
DXF	AutoCAD Format
EPS	Postscript and Encapsulated PostScript
GEM	GEM Draw Format
HPGL	Hewlett-Packard Graphics Language Plotter File
IMG	GEM Paint Format
MSP	Microsoft Windows (2.x) Paint Format
PCX	PC Paintbrush Format
PIC	Lotus 1-2-3 PIC Format
PNTG	Macintosh Paint Format
PPIC	PC Paint Plus Format
TIFF	Tagged Image File Format
WMF	Windows Metafile Format
WPG	WordPerfect Graphics Format

Creating Text Boxes

Text boxes are created in much the same way as figure boxes. First you set the Appearance and Size and Position options. Then:

1. Click on Graphics in the menu bar to open the Graphics menu.
2. Click on Text Box.
3. Click on Create to open the Text Box Editor window.
4. Type in the text for the text box. You can change fonts and attributes in the text box.
5. You can edit your size and position options by clicking on Box Position.
6. You can rotate the text in your box by selecting Rotate.
7. When you are finished, select Close.

Creating User Boxes

When you create a User box, you should first select your Appearance, Size, and Position options. Then:

1. Click on Graphics in the menu bar to open the Graphics menu.
2. Click on User Box.
3. Click on Create to display the Select Editor dialog box. If you are using a figure in the User box, select Figure Editor; if you are using text in the User box, select Text Editor; and if you are using equations in the box, select Equations Editor.
4. Click OK. You are in an Editor-User Box window for text, figures, or equations.
5. Proceed to create the information for the User box.
6. When you are finished, select Close.

Creating Equation Boxes

You can use the Equation Editor to create and edit mathematical or scientific equations. Only the basics of this feature are covered here; a full explanation of how this feature works is beyond the scope of this book. Refer to your WordPerfect manual or purchase an advanced users manual for more detailed help. To create an equation:

1. Click on Graphics in the menu bar to open the Graphics menu.
2. Click on Equation.
3. Click on Create to open the Equation Editor window, as shown in Figure 17.6. Your insertion point is in the editing pane. On the left side of the window is the Equation palette. In the bottom part of the window (separated by a line from the editing pane) is the Redisplay view panel.

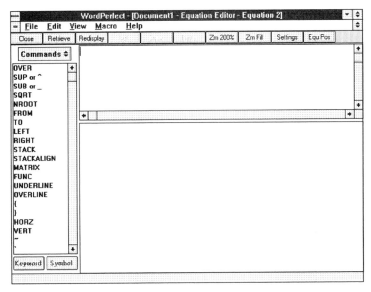

Figure 17.6—The Equation Editor.

4. Create an equation. You can move back and forth between the editing pane and the Equation palette. You can select commands in the palette by clicking on the command and choosing Symbol or Keyword (or by double- clicking on the command). If an item in the palette contains both a symbol and a keyword, choosing Keyword inserts the keyword text, and choosing Symbol inserts the symbol. The Equation palette contains several groups of commands and symbols. You can select a group from the Palette pop-up list. Appendix E has a complete list of all commands and symbols available in the Equation palette.

5. You can add and delete text in the editing pane.

6. To see how the equation will look when it is printed, choose Redisplay in the View menu, or use the Redisplay button in the button bar. The equation will display in the Redisplay view window.

7. Rework the equation until you are satisfied with its appearance.

8. Choose Close.

You can save an equation as a separate file and retrieve it later. To save the equation, use Save As from the File menu in the Equation Editor. When you retrieve an equation, WordPerfect looks for files with EQN extensions, so you should use this extension when naming the file.

To retrieve an equation you have saved, click on Retrieve and select an equation from the File list.

The Equation Editor allows you to enter and print equations. It does not calculate them for you.

Editing Graphics Boxes

To edit a graphics box:

1. Click on Graphics in the menu bar to open the Graphics menu.
2. Click on the box type you want to edit.
3. Click on Edit.
4. Type in the number of the box you want to edit.
5. You will be brought to the editing window for that box. Make your edits.
6. Choose Close when you are finished. Your edits are saved.

Editing Appearance Options

When you change appearance options a code is inserted into your document ([Fig Opt], [Txt Opt], and so on). You cannot edit these codes, but you can insert new ones. To do this, place the insertion point *after* the old code and insert a new code. When you are finished, delete the old code. Appearance options must always precede a graphics box to be effective for that box.

Using Graphics Lines

You can place horizontal and vertical lines in your document using the Graphics Lines feature. You can also change the thickness and shading of the lines.

To create graphics lines:

1. Click on Graphics in the menu bar to open the Graphics menu.
2. Click on Line.
3. To open the Create Line dialog box, click on Horizontal (Ctrl+F11) or Vertical (Ctrl+Shft+F11).
4. Choose a vertical and horizontal position for the line. The vertical position can be the baseline of your insertion point, or you can position the line on the top margin, bottom margin, centered between the top and bottom margins, or you can specify a position from the top edge of the page. Full vertical position extends the line from the top to the bottom margin. Horizontal position can be set at the left or right margin, centered between the left and right margins, or you can specify a position from the left edge of the page. A horizontal position set at Full extends the line from the left to the right margin. If you use this setting, you cannot enter a length in the Line Size box.
5. Type a length for your line in the Length text box.
6. You can increase the thickness of your line by entering a new number in the Thickness text box.
7. Set the shading from 0% to 100%, where 0% is no shading and 100% is black.
8. Choose OK.

Editing a Line

You can edit the line using the Edit Line dialog box, or you can use the mouse. To use the dialog box:

1. Click on Graphics in the menu bar to open the Graphics menu.

2. Click on Line.

3. Click on Edit Horizontal or Edit Vertical. WordPerfect searches for the line and the Edit Line dialog box opens.

4. Make any changes you want in the line.

5. Choose OK.

Shortcut: Position the tip of the mouse pointer directly on the line and click to select the line, then click the right mouse button. The Line cascading menu opens. Click on Edit Horizontal or Edit Vertical.

Editing a Line with the Mouse

Use the mouse to move or size a line the same way as with a box. Select the line by positioning the insertion point on it and clicking, then drag or size the line.

Using Line Draw

There are two ways to draw lines in WordPerfect. One is using graphics lines; the other is using Line Draw. The feature you use depends upon your needs. Line Draw lets you draw boxes, graphs, and borders using an array of pre-set characters. However, you cannot use proportional fonts in Line Draw, and you cannot change the thickness of the lines. When you use Line Draw, WordPerfect switches to draft mode.

To print lines created in Line Draw, you must select a fixed pitch font or a Line Draw font. Line Draw will not print properly if you do not. Do not use a proportional font with Line Draw. Use Left Justification only when using Line Draw.

To use Line Draw:

1. Press Ctrl+D to open the Line Draw dialog box. WordPerfect has switched you to draft mode and typeover mode.

2. Select one of the ten preset characters, or select your own character:

   a. Choose Character to open the Line Draw Character dialog box.

    b. Type a character in the box, or press Ctrl+W to open the WordPerfect Characters dialog box.

    c. Select a character and choose OK.

3. Using the arrow keys, draw your lines. Because you are in draft mode, the characters may not appear properly on the screen. When you return to normal mode, the characters will appear as they should.

4. To erase in Line Draw, Select Erase in the Line Draw Dialog Box and use the arrow keys to erase the lines.

5. Select Move to move the insertion point to another location.

6. When you are finished, select close.

You cannot use the mouse to drag lines created with Line Draw.

Review Exercises for Chapter 17

◆ Design a page layout for a graphics image with text above and below it on the page.

◆ Set the Appearance options any way you like.

◆ In a new window, create a Figure Graphics box.

◆ Retrieve a figure into the box.

◆ Set the size and position of the box.

◆ Close the Figure Editor and view the page using Print Preview.

◆ Add text to the page above and below the box.

◆ View the page again. Make changes if necessary. Use the mouse if you want to change the size or position of the box.

◆ Save and print the page.

Before You Go On...

Before you continue on to the next chapter, you should be able to create each type of graphics box and set the appearance options. You should be able to position and size a box with the dialog box and with the mouse. You should know how to use the graphics Line feature and Line Draw.

Chapter 18

Speeding Things Up with Button Bars and Macros

What You Will Learn in this Chapter

- How to display and hide button bars
- How to create button bars
- How to edit button bars
- How to assign a macro to a button
- How to change the position of button bars
- How to change appearance of button bars
- How to record and play macros
- How to edit a macro
- How to convert WordPerfect 5.1 macros
- How to assign macros to the macro menu

As you have realized by now, WordPerfect is the most sophisticated word processing program there is. This has its advantages and disadvantages. The major advantage is that it can accomplish virtually any word processing task that you can think of. A major disadvantage is that some of the more complex tasks involve multiple commands or keystrokes. You will be happy to learn that WordPerfect has two features—button bars and macros—that provide shortcuts to accomplish even the most intricate task.

What Are Button Bars?

Button bars are an exciting new feature in WordPerfect for Windows that give you quick access to commands and macros. When you click on a button bar, the command or macro is executed. Button bars can make WordPerfect for Windows the most user-friendly word processing program available. Any command can be executed with the click of a button. You don't even have to know how to read, since the buttons also have pictures (or **icons**) describing their functions.

You can create various button bars with different sets of commands or macros to accommodate specific sets of WordPerfect features. For example, you can create a Font button bar with special fonts, or you can create a Graphics button bar with graphics features. There is no limit to the number of button bars you can create.

The button bar can be used only with a mouse. You cannot use the keyboard to choose buttons on a button bar.

Displaying the Default Button Bar

WordPerfect is shipped with several button bars already created. If you have not selected a new button bar since WordPerfect was installed, the default button bar WP{WP}.WWB is automatically selected. To display the default button bar:

1. Click on View in the menu bar to open the View menu.
2. Click on Button Bar. The default button bar is displayed across the top of the window (see Figure 18.1).

Let's perform some commands using the default button bar

1. Click on the Open Button to display the Open File dialog box. Double-click on a file to open it.
2. Make a change in the document (type your name, or write a poem).
3. Click on the Save Button to save the document.
4. Click on the Print Button to print the document.

As you can see, this feature is a real time saver. You can use button bars to create shortcuts that were impossible before WordPerfect for Windows. The more you use button bars, the more ways you will think of to use them to further automate the program.

Some of the buttons on the button bar are dimmed. This occurs when the choice is not currently available. For example, in Figure 18.1 the Cut button is dimmed because no text has been selected to cut.

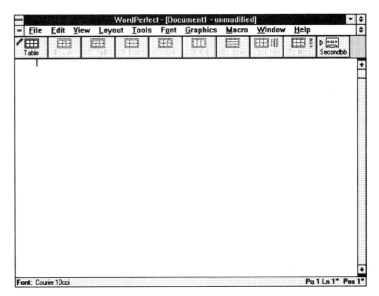

Figure 18.1—The Word Perfect Default button bar.

Hiding the Button Bar

To hide the button bar:

1. Click on View in the menu bar to open the View menu.
2. Click on Button Bar. The button bar is no longer visible.

When the button bar is displayed, a check appears next to the Button Bar menu item. When the button bar is not displayed (or is hidden), the check disappears.

Creating a New Button Bar

When you create a new button bar, you start with a blank bar and add buttons to it. Let's create a Font button bar containing buttons for commands found in the Font menu.

1. Click on View in the menu bar to open the View menu.
2. Click on Button Bar Setup to open the Button Bar Setup cascading menu.
3. Click on New to display the Edit Button Bar dialog box, as shown in Figure 18.2.

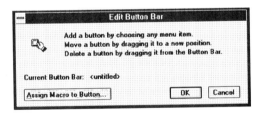

Figure 18.2—The Edit Button Bar dialog box.

Notice that the mouse pointer changes to a hand holding a button when it is positioned over the empty button bar or the menu area.

4. Click on Font in the menu bar to open the Font menu.
5. Click on Bold. A Bold button is now added to the button bar.
6. Add the following buttons to the button bar: Italic; Underline; Double Underline; Subscript; Superscript; WP Characters; Font; Large; Extra Large. If you make a mistake, delete the button by dragging it off the button

bar. Your new button bar should look like the one shown in Figure 18.3.

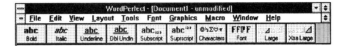

Figure 18.3—The new Font button bar.

7. When you are finished, choose OK to open the Save Button Bar dialog box, as shown in Figure 18.4.

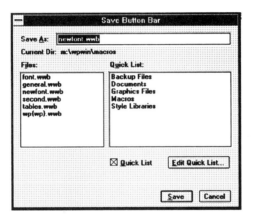

Figure 18.4—The Save Button Bar dialog box.

8. In the Save As text box, type "Font" for the new button bar. WordPerfect will automatically add the extension WWB to any button bar you save, unless you add your own extension. The Button Bar has now been saved to the name FONT.WWB.

You can add as many buttons as you like to a button bar. If you fill the visible space in the bar, arrows appear so that you can scroll to buttons that are not visible.

Selecting a Button Bar

When you have several button bars saved, you must select the one you want to use. To select a button bar:

1. Click on View in the menu bar to open the View menu.
2. Click on Button Bar Setup to open the Button Bar Setup cascading menu.
3. Click on Select to open the Select Button Bar dialog box.
4. Double click on the name of the button bar you want to select in the Files list box.
5. Choose Select.

The selected button bar remains active until you select another one. If you exit WordPerfect, the current button bar will remain selected.

Editing a Button Bar

You can make changes to a button bar even after it has been saved. To edit a button bar:

1. Select the button bar you want to edit.
2. Click on View in the menu bar to open the View menu.
3. Click on Button Bar Setup to open the Button Bar Setup cascading menu.
4. Click on Edit to display the Edit Button Bar dialog box.
   a. To add a button, choose any menu item (see instructions above in the "Creating a Button Bar" section).
   b. Move a button by dragging it to a new location on the button bar.
   c. Delete a button by dragging it off the button bar.
5. When you are finished, choose OK to save the edited button bar.

Let's edit the FONT.WWB button bar.

1. If it is not selected, select the button bar.
2. Click on View in the menu bar to open the View menu.
3. Click on Button Bar Setup to open the Button Bar Setup cascading menu.
4. Click on Edit to open the Edit Button Bar dialog box.
5. Add a new button (Normal font attribute).

a. Click on Font in the menu bar.

b. Click on Normal.

Notice that scroll arrow buttons have now appeared because there are too many buttons to be visible on the button bar.

6. Drag the buttons to rearrange them into alphabetical order. Your button bar should now look like the one shown in Figure 18.5.

7. When you are finished, choose OK to save the edited button bar.

Figure 18.5—The edited Font WWB button bar.

Assigning a Macro to a Button

In addition to menu commands, you can also assign macros to buttons in a button bar (macros are explained later in this chapter). To assign a macro to a button:

1. Click on View in the menu bar to open the View menu.

2. Click on Button Bar Setup to open the Button Bar Setup cascading menu.

3. Click on New to open the Edit Button Bar dialog box.

4. Choose Assign Macro to Button to display the Assign Macro To Button dialog box, as shown in Figure 18.6.

5. Select a macro from the Files list box by double-clicking on the macro.

6. Choose Assign.

Figure 18.6—The Assign Macro to Button dialog box.

    If you edit a macro that has been assigned to a button, the changes in the macro are not reflected in the button. You must add a new button for the edited macro.

Saving the Button Bar to a New Name

You can save a copy of the current button bar to a new name using the Save As dialog box:

1. Select the button bar you want to save to a new name.
2. Click on View in the menu bar to open the View menu.
3. Click on Button Bar Setup to open the Button Bar Setup cascading menu.
4. Click on Save As to open the Save Button Bar dialog box.
5. Type a new name in the Save As text box.
6. Choose Select. The current button bar has been saved to a new name.

Using the Options Feature

You can change the position and appearance of the button bar by using the Button Bar Options dialog box. When you change the settings in the Button Bar Options dialog box, they remain in effect for any button bar you select or create until you change the settings again. To change the Options settings:

1. Click on View in the menu bar to open the View menu.
2. Click on Button Bar Setup to open the Button Bar Setup menu.
3. Click on Options to open the Button Bar Options dialog box, as shown in Figure 18.7.
4. To change the position of the button bar, select one of the Position Option buttons (Left, Right, Top, or Bottom).
5. Choose a style by selecting a Style Options button.
6. Choose OK.

Figure 18.7—The Button Bar Option dialog box.

Category Markers

Category Markers appear on some of the buttons if you select Picture Only or Picture and Text in the Button Bar Options dialog box. They indicate that the buttons perform similar tasks. The following table lists each category marker and what it indicates:

Category marker	The Button Lets You:
[#1]	Create a document, button bar, graphics box or line, table, footnote, endnote, comment, overstrike, DDE (Dynamic Link Exchange) link, or spreadsheet link.
[#2]	Edit a button bar, graphics box or line, footnote, endnote, comment, overstrike, DDE link, or spreadsheet link.
[#3]	View the ruler, the button bar, Reveal Codes, Print Preview, Draft mode, comments, graphics, or short menus.

...continued

...from previous page

Category marker	The Button Lets You:
[#4]	Turn on the Columns or Outline feature.
[#5]	Turn off the Columns or Outline feature.
[#6]	Delete an outline family, columns and rows in a table, document compare markings, or DDE links.
[#7]	Select a sentence, paragraph, column, rectangle, printer, or button bar.
[#8]	Retrieve a document or graphics file.
[#9]	Save a document or button bar with a new name.
[#10]	Search for text or codes.
[#11]	Define the format for an outline, columns, date and time, index, list, table of contents, or table of authorities.
[#12]	Change options for tables, footnotes, endnotes, graphics boxes, spreadsheet links, or the button bar.
[#13]	Position a graphics box, a footnote, or an endnote.
[#14]	Edit a graphics box caption.
[#15]	Assign a new number to a graphics box, a footnote, or an endnote.
[#16]	Specify preferences for Location of Files, Backup, Environment, Display, Printing, Keyboard, Initial Codes, Document Summary, Date Format, Merge, Table of Authorities, or Equations.
[#17]	Update DDE links, spreadsheet links, or the date code.

What Are Macros?

A macro is a "mini-program" within WordPerfect that records commands and keystrokes and plays them back when accessed. A macro can consist of simple commands (changing line spacing, for example), commands and text (a margin change plus text), or very complex programming commands. Use macros to record tasks that you perform frequently. Any task you can perform in WordPerfect can be recorded into a macro.

A Note to WordPerfect 5.1 Users

The macro facility in WordPerfect for Windows is very different from that in WordPerfect 5.1. While the basic concept is the same—first you record a macro, then you play it back—the process is handled very differently. WordPerfect 5.1 records the keystrokes, while WordPerfect for Windows records only the results. For example, WordPerfect 5.1 would record a macro that executes a double-space command as follows:

```
{FORMAT}162{EXIT}{EXIT}
```

The same macro in WordPerfect for Windows would be:

```
(
Spacing:2.0
)
```

In addition, the programming command language is very different (see below for more information on WordPerfect for Windows programming language). As we will explain later in this chapter, these differences make converting complex macros from WordPerfect 5.1 to WordPerfect for Windows an unpredictable experience.

However, you will find editing macros much easier in WordPerfect for Windows. Since the program records only the results of keystrokes and not the keystrokes themselves, inserting new commands is much easier. You simply have to look up the command (see below) and insert it into the macro. This is much easier than trying to remember all of the keystrokes that go into a command, plus their macro formats. In addition, macros in WordPerfect for Windows are edited just as you would edit a regular file. You do not have to use a macro editor as you did in WordPerfect 5.1.

Recording Macros (Ctrl+F10)

When you record a macro, you type in the commands and/or text you want the macro to store. Later you can play them back. Macros are automatically placed in the directory specified for them during the installation process (see Appendix A).

To record a macro:

1. Click on Macro in the menu bar to open the macro menu.
2. Click on Record to open the Record Macro dialog box, as shown in Figure 18.8.
3. Type a Filename for the macro in the Filename text box. The filename may be up to eight characters. Do not add an extension; WordPerfect will automatically assign the WCM extension to all macros.
4. Type a brief description of the macro in the Descriptive Name text box (this is optional — it helps you to identify the macro later).

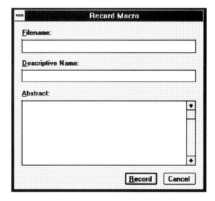

Figure 18.8—The Record Macro dialog box.

5. Type a longer description summarizing the macro's contents in the Abstract text box (this is also optional).
6. Choose Record to return to the document window.

   a. The Recording Macro prompt appears in the status bar. Every keystroke you type, as well as most mouse clicks, will be recorded until you tell WordPerfect to stop recording.

b. You will notice that the mouse pointer changes its appearance to remind you that certain mouse actions cannot be recorded (see below, "Using the Mouse With Macros", for restrictions).

c. Use WordPerfect as you normally would to type in commands and text. It is advisable to avoid using the mouse, and to use keystrokes only, since some mouse actions are not recognized when you record macros.

To stop recording the macro:

1. Click on Macro in the menu bar to open the macro menu.
2. Click on Stop (Ctrl+Shift+F10). The macro stops recording.

Let's record a simple macro to put a footer at the bottom of every page but suppress it for the first page. We are going to use keystrokes only to insert commands (see "Using the Mouse with Macros", below).

1. Click on Macro in the menu bar to open the macro menu.
2. Click on Record (Ctrl+F10) to open the Record Macro dialog box, as shown in Figure 18.8.
3. Type the Filename "Footer" in the Filename text box.
4. Type "Standard Footer" in the Descriptive Name text box.
5. Choose Record to return to the document window. The Recording Macro prompt appears in the status bar. We are now ready to record the keystrokes for our macro. If you make a mistake, correct it and continue.
6. Press Alt+L. This opens the Layout menu.
7. Press P for the Page cascading menu.
8. Press F to open the Footers dialog box.
9. Press A for Footer A.
10. Press C for Create to open the Footer window.
11. Press Enter twice. This will give you three lines between the end of the document and the beginning of the footer (WordPerfect automatically supplies one line).
12. Press Shift+F7 to center the footer.

13. Type the word "page," plus a space.
14. Press Alt+N to insert the page number code (^B).
15. Press Enter.
16. Press Alt+P to open the Placement dialog box.
17. Press E for Every Page.
18. Press Enter to close the Placement dialog box.
19. Press Alt+C to close the Footer window.
20. Press the right arrow key (→) once. (This is to be sure the insertion point is immediately after the footer code in Reveal Codes.)
21. Press Alt+L to open the Layout menu.
22. Press P to open the Page cascading menu.
23. Press U to open the Suppress dialog box.
24. Press F to choose Footer A.
25. Press Enter to close the Suppress dialog box.
26. Press Ctrl+Shift+F10 to stop recording the macro.

Pausing While Recording a Macro

You can pause while recording a macro, then, when you are ready, resume recording. For example, you might want to check a menu command or see how a feature is going to work before you record it. To pause while recording a macro:

1. Click on Macro in the menu bar to open the macro menu.
2. Click on Pause. Macro recording is paused. Now you can work in WordPerfect without your actions being recorded.
3. To resume recording, open the macro menu and click on Pause again.

Playing Macros (Alt+F10)

Once you have recorded a macro, you can play it back. To play (run) a macro:

1. Click on Macro in the menu bar to open the macro menu.
2. Click on Play to open the Play Macro dialog box.

3. Select the macro you want to play and click on Play or double-click on the macro you want to play.

The first time you play a macro, WordPerfect **compiles** it. This means WordPerfect converts it to a language that is processed very quickly by the computer. This makes your compiled macro play much faster. If you edit a macro, it will recompile the next time it is played.

Let's play our footer macro.

1. Click on Macro in the menu bar to open the macro menu.
2. Click on Play (Alt+F10) to open the Play Macro dialog box.
3. Double-click on FOOTER.WCM. The footer macro will play.

You can also play a macro by assigning it to a button in a button bar. When you click on the button, the macro is played.

Editing a Macro

To edit a macro, open it as you would any ordinary file. You can use the Quick List list box to switch to the directory containing your macro files. There are hundreds of commands that you can insert into macros when editing them.

Let's edit our footer macro.

1. Click on File in the menu bar to open the File menu.
2. Click on Open to display the Open File dialog box.
3. Double-click on Macros in the Quick List files box. The directory containing the macro files is opened.
4. Double-click on FOOTER.WCM. The file containing the footer macro is opened.
5. Edit the file so that the word "page" reads "Page."
6. Close and save the file. The next time you play the macro, the edited version will appear.

Programming and Command Language

There are hundreds of commands you can insert into macros when editing. In addition, WordPerfect for Windows has special programming commands that allow you to program sophisticated macros using advanced programming language and conditions. If you want to create or edit complex macros, you should order the WordPerfect Macros manual, which is available from WordPerfect Corp. or look for *Power Shortcuts: WordPerfect for Windows* (MIS:Press) at your local book store. Both the manual and the book contain detailed explanations and lessons using WordPerfect's macro command language.

Using the Mouse with Macros

It is advisable to use keystrokes only when recording macros. If you do use the mouse, keep in mind that the following mouse actions will not record: scrolling, selecting, and insertion point movements.

Converting 5.1 Macros

As mentioned earlier, WordPerfect for Windows uses a totally different macro language than WordPerfect 5.1. This makes macro conversion from WordPerfect 5.1 to WordPerfect for Windows very tricky indeed. Some commands translate without any problems, but if you have complex macros, many of the commands will not convert properly. To convert macros, you must use the Macro Facility, a special program that comes with WordPerfect for Windows.

The Macro Facility is not executed from within WordPerfect for Windows. When you install WordPerfect, an icon is added to the WordPerfect Program Group. Either exit WordPerfect to get back to the Windows Program Manager, or use the task list to switch programs (see Chapter 19). Bring up the WordPerfect Program Group and double-click on the Macro Facility Group icon. (You can also execute the Macro Facility in the File Manager. The execute file is named MFWIN.EXE, and it is found in the WPC directory.)

To convert a macro, choose Convert. The Convert dialog box appears. Select the macro you want to convert and choose Convert again.

When you play the macro in WordPerfect for Windows, a Syntax Error dialog box will appear each time a syntax error is encountered. Note the location of each error, and choose Continue Compilation. When you are done, edit the macro and correct all the errors.

The Syntax Error dialog box will appear when the macro being played has an error in syntax. It is not just a feature of the convert facility.

Assigning Macros to the Macro Menu

You can assign up to nine of your most commonly used macros to the macro menu. This gives you quick access to them. To assign a macro to the macro menu:

1. Click on Macro in the menu bar to open the macro menu.
2. Click on Assign to Menu to open the Assign Macro to Menu dialog box, as shown in Figure 18.9.
3. Choose Insert to open the Insert Macro Menu Item dialog box.
4. Type in the name of the macro in the Macro Name text box or click on the Select File button at the right of the Macro Name text box and select the macro.

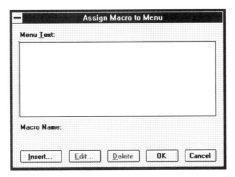

Figure 18.9—The Assign Macro to Menu dialog box.

5. Type in a description in the Menu Text text box. This is the way the name will appear as a menu item.

6. Choose OK to close the Insert Macro Menu Item dialog box.

7. The Assign Macro to Menu dialog box is still open. The macro you selected appears in the Menu Text list box.

8. Choose OK to return to your document.

You can now play the macro from the macro menu.
Let's assign our footer macro to the macro menu.

1. Click on Macro in the menu bar to open the macro menu.

2. Click on Assign to Menu to open the Assign Macro to Menu dialog.

3. Choose Insert to open the Insert Macro Menu Item dialog box.

4. Click on the Select File button at the right of the Macro Name text box, and select FOOTER.WCM.

5. Type "Standard Footer" in the Menu Text text box. This is the way the name will appear as a menu item.

6. Choose OK to close the Insert Macro Menu Item dialog box.

7. The Assign Macro to Menu dialog box is still open. The macro you selected appears in the Menu Text list box.

8. Choose OK to return to your document.

9. Open the macro menu. You will see Standard Footer listed as a menu item. You can now play the footer macro by clicking on the item.

Editing a Macro Menu Item

To change the menu item description of a macro:

1. Following the steps listed above, open the Assign Macro to Menu dialog box.

2. Select the macro menu item to be edited in the Menu Text list box.

3. Choose Edit to open the Edit Macro Menu Item dialog box.

4. Make any modifications you want in the text boxes.

5. Choose OK.

If you rename a macro listed in the macro menu, or change its location, you must edit the macro menu item to reflect these changes.

Deleting a Macro Menu Item

To delete a macro menu item:

1. Following the steps listed above, open the Assign Macro to Menu dialog box.

2. Select the macro menu item you want to delete in the Menu text box.

3. Choose Delete. The macro menu item is removed from the macro menu (the macro itself is not deleted from the directory).

4. If you change your mind before choosing OK, you can restore the macro menu item to the macro menu by choosing Cancel.

5. Choose OK. The macro menu item is deleted from the macro menu. However, you can still play the macro by choosing Play in the macro menu.

Review Exercises for Chapter 18

◆ Create a new button bar. Assign buttons for the following commands: Print, Open, Save, Center, and Margins. Assign FOOTER.WCM macro to a button.

◆ Arrange the buttons in alphabetical order.

◆ Save the button bar. Name it General.

◆ Change the position of the button bar to appear on the left side of the window.

◆ Change the position back to the top of the window.

◆ Record a macro to play a task you use frequently.

◆ Play the macro.

◆ Assign the macro to the macro menu.

Before You Go On...

Before you continue to the next chapter, you should be able to create and edit a button bar. You should know how to add, rearrange, and delete buttons and assign a macro to a button. You should know how to select, display, and hide button bars. You should be able to record, play, and edit macros. You should be able to assign a macro to the macro menu.

Chapter 19

Using WordPerfect
with Windows

What You Will Learn in this Chapter

- ◆ How to use the Windows Program Manager to track your open applications
- ◆ How to switch between two, three, or more open applications
- ◆ How to access DOS using the Windows shell
- ◆ Multitasking in Windows
- ◆ How to check for available memory
- ◆ What to do when you get an "Unrecoverable Application Error"

Windows is known as a graphical user interface (GUI) program. This means that instead of having to memorize DOS commands to do things like access a software program, you can click on an icon with your mouse. WordPerfect for Windows is designed the same way. Instead of having to memorize keystrokes to accomplish a task, you can click on either the menu bar or the button bars to access any feature. Because using a mouse is faster than using the keyboard, you can do most tasks more quickly. You can even cut, copy, and paste text at the flick of a click!

WordPerfect for Windows must be used with Windows. While it is not necessary for you to be a Windows expert, there are certain features you should know so that you can take advantage of the Windows environment. You should be familiar with the Windows Program Manager, and you should know how to switch between WordPerfect and Windows, how to switch between WordPerfect and other applications, how to access DOS from the Windows shell, and how to run applications in the background.

A Word About the Program Manager

When you enter Windows you are automatically in the Program Manager, which is responsible for the group windows that contain the icons you use to access your applications. Another one of the Program Manager's jobs is to keep track of all of the applications you are running at one time. When you open WordPerfect, the Program Manager adds this to its task list. Then when you open another application while you are still in WordPerfect, it adds the new application to the list. To see how the Program Manager works:

1. Double-click on the WordPerfect icon and execute the program. You are now in the WordPerfect document screen.

2. Press Alt+Esc. The Program Manager task list will pop up on your screen.

3. Double-click on Program Manager. You are back in the original Windows window.

4. Double-click on Thesaurus in the WordPerfect group window. The Thesaurus is now in your window.

5. Press Alt+Esc. The Program Manager task list is on your screen. Listed are WordPerfect, Program Manager, and Thesaurus, as shown in Figure 19.1. The Program Manager task list tells you at a glance what applications are running concurrently.

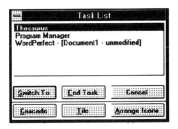

Figure 19.1—The Task List window.

6. Double-click on WordPerfect to return to WordPerfect.

Switching Between Two Open Applications

Once you have opened more than one application, there is a faster way to switch between them. To switch between only two applications (for example, WordPerfect and the Speller):

1. Open your first application.
2. Press Alt+Esc to access the Program Manager task list.
3. Click twice on Program Manager.
4. Open your second application.
5. Press Alt+Esc to return to the Program Manager.
6. Double-click on your first application.
7. To switch back and forth between the two applications without using the Program Manager, press Alt+Tab.
8. Exit the applications from within the programs themselves.
9. When you have exited both applications, you will be back in the Windows window.

Switching Between More than Two Open Applications

You can have more than two applications active at the same time in Windows. You can open as many applications as the memory in your computer will allow. If you have three or more applications open you cannot use Alt+Tab to switch between them; this works only when switching between the last two applications you accessed. If you do not want to have to go through the Program Manager every time you switch to another program, there is another way. Assume you have opened WordPerfect, the Thesaurus and File Manager. (Although the Thesaurus and File Manager can be accessed from within WordPerfect, let's pretend that they can't for this demonstration.) You are currently in WordPerfect and you want to switch to the Thesaurus.

1. Open your first application (WordPerfect).
2. Click on the inside down icon at the top-right of your window, as shown in Figure 19.2. You are back in Windows and there is a WordPerfect icon at the bottom of your screen.

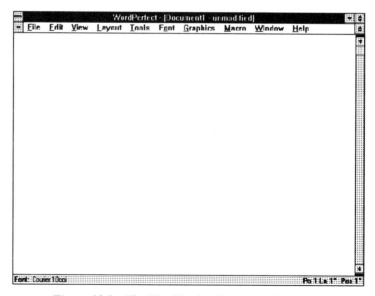

Figure 19.2—The WordPerfect Document1 window.

3. Double-click on Thesaurus in the WordPerfect group window.

4. When you have finished using the Thesaurus, click on the inside down icon at the top right of your window. You are back in the Windows window and you now have two icons at the bottom of your screen: WordPerfect and the Thesaurus.

5. Double-click on File Manager.

6. When you are finished using the File Manager, click on the inside down icon at the top right of your window. You now have three icons at the bottom of your screen.

7. Double-click on the WordPerfect icon. You are now in WordPerfect.

To access either the Thesaurus or the File Manager without going back to the Windows window:

1. While you are in WordPerfect click on the down icon at the top-right corner of your window, as shown in Figure 19.2. The WordPerfect window will shrink enough for you to see and access either the Thesaurus icon or the File Manager icon.

2. Click twice on either the Thesaurus icon or the File Manager icon.

3. To return to WordPerfect, click on the inside down icon at the top-right of the window. You are back in WordPerfect.

4. To return your WordPerfect window to full size, click on the up icon in the top-right corner of the window. You do not have to resize the window. If you like you can continue to work with the window this size.

5. You can exit from inside any application, or you can click once on the icon and select Close.

6. When you have exited all of the applications, you will be back in the Windows window.

Accessing DOS Using the Windows Shell

Occasionally you will need to access DOS from within Windows. You can do this from any application you are currently in. To access DOS:

1. Click on the inside down icon at the top-right corner of your window, or click on the icon bar at the top-left corner of your window and select Minimize. You will be in the Windows window.
2. Change windows to Program Manager.
3. Click on the DOS icon.
4. To return to Windows, type "Exit" and press Enter.
5. Double-click on the program icon.
6. If you have minimized your screen, click on the bar icon in the top-left corner and select Maximize. Otherwise, click on the up icon in the top-right corner of your screen.

Multitasking in Windows

Multitasking refers to the ability to perform several tasks simultaneously on your computer. If you want to multitask, you must have at least a 386 computer (your CPU chip is an 80386). If you have a 386 computer, your multitasking capabilities are limited only by the amount of memory your computer has available for each task. As an example of multitasking, assume you have a large database and you are going to sort and select several hundred names and addresses for a mailing, at the same time you need to generate your end-of-the-month bills. To add insult to injury you also have a letter that has to be in the mailbox for the last pickup of the day—one hour from now. If your computer has enough memory available, you can go into your database program, establish your sort and select criteria, then, while the database is sorting and selecting, you can switch to your billing program. You can give your billing program the information it needs to generate the bills and send them to the printer. You then switch to WordPerfect and begin to type your letter. While you are typing your letter, the database is sorting and selecting and the billing program is printing out your bills. By the time you have finished your letter and have dropped it in the mailbox, your database is sorted, your bills are printed, and you can take a much deserved break!

A Word About Memory Problems

Each application you open while you are in windows uses memory. In addition to the memory each opened application uses, memory is also used by DOS and Windows. You can check to see how much memory you have available in the WordPerfect File Manager. Click on Info. Select Windows Info, and the File Manager will tell you how much memory you have left after taking into account all of the applications you are currently running. If you are operating Windows on a 386 computer and have more than 2 megabytes of RAM, you should not encounter memory problems often. Windows should automatically manage and allocate enough memory for each application up to the limits of your RAM. If you are constantly getting messages that tell you there is not enough memory to run an application, check your Windows manual to find out how to remedy the problem.

The Windows Swap File Feature

Windows has a feature called Swap file. This is a file that uses available hard drive space when Windows needs more memory. Instead of holding an application in RAM, Windows writes it to the hard drive, thereby freeing up memory for another application. There are two kinds of Swap files, temporary and permanent. For more information on Swap files, consult your Windows manual.

When You Get an Unrecoverable Application Error Message

Any time you are working in a Windows application you might get an Unrecoverable Application error message. When this happens, you should exit all open applications, exit Windows, and reboot (press Alt+Ctrl+Del), or, you turn your computer off and then back on. You should reboot whenever you receive this message, even if the problem seems to resolve itself and everything appears to be running normally. This message may appear while you are working in WordPerfect and you may be popped out of the program. If this happens and your document hasn't been saved manually, you can still retrieve it if you have set your Preferences for a timed backup. See Chapter 3 for a complete explanation of how to set your WordPerfect Preferences for a timed backup.

Review Exercises for Chapter 19

- ◆ Open WordPerfect from within Windows.
- ◆ Use Ctrl+Esc to access the Program Manager.
- ◆ Open another application.
- ◆ Use your Alt+Tab keys to move between the two programs.
- ◆ Open another application.
- ◆ Use program icons to switch between applications.
- ◆ Go to DOS from the Program Manager.
- ◆ Type "Exit" and return to Windows.
- ◆ Exit all open applications from the program icons.

Congratulations!

You have completed the last chapter on learning WordPerfect for Windows. You should now be able to enjoy the many features it offers.

Installing and Configuring WordPerfect for Windows

T his appendix tells you what system requirements are necessary to run WordPerfect for Windows, and explains how to install the program on your computer, and how to configure it for your special needs.

System Requirements

WordPerfect for Windows will run on a personal computer with an 80286, 80386, or higher processor. Your video card and monitor should be capable of supporting graphics (EGA, VGA, 8514/A, or Hercules graphics card).

Hard Disk Requirements

You must have a hard disk to run WordPerfect for Windows. It will not run off of floppy disks. Your hard disk must have at least 9 megabytes of free space to install the program. The learning files take up a great deal of space on your hard disk, and are not necessary to run the program. If you want to save space, you can remove them after you are through working with them, or not install them at all. Although you can store your documents on floppy disks, it is advisable to keep them on the hard disk, which means that you should have enough additional space to store your files. When you run the Install program for WordPerfect for Windows, you will receive a message informing you of how much space is required to run the program, and how much space is available on your hard disk. If you do not have enough space left, you will have to delete files in order to free up space.

Floppy Disk Requirements

You must have at least one floppy disk drive to install the program from disks. If you are using a 5.25" floppy disk drive, it must be high-density (720 kilobytes). If you purchase the program on 3.5" floppy disks, you will automatically receive high-density (1.4 megabytes) disks. The program is available on 3.5" low-density disks (720 kilobytes), but they must be ordered specially from WordPerfect.

Memory Requirements

In order to run WordPerfect for Windows, you must also run Windows 3.0 and DOS. The minimum memory allocation for all of these programs is 2 megabytes. If you have any other programs running at the same time, or if you plan to multitask, you should have at least 4 megabytes of RAM in your computer. If you run out of memory while trying to use an application, Windows will prompt you with an Insufficient Memory error message.

Mouse Requirements

You should have a mouse to work with WordPerfect for Windows. Some features of the program will not work without one (such as button bars). WordPerfect will automatically recognize your mouse when the program is installed.

Software Requirements

To run WordPerfect, you must have Microsoft Windows, Version 3.0 or higher, running in standard or enhanced mode. You must also have Microsoft or IBM DOS, Version 3.0 or higher.

Installing WordPerfect for Windows

Before you install WordPerfect for Windows, you must install Microsoft Windows on your computer. Windows must be running in standard or enhanced mode.

When you install WordPerfect for Windows, a WordPerfect program group will be set up in the Windows Program Manager.

WordPerfect for Windows is installed from floppy disks. You *must* use the Install program on the disks. Because the files on the disks are compressed, you cannot just copy them onto the computer.

Insert the WordPerfect for Windows Install/Program 1 disk in floppy disk drive A or B. Then, if you are using drive A, type:

`A:INSTALL` Enter

If you are using drive B, type:

`B:INSTALL` Enter

You are asked whether you want to continue with the installation. Say Yes. A menu will appear with the installation choices. You should choose either Basic or Custom installation (this book does not cover network installation).

Basic Installation

If you are not experienced with computers, you should choose Basic Installation. This program will automatically create directories for the WordPerfect files and install all of the files from the disks. You will be prompted to insert the appropriate disks during the installation process. WordPerfect will ask if you want the installation program to check and modify your AUTOEXEC.BAT and CONFIG.SYS file. If you do not know how to do this yourself, answer Yes. If you want to do it yourself, say No. When installation is complete, type the path into the AUTOEXEC.BAT file and set the files and buffers in the CONFIG.SYS file for at least twenty-five.

Custom

If you use the Custom Installation program, you will have more control over the installation of WordPerfect. You can set the directories for the WordPerfect files and decide which files will be installed. WordPerfect will prompt you with information about what the program files are used for, and ask whether you want to install them. You can let the installation program modify your AUTOEXEC.BAT and CONFIG.SYS files, or you can do it yourself.

Printers

These instructions are for WordPerfect printer drivers only. If you choose to use a Windows printer driver, you must refer to your Windows manual for instructions on printer setup.

During the installation process, you will be asked which printer drivers you want to install. WordPerfect will then install the appropriate files to communicate with your printer(s). You may wish to modify the printer setup once the program has been installed. This will be necessary if you are using an I/O port other than LPT1, or if you are using cartridges or downloadable soft fonts with your printer. To modify your printer setup, you must start WordPerfect (click on the WordPerfect Group icon in the WordPerfect group). See Chapter 1 if you need more information about how to start WordPerfect from Windows.

Once you have started WordPerfect:

1. Click on File in the menu bar.
2. Click on Select Printer to display the Select Printer dialog box.
3. Highlight the printer driver you want to modify, and click on Setup to display the Printer Setup dialog box. The filename and name of the printer have been filled in.
4. Fill in the necessary information.

   a. If you are using downloadable soft fonts, fill in the entire path for the directory in which they have been installed (Example: C:\FONTS).

   b. If you are using a sheet feeder with your printer, click on the Sheet Feeder button and select the one you are using from the list.

   c. Tell WordPerfect which I/O Printer Port you are using. The default is LPT1. If you are using another port, click on the Port button, and make a selection from the list.

   d. If you are using a network printer, select Network Printer. If necessary, fill in the filename of the network printer.

   e. If you are using cartridges or soft fonts, tell WordPerfect which ones you are using and how to handle them. See the next section for more information on using cartridges and soft fonts.

   f. Select a current initial font by clicking on the Initial Font button. A list of all of the available fonts (including printer internal fonts, cartridges fonts, and soft fonts) appears. Select the font you want to be your initial font. This is the one that will be present each time you start WordPerfect.

   g. Click on OK to accept your printer setup. The Printer Setup dialog box closes and you are back in the Select Printer dialog box. Click on Close. Printer Setup is complete.

Cartridges and Soft Fonts

Cartridges

If you want to use cartridges with your printer, click on the Cartridges/Fonts button to open the Cartridges and Fonts dialog box. Highlight Cartridges, and click on Select to display the Select Fonts dialog box. The Quantity box tells you how many cartridges you can use for your printer, and how many selections are available. The list box contains the names of the cartridges available for your printer. Highlight a cartridge (if necessary, use the scroll buttons to view the entire list) and click in the Present When Print Job Begins box. The cartridge is selected and an asterisk appears next to its name on the list. (If you make a mistake, click on the Present When Print Job Begins box to deselect the cartridge.) Click on OK. The Select Fonts dialog box closes and you are returned to the Cartridges and Fonts dialog box. Click on Close. You will return to the Select Printer dialog box, and the status bar will show that the fonts are being updated. Repeat the procedure for every cartridge you want to select.

Soft Fonts

Soft fonts must be installed on your computer before they can be used with your printer. You must also tell WordPerfect where they are installed (see above, step 4a). Once they are installed on the computer, you can configure the WordPerfect printer driver to recognize them. Click on the Cartridges/Fonts button to open the Cartridges and Fonts dialog box. Highlight Soft Fonts and click on Select to open the Fonts Group dialog box. The list box contains the names of the soft font sets available for your printer. (If you are using a soft font package that is not on the list, call WordPerfect to find out about ordering a special Printer disk.) Highlight a soft font set and click on Select to open the Select Fonts dialog box, which contains a list of all of the fonts available in the set.

You must mark each font you want to use, telling WordPerfect whether you want to download the font with each print job or have the font present when printing begins. To do this, highlight the font and press the Plus key (+) if you want the font to download with the job, and the Asterisk key if you want the font present when the job begins. If you choose to have the font present when the job begins, you must **initialize** the printer before you print (see below). The advantage of choosing to have the font present when the job begins is that you do not have to wait for the font to download each time you print. However, you must have enough memory in your printer to hold all of the fonts that you select this way. When you are finished marking the fonts, click on OK. The Fonts Group dialog box closes and you are returned to the Cartridges and Fonts dialog box. Click on Close. You will return to the Select Printer dialog box, and the status bar will show that the fonts are being updated. Repeat the procedure for every soft font set you want to select.

Initializing Printer

If you choose to have soft fonts present when the job begins, you must download them to the printer before you print. This is done by initializing the printer. Once you initialize the printer, the fonts will remain in the printer's memory until you initialize again or turn off the printer. To initialize the printer, first turn the printer on and be sure it is on line. Then select Print from the File menu. In the Print dialog box, select Initialize Printer.

Configuring WordPerfect for Windows

When you install WordPerfect for Windows, system defaults are set up in the program. These defaults are present when you start WordPerfect, and they affect formatting, keyboard layout, the WordPerfect environment, display, and many other features of WordPerfect. You can change these defaults to customize the program to suit your needs by using the Preferences command. You might want to use the program for awhile to see how the default settings work, before you make changes. Any changes you make using Preferences will affect only documents that are started after the change has been made. Old documents will not be affected. Appendix C lists WordPerfect's default settings. To change the system settings:

1. From the document window, click on File in the menu bar.
2. Click on Preferences (Ctrl+Shift+F1) to open the Preferences menu. You can change the following:

Backup

Timed Backup and Original Backup are discussed in Chapter 3. You can change the default settings for these features in the Backup option.

Date Format

You can insert the date and time into your document using the Date and Time feature (see Chapter 4). The default setting inserts the date only in the following format: *month day, year.* You can change this default format in the Date Format option.

Display

This option affects the way your screen looks. You can change the document window, scroll bars, hard return character, units of measure, draft mode colors, and reveal code colors.

Document Summary

You can set document summary defaults that will automatically be in effect in every document summary you set up. For example, you can set up defaults for Subject Search Text, Default Descriptive Type, and Create Summary on Save/Exit. For information on Document Summary, see Chapter 8.

Environment

The Environment Settings dialog box allows you to change settings that affect your system environment. These settings include Auto Code Placement, Confirm Code Deletion, Fast Save, Allow Undo, whether to format retrieved documents for the printer, "beep" settings, menu settings, ruler and hyphenation features.

Equations

You can use this setting to change the way equations—including print, graphic font, keyboard, and alignment options—appear in your document. See Chapter 17 for information about equations.

Initial Codes

This option allows you to set system formatting changes. The following codes can be set as initial codes:

Column Definition	Letter Spacing
Column On	Line Height
Decimal/Align Character	Line Numbering
Endnote Number	Line Spacing
Endnote Options	Margins
Font	New Page Number
Footnote Options	Page Numbering Style
Footnote Number	Paper Size
Graphics Box Number	Suppress Page Format
Graphics Box Options	Tab Set
Hyphenation On/Off	Text Color
Hyphenation Zone	Underline Spaces and Tabs
Justification	Widow/Orphan On/Off
Kerning	Word Spacing
Language	

The codes you insert in the Preferences Initial Codes feature become the default codes for the system.

Keyboard

The Keyboard option allows you to select the keyboard layout you want to use (CUA or WP5.1) It also allows you to reassign or remap WordPerfect features, menus and submenus, and macros, and test to the keys on your keyboard.

Location of Files

When you install WordPerfect, the files are placed in specific directories. WordPerfect looks to the Location of Files option to determine where to look for these files. You can use this feature to change the default directories for backup, document, graphics, printer, spreadsheet, macro, keyboard, button bar, style, thesaurus, speller and hyphenation files.

Merge

This option allows you to specify beginning and ending field and record delimiters for a DOS text or pre-WordPerfect 4.0 file secondary merge file. See Chapter 12 for information about Merge.

Print

This option allows you to set options for your Print dialog box. You can set options for Multiple Copies, Document Settings (Binding Offset and Graphics and Text Quality), Redline Method, Percent of Normal, and Windows Printer Drivers. For information on Print, see Chapters 3 and 16.

Table of Authorities

This option allows you to add or remove dot leaders, underlining, and blank lines in a table of authorities. For information about tables of authorities, see Chapter 14.

Appendix B

Conversion

Files created by programs other than WordPerfect 5.1 cannot be read by WordPerfect for Windows (see "A Few Notes About Converting," later in this chapter, for converting macros from WordPerfect 5.1 to WordPerfect for Windows). Before these files can be used in WordPerfect, they must be converted. WordPerfect for Windows has come up with a very simple conversion process, and has made it equally easy to convert a WordPerfect file to another format.

If you want to convert more than one file at a time, you will have to call WordPerfect Information Services and order a file called CONVERT.EXE. (WordPerfect 5.1 users can use the CONVERT.EXE file that comes with the program; it is completely compatible with WordPerfect for Windows.)

Converting a File to WordPerfect Format

1. Click on File.
2. Click on Open to display the Open File dialog box.
3. Type the path and filename of the file you want to convert.
4. Choose OK.
5. When WordPerfect attempts to open the document, the Convert Format dialog box is displayed.
6. Select the format you are converting from using the drop-down list.
7. Choose OK.
8. Your file will now be in your document window. Files that have been converted into a WordPerfect format do not always look exactly the same; you will not lose any text, but you might lose some of your formatting. Check your files carefully.
9. Click on File.
10. Click on Save As to display the Save As dialog box.
11. Choose WordPerfect 5.1 in the Format List.
12. Choose Save.

Following is a list of formats that can be converted into the WordPerfect for Windows format. This list is current at the time of this writing. If you have a file that is not on this list, check the Convert File Format dialog box list in your copy of WordPerfect to see if it has been added.

ANSI Text (Windows)
Ami Pro versions 1.2, 1.2a, 1.2b
ANSI Delimited Text (Windows)
ANSI Generic Wordprocessing (Windows)
ANSI Text (Windows)
ANSI Text CR/LF to [SRt] (Windows)
ASCII Delimited Text (DOS)
ASCII Text (DOS)
ASCII Text CR/LF to [SRt] (DOS)
DisplayWrite versions 4.0, 4.2, 5.0

IBM DCA/FFT
IBM DCA/RFT
MS Word for Windows versions 1.0, 1.1, 1.1A
MS Word versions 5.0, 5,5
MultiMate versions 3.3, 3.6
MultiMate Advantage II version 3.7
MultiMate 4.0
OfficeWriter versions 6.0, 6.1, 6.11, 6.2
Rich Text Format (RFT)
WordPerfect 4.2, 5.0
XYWrite III Plus versions 3.55, 3.56

Converting WordPerfect Files to Another Format

1. Click on File.
2. Click on Save As.
3. Type the name of the file you want to save in the Save As text box.
4. Use the Format list to select the format you want to use for your file.
5. Choose Save.

The following is a list of formats into which you can convert your files. The list is current at the time of this writing.

Ami Pro versions 1.2, 1.2a, 1.2b
ANSI Delimited Text (Windows)
ANSI Generic Wordprocessing (Windows)
ANSI Text (Windows)
ASCII Text (DOS)
ASCII Delimited Text (DOS)
ASCII Generic Word Processor (DOS)
DisplayWrite versions 4.0, 4.2, 5.0
IBM DCA/FFT
IBM DCA/RFT
MS Word for Windows versions 1.0, 1.1, 1.1a
MS Word versions 5.0, 5,5

MultiMate versions 3.3, 3.7
MultiMate Advantage II version 3.7
MultiMate 4.0
OfficeWriter versions 6.0, 6.1, 6.11, 6.2
Rich Text Format (RTF)
WordPerfect versions 4.2, 5.0
WordStar versions 3.3, 3.31, 3.4, 4.0, 5.0, 5.5, 6.0
XYWrite III Plus versions 3.55, 3.56

A Few Words About Converting

If you want to save a file in DOS, save it to an ASCII text format, which strips all formatting codes but leaves the text intact.

Database records can be saved as ASCII delimited text in the database program and converted into WordPerfect format.

Most spreadsheets can be retrieved into WordPerfect without converting them. If you have a problem retrieving a spreadsheet, try converting it to ASCII delimited text in your spreadsheet application, then convert it into a WordPerfect format.

ANSI text is commonly used in Windows applications (such as the notepad). When you convert a document to ANSI Text, you leave the text but strip out the formatting codes.

If you want to convert a document from Word for Windows, you must save the document in that program with the Fast Save feature turned off.

As mentioned in Chapter 18, WordPerfect for Windows uses a totally different macro language than WordPerfect 5.1. This makes macro conversion from WordPerfect 5.1 to WordPerfect for Windows a very tricky affair indeed. Some commands translate without any problems, but if you have complex macros, many of them will not convert properly. To convert macros, you must use the Macro Facility, a special program that comes with WordPerfect for Windows.

The Macro Facility is not executed from within WordPerfect for Windows. When you install WordPerfect, an icon is added to the WordPerfect program group. Either exit WordPerfect to get back to the Windows Program Manager or use the Task List to switch programs (see Chapter 19). Bring up the WordPerfect program group and double-click on the Macro Facility Group icon.

To convert a macro, choose Convert to open the Convert dialog box. Select the macro you want to convert, and choose Convert.

When you play the macro in WordPerfect for Windows, a Syntax Error dialog box will appear each time a syntax error is encountered. Note the location of the error and choose Continue Compilation. Note all error locations. When you are done, edit the macro and correct all errors.

Appendix C

Initial Settings

T his appendix contains a list of the initial WordPerfect settings.

Feature	Initial Setting
Allow Undo	On
Auto Code Placement	On
Auto Redisplay in Draft Mode	On
Automatic Ruler Display	Off
Backup Options	
Minutes Between Timed Backups	20
Original Document Backup	Off
Timed Document Backup	On
Beep Options	
On Error	Off
On Hyphenation	On
On Search Failure	Off
Button Bar, default file	WP{WP}.WBB
Center Page (top to bottom)	Off
Comments Display	On
Confirm on Code Deletion	Off
Date Format	[Month] [Day #], [Year ####]

Feature	Initial Setting
Decimal Alignment Character	.
Display Columns Side by Side	On
Display Horizontal Scroll Bar	Off
Display Last Open Filenames	On
Display Merge Codes	On
Display Pitch	
Auto	On
Manual	Off
Manual Width	0.1"
Display Sculptured Dialog Boxes	On
Display Shortcut Keys	On
Display Vertical Scroll Bar	On
Document Summary	
Create Summary on Save/Exit	Off
Subject Search Text	RE:
Draft Mode	Off
Equation Options	
Graphical Font Size	Default
Horizontal Alignment	Center
Keyboard	Current WP
Print as Graphics	On
Vertical Alignment	Center
Fast Save	On
Footers	Off
Force Current Page (Odd/Even)	Off
Format Retrieved Documents for Default Printer	On
Graphics, show in document	On
Hard Return Display Character	None
Headers	Off
Hyphenation (feature)	Off
Hyphenation Dictionary	External
Hypenation Zone	
Left	10%
Right	4%
Justification	Full
Kerning	Off
Keyboard layout	CUA Keyboard

Feature	Initial Setting
Language	US
Letter Spacing	WordPerfect Optimal
Line Height	
Auto	**On**
Fixed	**Off**
Fixed Height	**.167"**
Line Height (Leading) Adjustment	
Between Lines [SRt]	0"
Between Paragraphs [HRt]	0"
Line Numbering	Off
Line Spacing	1
Location of Files	Set by Install Program
Margins	
Bottom	1"
Top	1"
Left	1"
Right	1"
Merge Fields Delimiters	
Begin	None
End	,
Record Delimiters	
Begin	None
End	[CR]
Merge Codes Display	Yes
Page Numbering	
Accompanying Text	[^B]
New Page Number	1
Numbering Type	Arabic
Page Number Position	No Page Numbering
Paper Size	8.5" x 11"
Paper Type	Standard
Place Ruler Buttons on Top	Off
Print Options	
Binding Offset	0"
Graphics Quality	Medium
Multiple Copies Generated By	WordPerfect
Number of Copies	1
Text Quality	High

Feature	Initial Setting
Prompt for Hyphenation	
Never	Off
When Required	On
Always	Off
Quick List	Off
Redline Method	Printer Dependent
Ruler Display	Off
Show Ruler Guides	On
Size Attribute Ratios (% of Normal)	
Fine	60%
Small	80%
Large	120%
Very Large	150%
Extra Large	200%
Superscript/Subscript	60%
Suppress	
Header A	Off
Header B	Off
Footer A	Off
Footer B	Off
Page Numbers	Off
Print Page Number at	
Bottom Center	Off
Tab Set	Relative to Left Margin, every 0.5"
Tabs Snap to Ruler Grid	On
Table of Authorities	
Blank Line Between Authorities	On
Dot Leaders	On
Underlining Allowed	Off
Units of Measure	
Display and Entry of Numbers	Inches (")
Status Bar Display	Inches (")
Widow/Orphan Protection	Off
Word Spacing	Optimal
Word Spacing Justification Limits	
Compressed To	60%
Expanded To	400%

—————Appendix D

Codes in Reveal Codes

The following is a list of all of the codes you can insert in your documents and how they appear in Reveal Codes.

Code	Name of Code
[-]	Hyphen
-	Soft Hyphen
[Adv]	Advance
[Bline:Off]	Baseline Placement Off
[Bline:On]	Baseline Placement On
[Block Pro]	Block Protection
[Bold Off]	Bold Off
[Bold On]	Bold On
[Box Num]	Box Number
[Cell]	Table Cell
[Center]	Center
[Center Pg]	Center Page Top to Bottom
[Cndl EOP]	Condition End of Page
[Centr Tab]	Centered Tab

Code	Name of Code
[Col Def]	Column Definition
[Col Off]	End of Text Columns
[Col On]	Beginning of Text Columns
[Color]	Print Color
[Comment]	Document Comment
[Date]	Date/Time Function
[Dbl Indent]	Double Indent
[Dbl Und On]	Double Underline On
[Dbl Und Off]	Double Underline Off
[DDE Link Begin]	DDE Link Begin
[DDE Link End]	DDE Link End
[Dec Tab]	Decimal Aligned Tab
[Decml/Algn Char]	Decimal Character/Thousands Separator
[Def Mark:Index]	Index Definition
[Def Mark:List]	List Definition
[Def Mark:ToA]	Table of Authorities Definition
[Def Mark:ToC]	Table of Contents Definition
[Dorm HRt]	Dormant Hard Return
[DSRt]	Deletable Soft Return
[Embedded]	Embedded Code for Macro
[End C/A]	End of Centering/Alignment
[End Def]	End of Index, List, or Table of Contents
[End Mark]	End of Marked Text
[End Opt]	Endnote Options
[Endnote]	Endnote
[Endnote Placement]	Endnote Placement
[Equ Box]	Equation Box
[Equ Opt]	Equation Box Options
[Ext Large Off]	Extra Large Print Off
[Ext Large On]	Extra Large Print On
[Fig Box]	Figure Box
[Fig Opt]	Figure Box Options
[Fine Off]	Fine Print Off
[Fine On]	Fine Print On
[Flsh Rgt]	Flush Right
[Font]	Base Font

Code	**Name of Code**
[Footer A]	Footer A
[Footer B]	Footer B
[Footnote]	Footnote
[Force]	Force Odd/Even Page
[Ftn Opt]	Footnote Options
[HdCntrTab]	Hard Centered Tab
[HdDecTab]	Hard Decimal Aligned Tab
[HdRgtTab]	Hard Right Aligned Tab
[HdSpc]	Hard Space
[HdTab]	Hard Left-Aligned Tab
[Header A]	Header A
[Header B]	Header B
[HLine]	Horizontal Line
[HPg]	Hard Page Break
[Hrd Row]	Hard Row
[HRt]	Hard Return
[HRt-SPg]	Hard Return-Soft Page
[Hyph Ign Wrd]	Hyphenation Ignore Word
[Hyph Off]	Hyphenation Off
[Hyph On]	Hyphenation On
[HyphSRt]	Hyphenation Soft Return
[HZone]	Hyphenation Zone
[Indent]	Indent
[Index]	Index Entry
[Insert Pg Num]	Insert Page Number
[Italc Off]	Italics Off
[Italc On]	Italics On
[Just Lim]	Word spacing Justification Limits
[Just: Center]	Center Justification
[Just: Full]	Full Justification
[Just: Left]	Left Justification
[Just: Right]	Right Justification
[Kern]	Kerning
[L/R Mar]	Left and Right Margins
[Lang]	Language
[Large Off]	Large Print Off
[Large On]	Large Print On
[Line Height Adj]	Line Height Adjustment

Code	Name of Code
[Link]	Spreadsheet Link
[Link End]	Spreadsheet Link End
[Ln Height]	Line Height
[Ln Num Off]	Line Numbering Off
[Ln Num On]	Lin Numbering On
[Ln Spacing]	Line Spacing
[Mar Rel]	Left Margin Release
[Mark:List]	List Entry
[Mark:ToC]	Table of Contents Entry
[New End Num]	New Endnote Number
[New Equ Num]	New Equation Box Number
[New Fig Num]	New Figure Box Number
[New Ftn Num]	New Footnote Number
[New Tbl Num]	New Table Number
[New Txt Num]	New Text Box Number
[New Usr Num]	New User Box Number
[Note Num]	Note Number
[Open Style]	Open Style
[Outline Lvl Open Style]	Open Outline Style
[Outline Lvl Style Off]	Paired Outline Style Off
[Outline Lvl Style On]	Paired Outline Style On
[Outline Off]	Outline Off
[Outline On]	Outline On
[Outln Off]	Outline Off (Attribute)
[Outln On]	Outline On (Attribute)
[Ovrstk]	Overstrike
[Paper Sz/Typ]	Paper Size and Type
[Par Num]	Paragraph Number
[Par Num Def]	Paragraph Numbering Definition
[Pg Num]	New Page Number
[Pg Num Style]	Page Number Style
[Pg Numbering]	Page Numbering
[Ptr Cmnd]	Printer Command
[Redln Off]	Redline Off
[Redln On]	Redline On
[Ref]	Reference (Cross-Reference)
[Rgt Tab]	Right Tab
[Row]	Table Row

Code	Name of Code
[Select]	Beginning of Selection
[Shadw Off]	Shadow Off
[Shadw On]	Shadow On
[Sm Cap Off]	Small Caps Off
[Sm Cap On]	Small Caps On
[Small Off]	Small Print Off
[Small On]	Small Print On
[SPg]	Soft Page Break
[SRt]	Soft Return
[StkOut Off]	Strikeout Off
[StkOut On]	Strikeout On
[Style Off]	Style Off
[Style On]	Style On
[Subdoc]	Subdocument (Master Documents)
[Subdoc End]	End of Subdocument
[Subdoc Start]	Beginning of Subdocument
[Subscpt Off]	Subscript Off
[Subscpt On]	Subscript On
[Suppress]	Suppress Page Format
[Suprscpt Off]	Superscript Off
[Suprscpt On]	Superscript On
[T/B Mar]	Top and Bottom Margins
[Tab]	Left-Aligned Tab
[Tab Set]	Tab Set
[Target]	Target (Cross Reference)
[TBl Box]	Table Box
[Tbl Def]	Table Definition
[Tbl Off]	Table Off
[Tbl Opt]	Table Box Options
[Text Box]	Text Box
[ToA]	Table of Authorities Entry
[Txt Opt]	Text Box Options
[Und Off]	Underline Off
[Und On]	Underline On
[Undrln]	Underline Spaces/Tabs
[Unknown]	Non-WPWin 1.0 Code
[Usr Box]	User-Defined Box
[Usr Opt]	User-Defined Box Options

Code	Name of Code
[VLine]	Vertical Line
[Vry Large Off]	Very Large Print Off
[Vry Large On]	Very Large Print On
[W/O Off]	Widow/Orphan Protection Off
[W/O On]	Widow/Orphan Protection On
[Wrd/Ltr Spacing]	Word and Letter Spacing

Equation Palette

This appendix lists all of the commands and symbols available in the Equation Editor.

The first column in each list below contains the command or symbol as it is listed on the Palette. Other columns show the complete name of the command or symbol or additional information about its use (this information may also be displayed in the status bar in the Equation Editor when each command or symbol is selected).

In all of the lists except Arrows, there is a column labeled *Keyword*. When a keyword is available, you can type the word or symbol into the Editing pane using the keyboard or insert it using the Equation Palette.

If no keyword is available, you must insert the word or symbol from the Equation Palette. To insert a word or symbol from the Equation Palette into the Editing pane, choose a group from the Palette pop-up list, select the item you want on the palette, then choose Keyword or Symbol or else double-click the item to insert it into your equation text.

For items in the palette that contain both a symbol and a corresponding keyword (such as, ∫ and INT), choosing Keyword puts the keyword (INT) in your equation in the Editing pane. If you prefer to have the symbol (∫), choose Symbol. Choosing Keyword or Symbol only affects what is inserted in the Editing pane. In both cases, when you choose Redisplay, or when you print the equation, the appropriate symbol appears. If there is only a keyword or a symbol (not both) one of the buttons (Keyword or Symbol) will be dimmed.

WordPerfect Characters

Many of the symbols available on the Equation Palette are in the WordPerfect character sets. You can insert any of these symbols directly into the Editing pane using the WordPerfect Characters dialog box. To do so, choose WP Characters from the Equation Editor Edit menu, or press WordPerfect Characters (Ctrl+W).

Arrows

The Arrows menu contains a variety of arrows and several hollow and solid figures such as triangles, squares, and circles. There are no keywords for this group, but each symbol can be inserted from the Equation Palette or using the WordPerfect Characters dialog box (see *WordPerfect Characters* above).

Symbol	Description
←	Left Arrow
→	Right Arrow
↑	Up Arrow
↓	Down Arrow
↔	Left & Right Arrow
↕	Up & Down Arrow
⇇	Two Left Arrows
⇉	Two Right Arrows
⇆	Left & Right Arrows
⇄	Right & Left Arrows
⇐	Double Left Arrow
⇒	Double Right Arrow
⇑	Double Up Arrow
⇓	Double Down Arrow
⇔	Double Left & Right Arrow
⇕	Double Up & Down Arrow
↗	North East Arrow
↘	South East Arrow
↙	South West Arrow
↖	North West Arrow
↝	Curly Right Arrow
↼	Left Harpoon Up
↽	Left Harpoon Down
⇀	Right Harpoon Up
⇁	Right Harpoon Down
⇋	Left & Right Harpoons
⇌	Right & Left Harpoons
↿	Up Harpoon Left
↾	Up Harpoon Right
⇃	Down Harpoon Left
⇂	Down Harpoon Right
↩	Hook Left Arrow
↪	Hook Right Arrow
↦	Maps To

Symbol	Description
◁	Triangle Left
▷	Triangle Right
△	Triangle Up
▽	Triangle Down
◄	Small Triangle Left
►	Small Triangle Right
△	Big Triangle Up
▽	Big Triangle Down
◀	Solid Triangle Left
▶	Solid Triangle Right
▲	Solid Triangle Up
▼	Solid Triangle Down
≙	Defined As
≙	Corresponds To
⋈	Bow Tie
★	Solid Star
★	Big Solid Star
◇	Diamond
◆	Solid Diamond
◊	Hollow Diamond
○	Big Circle
○	Circle
○	Small Circle
•	Small Solid Circle
□	Square
■	Solid Square

Commands

The following are keywords that the Equation Editor recognizes as commands. Most require a specific syntax when using the command. All have some formatting function, such as drawing a line or arranging variables in the equation. All commands can be typed from the keyboard and can be in either uppercase or lowercase.

Keyword	Function	Syntax
OVER	Fraction	x OVER y
SUP or ^	Superscript	x SUP y or x^y
SUB or _	Subscript	x SUB y or x_y
SQRT	Square root	SQRT x
NROOT	Nth root	NROOT n x
FROM	Limits	x FROM y TO z
TO	Limits	x FROM y TO z
LEFT	Left delimiter	LEFT x
RIGHT	Right delimiter	RIGHT x

Keyword	Function	Syntax
STACK	Vertical stack	STACK {x#y}
STACKALIGN	Vertical stack with character alignment	STACKALIGN {x&y # a&b}
MATRIX	Matrix	MATRIX {x&y # a&b}
FUNC	User function	FUNC name
UNDERLINE	Underline	UNDERLINE x
OVERLINE	Overline	OVERLINE x
{	Start group	{x+2}
}	End group	{x+2}
HORZ	Horizontal move	HORZ n
VERT	Vertical move	VERT n
~	Normal space	x~y
`	Thin space (¼ normal space)	x`y
BINOM	Binomial	BINOM x y
&	Column separator	x & y
#	Row separator	x # y
MATFORM	Matrix column format	MATFORM {ALIGN*x* & ALIGN*x* &...& ALIGN*x*}
ALIGNL	Align left	ALIGNL x
ALIGNR	Align right	ALIGNR x
ALIGNC	Align center	ALIGNC x
PHANTOM	Place holder	PHANTOM x
.	No delimiter	LEFT .
\	Literal	\ x
BOLD	Bold attribute	BOLD x
ITAL	Italic attribute	ITAL x
OVERSM	Fraction small	x OVERSM y
BINOMSM	Binomial small	BINOMSM x y
LINESPACE	Vertical Spacing	LINESPACE n
LONGDIV	Long Division	LONGDIV x
LONGDIVS	Long Division (squared)	LONGDIVS x
SCALESYM	Scale symbol	SCALESYM n x

Functions

The following commands are recognized as mathematical functions by the Equation Editor. These function names will be formatted in the current font (non-italic). All functions can be typed from the keyboard and retain the case in which they are typed.

Keyword	Description
cos	Cosine
sin	Sine
tan	Tangent
arccos	Arc Cosine
arcsin	Arc Sine
arctan	Arc Tangent
cosh	Hyperbolic Cosine
sinh	Hyperbolic Sine
tanh	Hyperbolic Tangent
cot	Cotangent
coth	Hyperbolic Cotangent
sec	Secant
cosec	Cosecant
exp	Exponent
log	Logarithm
ln	Natural Logarithm
lim	Limit
liminf	Limit Inferior
limsup	Limit Superior
min	Minimum
max	Maximum
gcd	Greatest Common Denominator
arc	Arc Function
det	Determinant
mod	Modulo

Greek

The following Greek characters and variants are supported with keyword commands. Greek character keywords are case sensitive; if any letter in the keyword is uppercase, the Greek character is printed in uppercase; otherwise, it is printed in lowercase. All the Greek characters available in the WordPerfect character set are also available using the WordPerfect Characters dialog box (see *WordPerfect Characters* above).

Symbol	Keyword
α	alpha
β	beta
γ	gamma
δ	delta
ε	epsilon
ε	varepsilon—epsilon (variant)
ζ	zeta
η	eta
θ	theta

Symbol	Description
ϑ	vartheta—theta (variant)
ι	iota
κ	kappa
λ	lambda
μ	mu
ν	nu
ξ	xi
o	omicron
π	pi
ϖ	varpi—pi (variant)
ρ	rho
ϱ	varrho—rho (variant)
σ	sigma
ς	varsigma—sigma (variant)
τ	tau
υ	upsilon
φ	phi
φ	varphi—phi (variant)
χ	chi
ψ	psi
ω	omega
A	ALPHA
B	BETA
Γ	GAMMA
Δ	DELTA
E	EPSILON
Z	ZETA
H	ETA
Θ	THETA
I	IOTA
K	KAPPA
Λ	LAMBDA
M	MU
N	NU
Ξ	XI
O	OMICRON
Π	PI
P	RHO
Σ	SIGMA
T	TAU
Υ	UPSILON
Φ	PHI
X	CHI
Ψ	PSI
Ω	OMEGA

Large

The following commands insert an operator that takes on one of two sizes—small or large. When you use commands from the Large group, delimiters used with the LEFT and RIGHT commands (such as parentheses, brackets, and so forth) are sized accordingly. The Large commands can be typed from the keyboard as either keywords or symbols, or inserted using the WordPerfect Characters dialog box (see *WordPerfect Characters* above). Keywords for large symbols are not case sensitive.

Symbol	Keyword	Description
$\sum$	SUM	Summation
	SMALLSUM	Small Sum
$\int$	INT	Integral
	SMALLINT	Small Integral
	OINT	Contour Integral
	SMALLOINT	Small Contour Integral
$\prod$	PROD	Product
	SMALLPROD	Small Product
	COPROD	Coproduct
	SMALLCOPROD	Small Coproduct
$\cap$	CAP	Intersection
	BIGCAP	Big Intersection
$\cup$	CUP	Union
	BIGCUP	Big Union
	UPLUS	Multiset Union (U Plus)
	BIGUPLUS	Big U Plus
	SQCAP	Square Intersection
	BIGSQCAP	Big Square Intersection
	SQCUP	Square Union
	BIGSQCUP	Big Square Union
$\vee$	OR	Logical Or
	BIGVEE	Big Vee
$\wedge$	AND	Logical And
	BIGWEDGE	Big Wedge
$\oplus$	OPLUS	Circle Plus
	BIGOPLUS	Big Circle Plus
$\ominus$	OMINUS	Circle Minus
	BIGOMINUS	Big Circle Minus
$\otimes$	OTIMES	Circle Multiply
	BIGOTIMES	Big Circle Multiply
$\oslash$	ODIV	Circle Divide
	BIGODIV	Big Circle Divide
$\odot$	ODOT	Circle Dot
	BIGODOT	Big Circle Dot
(	(	Left Parenthesis
)	)	Right Parenthesis
[	[	Left Bracket
]	]	Right Bracket
[	LDBRACK	Left Double Bracket

Symbol	Keyword	Description
⟧	RDBRACK	Right Double Bracket
{	LBRACE	Left Brace
}	RBRACE	Right Brace
⌊	LFLOOR	Left Floor
⌋	RFLOOR	Right Floor
⌈	LCEIL	Left Ceiling
⌉	RCEIL	Right Ceiling
⟨	LANGLE	Left Angle
⟩	RANGLE	Right Angle
|	LINE	Vertical Line
‖	DLINE	Double Vertical Line

Other

The Other group contains diacritical marks and different orientations of ellipses. Each item has a keyword and the keywords are not case sensitive.

Symbol	Keyword	Description
$\vec{x}$	VEC	Vector Above: x VEC
$\bar{x}$	BAR	Bar (Overline): x BAR
$\hat{x}$	HAT	Hat Above: x HAT
$\check{x}$	CHECK	Check Above: x CHECK
$\acute{x}$	ACUTE	Acute Accent: x ACUTE
$\grave{x}$	GRAVE	Grave Accent: x GRAVE
$\breve{x}$	BREVE	Breve Accent: x BREVE
$\dot{x}$	DOT	Dot Above: x DOT
$\ddot{x}$	DDOT	Double Dot Above: x DDOT
$\dddot{x}$	DDDOT	Triple Dot Above: x DDDOT
$\mathring{x}$	CIRCLE	Circle Above: x CIRCLE
$\tilde{x}$	TILDE	Tilde Above: x TILDE
$\ddot{x}$	DYAD	Dyad Above: x DYAD
⋯	DOTSAXIS	Ellipsis (centered)
...	DOTSLOW	Ellipsis (on baseline)
⋮	DOTSVERT	Ellipsis (vertical)
⋱	DOTSDIAG	Ellipsis (diagonal)

Sets

This menu contains set symbols, relational operators, and some commonly-used Fraktur and hollow letters. There are keywords for some of the set symbols. These commands are not case sensitive. All symbols are available using the WordPerfect Characters dialog box (see *WordPerfect Characters* above).

Symbol	Keyword	Description
\\	SETMINUS	Set Minus (Figure Backslash)
⊂	SUBSET	Proper Subset
⊃	SUPSET	Proper Superset
⊆		Reflex Subset (Contained In)
⊇		Reflex Superset (Contains)

Symbol	Keyword	Description
⊊		Subset But Not Equal
⊋		Superset But Not Equal
⊏	SQSUBSET	Square Proper Subset
⊐	SQSUPSET	Square Proper Superset
⊑		Square Reflex Subset
⊒		Square Reflex Superset
⊊		Square Subset, Not Equal
⊋		Square Superset, Not Equal
∈	IN	Member (Element)
∉	NOTIN	Not a Member
∋	OWNS	Owns (Contains As A Member)
∅	EMPTYSET	Empty Set
⋓		Double Union
⋒		Double Intersection
⋐		Double Subset
⋑		Double Superset
⊄		Not Subset
⊅		Not Superset
⊈		Not Reflex Subset
⊉		Not Reflex Superset
⋢		Square Not Subset
⋣		Square Not Superset
⋢		Square Not Reflex Subset
⋣		Square Not Reflex Superset
≮		Not Less Than
≰		Not Less Than or Equal
≯		Not Greater Than
≱		Not Greater Than or Equal
≁		Not Similar
≄		Not Similar or Equal
≇		Not Congruent
≉		Not Approximately Equal
⊀		Does Not Precede
⋠		Neither Precedes nor Equals
⊁		Does Not Follow
⋡		Neither Follows nor Equals
∦		Not Parallel
∤		Does Not Divide
∄		There Never Exists
ℜ	REAL	Real (R Fraktur)
ℑ	IMAG	Imaginary (I Fraktur)
ℭ		C Fraktur
ℨ		Z Fraktur
℘		Weierstrass
℘		Capital Weierstrass
ℏ		Planck's Constant
ℒ		Laplace Transform (Script L)

Symbol	Keyword	Description
𝓔		Script E
𝓕		Fourier Transform (Script F)
C		Complex Number (Hollow C)
I		Integer (Hollow I)
N		Natural Number (Hollow N)
R		Real Number (Hollow R)
℧	MHO	Mho
Å	ANGSTROM	Angstrom

Symbols

Miscellaneous symbols are listed below. Keywords exist for each symbol. The keywords are not case sensitive. You can also use the WordPerfect Characters dialog box to insert the symbol into your equation (see *WordPerfect Characters* above).

Symbol	Keyword	Description
'	'	Prime
"	"	Double Prime
‴	‴	Triple Prime
∞	INF (INFINITY)	Infinity
∂	PARTIAL	Partial Derivative
∇	GRAD	Nabla (Gradient)
×	TIMES	Multiplication Sign (x)
÷	DIV	Division Sign
±	+- (PLUSMINUS)	Plus Or Minus
∓	-+ (MINUSPLUS)	Minus Or Plus
•	CDOT	Center Dot
⊻	XOR	Logical Exclusive Or
≤	<=	Less Than Or Equal
≥	>=	Greater Than Or Equal
≪	<<	Much Less Than
≫	>>	Much Greater Than
⋘	LLL	Much Much Less
⋙	GGG	Much Much Greater
≠	!=	Not Equal
¬	NOT	Logical Not
≺	PREC	Precedes
≻	SUCC	Succeeds (Follows)
≼	PRECEQ	Precedes Or Equals
≽	SUCCEQ	Succeeds (Follows) Or Equals
≡	==	Equivalent
≢	NEQUIV	Not Equivalent
∼	SIM	Similar
≃	SIMEQ	Similar Or Equal
≈	APPROX	Approximately Equal
≅	CONG	Congruent
∝	PROPTO	Proportional To

Symbol	Keyword	Description
≐	DOTEQ	Equal by Definition
∥	PARALLEL	Parallel
⊥	PERP	Perpendicular To
∀	FORALL	For All
∃	EXISTS	There Exists
∴	THEREFORE	Therefore
∵	BECAUSE	Because
::	IDENTICAL	Identical
∔	DSUM	Direct Sum (Dot Plus)
≟	QEQUAL	Questioned Equality
≒	IMAGE	Image (Falling Dots Equals)
≓	RIMAGE	Reverse Image
≎	ISO	Isomorphic
≇	NISO	Not Isomorphic
≍	ASYMEQ	Asymptotically Equivalent
≭	NASYMEQ	Not Asymptotically Equivalent
⌣	SMILE	Smile
⌢	FROWN	Frown
∮	BETWEEN	Between (Quantic)
≀	WREATH	Wreath Product
⊤	TOP	Top
⊢	ASSERT	Assertion
⊣	MASSERT	Mirrored Assertion
⊨	MODELS	Models

Selection Keystrokes

The table below lists the keystrokes you can use to make table selections. Before you can use these keystrokes, you must place the insertion point inside the table and activate cell select mode by pressing Shift+F8 (which selects the current cell). The keystrokes let you extend the selection to include another cell, row, column, or even text outside of the table.

Table Select Keystroke(s)	Result
Shift+F8	Selects cell and turns on cell select mode.
Shift+Arrow (↓↑→←)	Extends selection one cell, row, or column at a time. Can extend selection outside of table.
Shift+Alt+Arrow (↓↑→←)	Same as Shift+Arrow except selection does not extend outside of the table.
Shift+Home	Extends selection to beginning of current row.
Shift+End	Extends selection to the end of current row.
Shift+Ctrl+Home	Extends selection outside of table to beginning of document.
Shift+Ctrl+End	Extends selection outside of table to end of document.
Ctrl+Left or Right Arrow (← →)	Extends selection to include the current row.
Ctrl+Up or Down Arrow (↑ ↓)	Extends the selection to include the column

Some keystrokes extend selections outside of the table. When this happens, the selection's highlighting changes. Normally, the selection highlighting fills the entire cell. But when the selection extends outside of the cell, the selection only highlights the text in the cell.

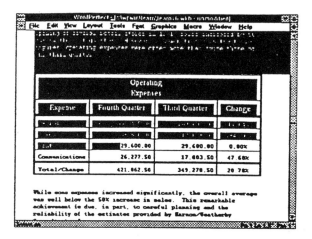

This type of selection includes the Table definition code [Tbl Def], meaning that if you were to press Delete or choose Cut from the Edit menu, your table would be deleted.

Shaded Check Boxes and Unknown Settings

When you select one or several columns or cells that contain various appearance, size, attribute, justification, or alignment settings, WordPerfect shades check boxes in the Format Cell or Format Column dialog boxes. It also uses "Unknown" for the Justification and Alignment setting in these dialog boxes. This is to remind you that the settings throughout the selection are not consistent.

To turn on options with shaded check boxes, you must click them so that an "x" appears in their check boxes. Clicking a check box until it's neither shaded nor checked turns off the option in all selected cells.

Index

Symbols

{END FIELD} code
274-277, 286
{END RECORD} code
274-277
{PAGE OFF} code   286-287
{PRINT} code   286-287

A

Absolute Tab Settings   153
    Help Window   153
Abstract text box   412
Accompanying Text text
    box   125
Active style   342
Active window   140
Add
    and Speller   163
    Markings   336
        Dialog box   336
    Paper Size dialog box
        356-358
    Quick List Item dialog box
        193-194
Advance   364-366
    Dialog box   365
    Text box   365
Alignment code   89, 90
Allow Undo   438, 447
Anchor to   385
Annotate   154
Append
    to Clipboard   179, 191
    to File   142

Applications
    Dialog box   196
    Feature   195-196
    Menu   196
    Switching between
        423-426
Arabic numerals   124, 203
Arrow buttons   407
Ascending   306, 308, 313, 314
Assign
    Applications to menu   195
    Fonts to ruler   372
    Macros
        to button   407-408
        to Button dialog box   408
        to menu   417-418
            Dialog box   417
    Numbers
        to graphics boxes   382
        to lists   324
    Short form, for Table of
        Authorities   328
Attach Previous Level   203
Auto Code Placement   76, 77,
    79, 93, 103, 104, 116,
    122, 128, 375

B

Backup   438
    Original   58
    Timed   59
Base font   452
Baseline   374-375, 387,
    397, 451
Beep options   447

Begin link code   264, 266
Bin, printer   359-360
Bin text box   359
BK! extension   58
BK# extension   59-60
Blank field   288-295
Block Protect   132
    Code on   132, 255
    Parallel with, columns
        225-226
    Preventing page breaks in
        tables   255
Boilerplate document
    301-303
Boilerplating   57, 301-303
Bold   94
    Codes, deleting   94
Bookmark
    and Help   155-156
    Define dialog box   155
    Name text box   155
Border spacing, and graphics
    boxes   382
Border style, and graphics
    boxes   381
Bottom margins   127-129
Box
    Number, and graphics
        boxes   389-390
    Position   384, 385-387,
        388-389
        Size dialog box   384
    Type, and graphics
        boxes   384

Browse, and Help 153
Bullets, and outlining 202
Button Bar
    Assign Macro to 407
    Category markers 409-410
    Create 404-405
    Default 402-403
    Edit 406-407
    Hide 404
    Options 408-409
        Dialog box 409
    Save 405, 408
    Select 405-406
    Setup 404

C

Calculate 250
Cancel 21
Cannot Print dialog box 353
Caption numbering 382-383
Caption style 382-383
Caption Editor 389
Caption position 383
Caption, and graphics boxes
    382-383
Cartridges, font 368, 436
Cascade 141
Cascading menu, defined 18
Category markers, and button
    bars 409-410
Cell (see also Tables)
    Addresses 243
Center
    At specific location on line
        87-88
    Between left and right
        margin 87
    Code 88
    Ending centering 88-89
    Existing text 89
    Justification 92
    Lines 89
    Multiple lines of text 89
    Page 128-129
        Code 129
    Tabs 80
    Text with leader dots 88
Certificate of License
    Registration 15
Change Default
    Directory 197,
    439-440
Change Dictionary 172
Character Set dialog box 367

Characters text box 209
Check box, defined 20
Checkmark, defined 18
Clear All Tabs 82
Clear tabs 82
Clipboard 188, 190-191
Close document 17, 55-56
Codes
    Dialog box 144
    Reveal Codes and 44-46,
        451-456
    Searching for 144-145
Column(s) 216-228
    Changing the number
        of 225
    Copy text between 219
    Margin markers 228
    Converting into tables
        258-259
    Cut and paste text
        between 219
    Define, dialog box 218
    Dialog box 240
    Distance between 218,
        222, 225
    Drop down list 226-227
    Entering text in 219
    Groups 220
    Moving insertion
        point 220
    Newspaper 216-220
        Adjusting width using the
            ruler 227-228
        Creating 218
        Defining using the
            ruler 226
        Turning on and off using
            the ruler 227
    Numeric 232-233
    Parallel 220-225
        Adjusting width
            223-224
        Copying, deleting, or
            moving groups 225
        Creating 221-224
        Redefining 225
        with Block Protect
            225-226
    Ruler and 226-228
    Tables within 238,
        260-261
    Turning on and off
        218, 220

    Width text box 247
    (see also, Tables)
Command buttons,
    defined 21
Command Line text box 196
Comments 147-149
    Creating 148
    Converting to text 149
    Converting text into
        148-149
    Display 147-148
    Editing 149
Concordance file 321
Condense Master 339
    Dialog box 339
Conditional end of page
    130-131
    Dialog box 131
Configuring WordPerfect for
    Windows 437-440
Control Printer dialog
    box 352-354
Conversion
    Files 441-443, 443-445
    Macros 416-417, 444-445
Convert comments to
    text 149
Convert Format dialog
    box 442
Convert Case 97
Converting text to comments
    148-149
Copy File(s) dialog box
    184-185
Copy
    All (files) 185
    Between documents 142
    Calculations between
        cells 249
    Column groups 225
    Data between cells 238
    File 183-184, 188
    Footnotes 211-212
    Multiple files 184-185
    Paper size definition 359
    Rectangle 140
    Selected text 17, 139-140
    Tabular column 233
    to clipboard 139-140
CPU (Central Processing
    Unit) 7
Create
    Comment 148
    DDE Link dialog box 269

Directory   180
    Dialog box   180
    Line dialog box   397
    Link   265
    Spreadsheet Link dialog
        box   265
    Summary   195, 438, 448
    Table   237-238
        Dialog box   237
Cross-Referencing
    Generating   334-335
    Marking
        Reference only   332-333
        Reference and
            target   334
        Target only   333
        Text for   332
    Multiple targets   334
CUA Keyboard
    (see keyboards, CUA)
Current copy, and Print dialog
        box   66-67
Current outline style   202-203
Current Page option   67
Current Print Job dialog
        box   66
Custom installation   464
Cut
    Between documents   142
    Rectangle   140
    Selected text   138-139
    Tabular column   233
    Text   17, 138-139
        In columns   233

D

Date
    Code   98-99
    Format   99-100, 438
        Default   99
        Preview   100
    Text code   98
DDE link   269-270
    Begin   452
    End   452
Decimal align character
        234-235
    Text box   234
Decimal align tabs   81,
        232-235
Decimal tab shortcut key
        84, 234
Default date format   98
Default button bar   402-403

Define
    Columns dialog box   218
    Date/Time format   100
    In Help   155
    Index dialog box   323
    List dialog box   325
    Paragraph Numbering dialog
        box   202
    Table of Authorities dialog
        box   330-331
    Table of Contents dialog
        box   327
Delete
    2nd option, and Speller   166
    All   183
    Characters   34-35
    Codes   46
    Column groups   225
    Columns/Rows dialog
        box   247
    Files   182-183
    File(s) dialog box   182
    Footnotes   211
    Outline family   410
    Paragraphs   39-40
    Selected text   37-42
    Sentences   38-39
    Style dialog box   348
    to end of line   40
    Words   37-38
Description text box   344, 345
Descriptive Name text box
        196, 412
Dictionary dialog box   164
Dictionary   164
Dimmed
    Buttons   403
    Menu items   17
Direction pop-up list   143-145
Directory/Filename text
        box   62, 64
Directory Names   176,
        180-181
Disable Cell Locks   256-254
Disable Checking, and
        Speller   166
Discontinue
    Code   120
    Header or Footer   120
    Page Numbering   126
Disk Operating System
        (see DOS)
Disk window   195
Display pitch   150-151, 448

Document
    Comments
        (see Comments)
    Compare   335-336, 372
        Removing markings   336
    Copying   183-184, 188
    Close   17, 55-56
    Creating   29, 65
    Date/Time Format dialog
        box   100
    Initial codes   150
    Initial Settings   149
    Naming   51
    On Disk option   68-69
    Open   61-62
    Printing   65-69
    Redline dialog box
        335-336
    Retrieve   63-64
    Saving   50, 52-55
    Scrolling through   15, 22,
        33-34, 134
    Summary   195, 438, 448
        Dialog box   195
DOS (Disk Operating
        System)   6, 11-12
Dot leaders   (see Leader dots)
Double indent   86
Double sided printing   357
Double underline   96
Downloadable soft fonts
        368-369, 436-437
Draft mode   147
Drop-down list boxes,
        defined   21
Duplicate words, and
        Speller   166

E

Edit
    All, and graphics
        boxes   369
    Button bar dialog box   404
    Comment 149
        Dialog box   149
    Dialog box   172, 190-191
    Footnote dialog box
        210-211
    Full form, and Table of
        Authorities   329-330
    Headers and footers
        119-120
    Horizontal   398
    Line dialog box   397-398

Link   265-266
Paper Size dialog box   358
Quick list   194
   Dialog box   194
   Short form, and Table of
      Authorities   329-330
   Spreadsheet   Link   dialog
      box   266
   Vertical   398
Ellipses   18, 19
End link code   264, 266
End Centering/Alignment
   88-89
Endnotes   (see Footnotes and
   Endnotes)
Enlarge Area   392
Enter Field text box   291
Enter Key Inserts option
   344-347
Environment   438
   Settings dialog box   438
Equation(s)   439
   Boxes   394-396
   Editor window   394-396
   Palette   457
Evenly spaced tabs   83
Exit
   Document   56
   Using Exit to Save and
      Exit   56
   WordPerfect   25, 47
Expand Master   338
Extra large   404, 450, 452

F

Facing Pages   364
Figure boxes (see graphics
   boxes)
Figure Editor   390-392
Figures, graphics
   (see graphics boxes)
Figure Options dialog
   box   381
File Manager   176-198
   Access clipboard from
      190-191
   Appending to the clipboard
      from   191
   Applications menu   196
   and directories   177-178,
      180-182, 193-194, 197
   Copying files in   186-185
   Copy File(s) dialog
      box   185

Copying text to clipboard
   from   190-191
Deleting files in   182-183
Document Summary   195
Environment dialog
   box   197
File viewer   177-179, 190,
   194-195
Find File feature
   (see search features)
Find Words text box   192
Info windows   195
Moving files in   185-187
Move/Rename File(s) dialog
   box   187, 188
Navigator   177-179
Opening or retrieving
   documents from floppy
   disks   198
Passwords in   198-199
Printing in   188-189
Quick list   193-194
Renaming files in   185-187
Running another application
   in   189-190, 195-196
Run dialog box   190
Saving in   198
Search features   191-193
Set preferences in   196-197
Filename(s)
   Extensions   51
   Text box   62, 64
File(s)
   Backup   58, 59, 438
   Conversion   441-445
   Copying   183-184
   Creating   29, 65
   Cutting   142
   Deleting   182-183
   Finding   63
   List box   54
   List dialog box   181, 189
   Menu   53
   Naming   51, 185-187
   Pattern text box   193
   Renaming   51
   Retrieving   63-64
   Saving   50, 52-55
   Searching for   191-193
   Text box   189
   to Compare text box   336
   to Copy text box   184
   to Delete text box   182

to Move/Rename text
   box   86
Viewer   178-179
Viewing   62-63
Find
   and File Manager   191-193
   Files   193
      Dialog box   193
   Words, and File Manager
      191-192
      Dialog box   192
Fine Print   452
First Baseline at Top of Margin
   374-375
Fixed text box   376
Floppy drive   9
Floppy Disk   7, 9-10, 50
Flush Right   89-90
Font(s)
   Attributes   370-372
   Button bar   404-407
   Dialog box   369
   Downloadable soft fonts
      368-369, 436-437
   Fixed   33
   List box   369
   On print cartridges
      368, 436
   Proportional   33
   Ruler   372
   Scalable   369
   Selecting   369, 372
   Using with Line Draw   398
Footers (see Headers and
   Footers)
Footnote(s) and Endnote(s)
   Copying or moving
      211-212
   Creating   210
   Deleting   211
   Edit   210-211
      Dialog box   211
   Endnotes (differences from
      Footnotes)   212
   Number text box   210-211
   Options
      Code   208
      Dialog box   208-209
      Setting   208-209
   Window   211
Force
   Current page   125
   Odd/even page   125

Format
    Cell dialog box   240
    Column dialog box
        239, 247
    Column justification   259
    Row dialog box   241
Formula text box   248
Full form, Table of Authorities
        329-330
    Editing window   329-330
Full Document Option
        button   67
Full justification   92
Full Page, and Print
        Preview   362

G

Generate
    Indexes   324
    Marked text   324-325
    Table of Authorities   331
    Table of Contents   327
Global
    Select   316
    Sort   315-316
Glossary, and Help   157
Go To   134-135
    Dialog box   134-135
Graphics boxes
    Anchoring   385
    Assigning new
        number   389-390
    Border
        Spacing   382
        Style   381
    Caption
        Editing   389
        Numbering   382-383
        Position   383
    Changing options
        380-383, 396
    Creating   390-392
    Editing   396
    Editing a graphics
        image   392
    Gray shading   382
    Invert   392
    Minimum offset from
        paragraph   382
    Mirror Image   392
    Moving   388
    Numbering   389-390
    Positioning   384, 385-387,
        388-389

Rotating graphics
    image   392
Rotating text   393
Scaling graphics
    image   387, 392
Shading   382
Sizing   384, 387, 388-389
Type   387
Wrapping text around
    385, 389
Graphics
    Button bar   390-392
    Formats   392-393
    Line Draw   398-399
    Lines   397-399
        Editing   397-398
Gray shading, graphics boxes
    and lines   382

H

Hanging indent   86
Hard drive   7-8, 50
Hard decimal align   84
Hard page break   130, 219
Hard return   45, 76, 306, 374
Hard row   453
Hard space   453
Hard tab codes (see Tabs, Hard)
Hardware   6-11
Header Rows text box   254
Headers and footers
    Codes   116-117, 119,
        120, 121
    Creating   117-118
    Discontinuing   120
    Editing   119-120
    Odd and even pages   119
    Suppressing   120-122
Heading text box   321-322
Help
    About WordPerfect   157
    Annotation dialog box   154
    Back   153
    Bookmark   155-156
        Define dialog box   155
    Browse   153
    Command buttons
        152-154
    Edit   154-155
    File   154
    Glossary   157
    Help   156
    How Do I   156
    Index   152

Keyboard   156
Menu   151
Paper clip   154-155
Search   153
Using   157
What Is   157
Hide ruler   111
History dialog box   172
Horizontal position   385,
        388-389
    Text box   385
How Do I, Help   156
Hyphenation   101-104
    Zone   103-104

I

Icon   12-15
Import Spreadsheet dialog
    box   262
Importing spreadsheets
        261-265
    Linking   264-270
Include Subdocument dialog
    box   338
Indent
    Keys   85-87
    Left   85-86
    Double   86
    Hanging   86
Index
    Creating   320-323
    Defining   322-323
    Entry   320-322
    Generating   324
    Marking   322
Info windows   195
Initial
    Codes   150, 439
    Settings   149, 447-450
    Font   150, 435
Initialize printer   437
Input   257
Insert
    Columns/Rows dialog
        box   245, 247
    Date code   98-99
    Date text   98-100
    Hyphen   102-103
    Macro Menu Item dialog
        box   418
    Merge Codes dialog
        box   278
    Mode   35-36
    Page numbering   124-125

Soft hyphens   102-103
Special codes   83-84,
     234-35
   Dialog box   83-84, 234
Installing WordPerfect   13,
     431-437
Invert, and graphics boxes   392
Irregular capitalization, and
     Speller   166
Italic   95

J

Join Cells   251
Justification   90-91, 110
   Cascading menu   92
   Center   92
   Code   92-93
   Full   92
   Left   91
      Using with Line
         Draw   398
   Right   91
   Setting   92-93
Kerning   374
Key definitions   307-308
Keyboard(s)   439
   CUA   24-25, 33-34,
      156, 439
   Enhanced   10, 134, 439
   Help window   156
   Merge   256-258, 298-300
      In tables   256-258
   Numeric keypad   134
   Standard   10
   WP5.1   24-25, 156
Keyword   395

L

Landscape
   Orientation   354-355
   Paper size   355-358
Last Level in Wrapped
   Format   327
Last position   135
Leader dots
   Centering text   88
   Tabs   81, 235-236
Leave Redline Marks   336, 372
Left align tabs   80
Left indent   85-86
Left justification   91
Left margin
   Columns   218, 222-224
   Set   74-76

Legal paper size   356
Length text box   397
Letterspacing   374
Level Style box   202-203
Line
   Deleting to the end of   40
   Draw   398-399
      Character dialog box
         398-399
      Dialog box   398
   Flush right   89-90
   Graphics   397-399
   Height
      Adjustment   374,
         375-376
      Dialog box   376
   Numbering   360-362
      Dialog box   361
   Sort   306-309
      Fields, definition   307
   Spacing   77-78, 109-110
      Dialog box   77
   Status   15, 32
Link
   Deleting   266
   DDE   269-270
   Edit   265
   Importing   265
   Manually updating
      266-267
   Options   267
      Dialog box   267
   Spreadsheet   264-270
      Three-dimensional   268
List boxes, defined   21
Lists
   Creating 324-325
   Defining   324-325
   Generating   325
   Marking text for   324
Ln #   32-33
Lowercase, convert text to   97
Lowercase roman numerals
   124, 203

M

Macro(s)   411-419
   Assign to button   407-408
   Assign to Menu   417-419
   Converting from
      WordPerfect 5.1   416-417
   Deleting from menu   419
   Differences from
      WordPerfect 5.1   411

Editing   415, 418-419
Facility   416-417
   Group icon   416
Name text box   418
Programming and command
   language   416
Playing   414-415
Recording   412-414
Using mouse with   414
Main, and Dictionary   164
Margin(s)
   Bottom   127-129
   Centering text between top
      and bottom   128-129
   Dialog box   75, 128
   Codes   76
   Left   74-76, 107
   Markers   106-107
   Release key   79, 84-85
   Right   74-76, 107
   top   127-129
Mark
   Cross-Reference dialog
      box   333
   Index dialog box   322
   Table of Contents dialog
      box   326
   Text
      Index   322
      Lists   324
      Table of Authorities
         328-329
      Table of Contents   326
   ToA Full Form dialog
      box   328
   ToA Short Form dialog
      box   329
Master document   336-339
Match dialog box   167-168
Match, and Speller   167-168
Math formulas, in tables
   248-250
Maximize   15, 22, 140
   Button   15, 141
Memory   427
Menu bar, defined   16, 32
Menu name   16
Merge   273-300, 440
   Cascading menu   275
   Codes   274-276, 278-282,
      286-287, 290-300
   Date, inserting
   Dialog box   258, 282

Eliminating blank lines 288-292
Fields 274-282, 285-287, 289-297
Forms (see Merge, Keyboard)
Keyboard 256-258, 298-300
Lists 295-298
Preventing extra spaces 292-295
Primary file 277-282, 300
Records 311-312
Secondary file 274-277
Sort 312-313
Stopping a merge 287
Microsoft Windows (see Windows 3.0)
Minimize 15, 22
Minimum offset from paragraph, graphics 382
Minimum Note Height text box 209
Mirror Image 392
Modified open files, saving 55-56
Monitor 10
Mouse 10-11, 22-24
Clicking 23
Dragging 23
Double clicking 23
Positioning graphics boxes and lines 388-389, 398, 399
Quadruple clicking 23
Scrolling with 33
Selecting with 23-24
Sizing graphics boxes and lines 388-389, 398
Triple clicking 23
Move
/Rename dialog box 186-187
/Rename 186-187
All 187
Files 185-187
Graphics boxes 384, 385-386, 388-389, 390-392
Graphics lines 397-398
Movement keys 133-134
Multi-bin printers 359-360
Multiple pages option 67-68
Multiple characters, and Match dialog box 168

Multitasking 8, 426

N

Naming documents 51
Navigator, File Manager 177, 179
Network 66
Network Printer 66
New
Directory 180-181
Text box 180
Document 17, 65
Page number 124-125
Window 31-32
Newspaper columns (see Columns, Newspaper)
Next
Command 43
Document key 141
Page 362-363
No Numbering 323
No Page Numbering 123
No Sort 315-316
Normal font attribute 370
Note text box 209
Number of Columns text box 218, 222
Number of Levels text box 327
Number of Pages to Skip 385
Numbering format 322
Numbering Method list box 209
Numeric columns 232-233
NumLock key 34, 134

O

Offset position 387
Open
File 61-62
Dialog box 19, 62
Or Retrieve File dialog box 63
Outline style 454
Styles 345
Operators 248-249
Option buttons, defined 20
Optional Concordance File text box 323
Original backup 58
Orphans 132-133
Outlining 202-206
Changing the order and turning on 205

Creating 203-206
Define Paragraph Numbering dialog box 202
Numbering style 202-203
Turning off 206
Overstrike 409

P

Page(s)
Breaks 130, 219
Centering from top to bottom 128-129
Conditional end of 130-131
Force odd/even 125
Down 34, 134, 135
Multiple, printing 67-68
Number(ing) 122-127
Accompanying text 125
Code 122-123, 125
Dialog box 123
Discontinuing 126
Force current 125
Inserting 126
New 124-125
Position 123-124
Styles 124
Suppressing 127
Specific, printing 67-68
Up 34, 133, 135
Paired styles 343-345
Palette, Equation 457
Paper Orientation box 357
Paper size 354-359
Codes 355
Definition
Adding 356-358, 359-360
Copying 359
Deleting 359
Editing 358
Dialog box 356
Paper type 356-357
Paper clip, and Help 154-155
Paragraph(s)
Adjusting space between 374
Deleting 39-40
Indent 85-86
Double 86
Hanging 86
Margin release 87-85
Number dialog box 202
Numbering 206-207
Changing format of 207

Selecting   39-40
Sort   309-312
    Fields, defined   307
Parallel columns
    (see Columns, Parallel)
Parallel columns with Block
    Protect   (see Columns,
    Parallel, with Block
    Protect)
Password
    Deleting   199
    Setting   198-199
Paste
    Rectangle   140
    Selected text 17, 139
    Tabular column   233
    Text   139
    Text in columns   219
Pause, and Macros   414
Percent of Optimal
    Letter spacing   374
    Word spacing   373
Picture and Text, and Button
    Bars   409
Picture Only, and Button
    Bars   409
Placement dialog box   118
Play   414-415
    Macro dialog box   414-415
Portrait orientation   354-355
Pos#   32-33
POS   33
Position
    Footnotes   208-209
    From Left Edge text
        box   361
    Go to   135
    Hyphen
    Last   135
Preferences
    Backup   438
    Date format   438
    Display   438
    Document summary   438
    Environment   438
    Equations   439
    Initial codes   439
    Keyboard   439
    Location of files   439-440
    Merge   440
    Print   440
    Table of Authorities   440

Previous
    Document key   141
    Page   364
Primary
    File   277-282, 300
    File text box   282, 287,
        297, 300
    Merge document
        277-282, 300
    Merge file   277-282, 300
Print
    Cartridges   368-436
    Color   452
    Current Page   67
    Dialog box   21, 66-67,
        188-189
    Document on Disk   68-69
    Double-sided   357
    From File Manager
        188-189
        List of files   189
    Full Document   66
    Info Report   195
    Location box   357
    Manager   66
        Dialog box   353-354
        In Windows   352,
            353-354, 356
    Multiple pages   67-68
    Navigator dialog box   189
    Number of Copies   69
    Options   440
        Box   357
    Preview   362-364
        Menu bar   362-364
        Window   362
    Problems, common
        376-377
    Three ways to   352
    Topic, in Help   154
    Window   189
    (see also Control Printer
        dialog box)
Printer
    Codes   65
    Driver   11, 65-66, 434-435
    Enhancements   351-378
    Initializing   437
    Installation   434-437
    Setup   188
    Memory buffer of   377
Program Manager
    Task list   422-423

Windows   (see Windows
    Program Manager)
Prompt for Hyphenation   102
Prompt to Load Paper   357
Properties, Style
    343-345, 347
PRS file   377

Q
Quick List   193-194

R
Random Access Memory
    (RAM)   8-9, 50
Range Name text box   262
Range text box   68, 262
Reboot system   428
Record
    Macro(s)   412-414
        Dialog box   412
Record(s)
    Selection text box   307,
        309, 311, 315-316
    Merge   312-313
    Type   306, 310-311
Recover Backup File   59-60
Rectangle   140
Redisplay   394-395
    Button   395
    View
        Panel   394
        Window   395
Redline   335-336, 371-372
    Method   335
Reference Aids
    Defined   320
    Editing   332
Reference type   333, 334
References, relative cell   249
Remove
    Command   199
    Markings   336, 372
        Dialog box   336, 372
Rename   185-188
Replace
    Codes   145-146
    Replace All   146
    Text   145-146
Restart Each Page
    Footnotes   209
    Line Numbering   361
Restart Numbering on Every
    Page   210
Restore command   43

Resume command button   162
Retrieve
    Figure   391
    Figure dialog box   391
    File   61-64
    In File Manager   198
Return
    Hard   45, 76, 306, 374
    Soft   306
Reveal codes   44-46, 451-456
    Bar   15, 45
    Definition   44
    Ruler   110
Right align tabs   80-81
Right justification   91
Right margin, column
    223-224, 227-228
Right margin, set   74-76, 107
Right text box   249
Rotate, and graphics boxes
    392, 393
Rotated font   355
Row(s)
    Adding and deleting
        243-246
    Height   241-242
    Text box   237, 244, 245,
        252, 254
Ruler   105-111
    Adjusting column widths
        227-228
    Defining columns   226
    Defining tables   111
    Delete tabs   108
    Display   106
    Hide   111
    Selecting
        Fonts   110
            Scalable   372
        Styles   110
    Set
        Line spacing   109-110
        Margins   107
        Justification   110
        Tabs   108
    Turning columns on and
        off   227
Run dialog box   190
Run, and File Manager
    189-190, 195-196

S

Save
    Button   53
    Button Bar dialog box   405

Document   46-47, 50-60
    In File Manager   198
    Selected text   57
    Style dialog box   345
Save As
    Command   54-55
    Dialog box   46-47
    Text box   47
Scalable fonts   369
Scale   387, 392
Scroll
    Bars   15, 22, 134
    Boxes   15, 22
    Buttons   15, 22
Search
    and Replace   145-147
        Dialog box   145
    Codes   144-145
    Dialog box   143
    Document Body Only   145
    Files   191-193
    For text box   143-144
    In File Manager   191-193
    Next   144, 145
    Previous   144, 145
    Results window   192-193
    Reverse   143-144
    Text   143-144
    Words   191-193
Secondary
    File   274-277
        Text box   282, 287,
            297, 300
    Merge File   274-277
Select
    All   183, 185, 187, 189
    Criteria   315-316
    Editor dialog box   260, 394
    File dialog box   69, 323
    Printer   69-70
    Text   37-42, 138
    with keyboard   38, 39, 40,
        41-42
    with mouse   37, 38, 39,
        40-41, 138
    Using Sort   315-316
    WordPerfect Thesaurus
        dialog box   172
Selected text
    Apply font attributes   370
    Center   89
    Check spelling of   162
    Copy   17, 139-140
    Cut   17, 138-139
    Paste   17, 139

Selection statement   318
Separator   209
Set
    Justification   92-93
    Pitch text box   373, 374
    Tabs   81-82
        Default   82
Shading, graphics boxes   382
Short form
    and Table of Authorities
        328-329
    Text box   329
Shortcut keys   19, 44, 88
Show Ruler   106
Size
    Graphics boxes   384, 687,
        388-389
    Graphics lines   397-399
Skip Always, and Speller   163
Skip, and Speller   163
Skip Once, and Speller   163
Soft return   306
Soft hyphen   102-103
Soft page break   130
Software   6
Solitaire   196
Sort
    By date   315
    Dialog box   307, 309, 311
    Line   306-309
    Merge   312-313
    Paragraph   309-312
    Table   314-315
    Order   306, 608, 313,
        314, 315
    Status dialog box   307, 309
    Using to select   315-316
Spacing between
    Lines   77-78
    Letters   374
    Notes text box   209
    Paragraphs   374
    Words   373
Special codes   83-84, 89,
    103, 234
Speller   160-168
    Add   163
    Check list box   162
    Delete 2nd   166
    Dialog box   161
    Dictionary   164
    Disable checking   166
    Duplicate Words dialog
        box   166
    Edit   165

Icon 160
Irregular Capitalization
   Found dialog box 166
Looking up a word
   using 163
Manually editing a word
   while using 162
Match 167-168
Menu bar 164-168
Options menu 165
Skip Once 163
Skip Always 163
Suggest 163
Suggestion box 161,
   162, 168
Supplementary Dictionary
   dialog box 164
Split 252
Row/Column dialog
   box 252
Spreadsheets
DDE links 269-270
Importing 261-264
Linking 264-270
Three-dimensional 268
Start WordPerfect 13-16
Starting Number text box 203
Starting outline number
   202-203
Status bar 15, 32
Strikeout 371-372
Style(s)
Changing types of
   346-347
Defined 342
Delete 347-348
Dialog box 343
Edit 346
Editor window 344,
   345, 347
Library 348
   Retrieving different 349
Off Code 342-343, 344
On Code 342-343
On/Off 344, 346
Open 345
Paired 343-345
Properties 343-345, 347
   Dialog box 344, 347
Text box 202-203, 383
Types of 342-343
Versus macros 342
Subboxes, defined 19

Subdirectories 176, 178
Subdocument links, and master
   document 337-339
Subheading(s) 321-322
   Text box 321-322
Submenus, defined 19
Subscript 371, 404, 450
Subtree 193
Suggest, and Speller 163
Suggestion list box 161,
   162, 168
Summary (see Document,
   Summary)
Superscript 208, 371,
   404, 450
Supplementary 164
Suppress
Dialog box 121-122, 127
Headers and footers
   120-122
Page numbering 127
Swap files, Windows 427
Switching between Windows
   applications 423-425
Symbol
Equation palette 395
Selection statement 315
Synonym and Antonym display
   area 170-172
Syntax Error dialog box 417
System initial codes 150

T

Table of Authorities
   328-331, 440
Defining 330-331
Editing the full form
   329-330
Generating 331
Marking text for 328-329
Table of Contents 326-327
Defining 326-327
Generating 327
Marking text for 326
Table(s)
Adding rows and
   columns 243-249
Aligning in 238-240
Box, and graphics 260-261
Cell addresses 243
Changing
   Column width 247-248
   One cell 240-241

Controlling page
   breaks 255
Converting
Existing columns into
   258-259
   to text 259-260
Copying 233, 238
Create 237-238
Dialog box 237
Within a graphics box
   260-261
Cutting 238
Delete dialog box 259
Deleting rows and
   columns 243-249
Designing formats 255
Entering math
   formulas 248-50
Entering text 238
Formatting data in 238-240
Formula dialog box 248
Icon 237
Joining cells 251
Lines 255
Dialog box 255
Locking and unlocking cells
   252-254
Merging into 256-258
Making changes 238-255
Naming cells by
   position 243
Options dialog box
   244, 246
Pasting 238
Recalculating totals 250
Row 314
Setting lines per row and
   row height 241-242
Setting up a keyboard merge
   256-258
Sort 314-315
Splitting cells 251-252
Structure 237
Subtotal, total and grand
   total functions 250-251
within newspaper or parallel
   columns 238, 260-261
Tab(s)
Absolute 153
Center 80
Clear all 82
Clear tabs 82
Codes 79

Decimal 81, 232-235
Default 82
Dot leaders (see Tabs, Leader dots)
    Hard 84
    Left align 80
    Leader dots 81, 235-236
    Markers 106, 108-109
    Relative to left margin 79-80
    Right align 80-81
    Set 81-82
    Dialog box 82
    Underlining 96-97
Tabular columns 233
Target, and Cross-reference 332-334
Target Name text box 333-334
Task List, Windows 422-423
Template 24-25
Temporary backup file 58-59
Text offset, and graphics boxes 382, 385, 389
Text Adjustments box 357
Text box
    Creating 393
    Defined 20
Text Editor text box 260
Thesaurus 169-172
    Dialog box 169-171
    Dictionary 172
    Edit 172
    History 172
    How it is organized 170
    Icon 425
    Looking up a word before you type it 170
    Menu Bar 172
    References 171
Thickness text box, and line graphics 397
Three dimensional spreadsheets 268
Tile 141
Time, and Date and Time feature 98-100
Timed backup 59
Title bar
    Defined 16, 31
To Cell text box 249
To End of Selection, and Speller 162
To End of Page, and Speller 162

To End of Document, and Speller 162
ToA Edit Full Form 330
ToA Full Form 328
ToA Short Form 329
Toggle 18, 165
Tool dialog box 169, 170
Top margins, set 127-129
Transmitting printer instructions 65
Typeover mode 36-37
Typesetting dialog box 97, 373
Typesetting 97, 373-375

U

Undelete 42-44
Underline
    Codes, deleting 96
    Double 96
    Spaces 96-97, 374
    Tabs 96-97, 374
Undo 44
Units of measure 438, 450
Unlock Cell 252-254
Unrecoverable Application Error 428
Unsaved open files 61-62
Unselect All 183, 185, 187, 189
Update All Spreadsheet Links dialog box 266
Update All Links 266
Uppercase, convert text to 97
Uppercase roman numerals 124
User Defined format 202
User Defined number format 202
User boxes 397
Using Help 151-157

V

Vertical
    Command 397
    Position 386, 388-389
    Text box 384
View Options dialog box
Viewer 178-179, 194-195
View Reset 363-364
Viewing a document 62-63

W

What IS, and Help 157
Wide form 357

Widow/Orphans 132-133
Widows 132-133
Width text box 260
Windows (3.0) 12-13, 421-429
    Accessing DOS from 426
    Clipboard 188, 190-191
    Memory 427
    Multitasking 8, 426
    Program Manager 13, 15, 422-423
    Swap File feature 427
    Switching between applications 423-425
    Unrecoverable application error 428
Word and letter spacing 373-347
Word search 191-193
Word spacing 373
    Justification limits 92, 374, 450
Word text box 162, 163, 167-168, 170
WordPerfect (for Windows)
    Characters dialog box 367, 399
    Configuring 437-440
    Differences from WordPerfect 5.1 411
    Exiting 25, 47
    Group icon 13, 15, 29
    Installing 13, 431-437
    Printer driver 11, 65-66, 434-435
    Program group 13, 16, 29
    Starting 13-16
    System requirements for 431-433
Wordwrap 28
WP Characters 367-368
Wrap Text Around Box 385, 389

Z

Zoom 363

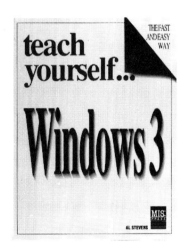

Welcome to Personal Computers

by Kris Jamsa

L et the publishers of the *Teach Yourself ...* series introduce you to the world of personal computers with this thoroughly unintimidating guide. Whether you're shopping for a computer or find yourself in a position to use one at work or at home, *Welcome to Personal Computers* is exactly the book you need. Written for the novice and fully illustrated, it is an easy-to-understand introduction to the complex world of personal computers. Author Kris Jamsa has written more than thirty computer books. His clear writing style presents new concepts in short, non-technical sentences so you'll quickly learn key PC concepts.

The book includes:

- Choosing, purchasing, and setting up your computer

- Understanding computer hardware

- Using common software programs such as spreadsheets, databases, and word processors

- Understanding operating systems

- The essential personal computer buyer's guide

A must for the beginning and intermediate computer user.

ISBN: 1-55828-188-6 $19.95

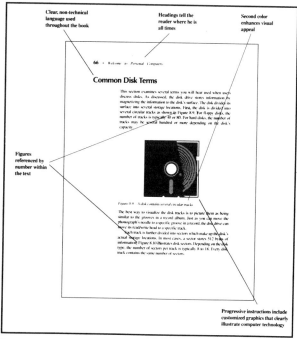

Design and content combine to make the most accessible beginner's book ever!

Available at your local book store or call (212) 886-9261

MIS: *PRESS*
A subsidiary of Henry Holt and Company
115 W. 18th Street
New York, NY 10011